NYINGMA
ANCIENT ONES
གསང་ཆེན་སྔ་འགྱུར་རྙིང་མ་པ།

The rNam-chos-dbang-ldan symbol:
Myriad forms~ten to the tenth power~be sealed.

Ways of Work

WAYS OF WORK

DYNAMIC ACTION

NYINGMA IN THE WEST

Dharma  Publishing

Nyingma in America Series

Annals of the Nyingma Lineage in America I
Annals of the Nyingma Lineage in America II
Annals of the Nyingma Lineage in America III
Copper Mountain Mandala: Mystic Land of Odiyan
Ways of Work: Dynamic Action

ISBN: 0-89800-178-1; 0-89800-135-8 (pbk.)

Typeset in Mergenthaler Sabon
Printed and bound by Dharma Press, California

9 8 7 6 5 4 3 2 1

In gratitude for
the wealth of opportunities offered by the West,
this volume is dedicated
to all the past, present and future supporters
of the Nyingma tradition.

Contents

Preface xv

Introduction xvii

Working at Nyingma

Implementing A Vision 5

Preserving and Sharing Knowledge 13

Seeds for Accomplishment 19

Working with Challenges 29

A Precious Education for Life 39

Tibetan Nyingma Meditation Center

Approaching Unfamiliar Knowledge 49

Preservation of Traditional Culture 63

Ritual Arts and Traditional Crafts 73

The Study of Tibetan Art 85
Developing Business Sense 93
Creating Art for Odiyan 103

Dharma Publishing

The First Publications 115
Reaching a Wider Audience 127
Opportunities for Learning 137
The Nyingma Edition of the Tibetan Canon 145
Creating Beauty for the Dharma 157
Translations and Research Projects 163

Dharma Press

Setting Up the Press 177
Management Changes 189
Innovation and Teamwork 199
Working in the World 209
Developing Efficient Strategies 221
Skillful Means at Work 233

Nyingma Institute

Opening New Horizons 247
Study and Practice 255

Opening Up Limitations 265
Focus on Long-term Programs 275
Making Transitions 285
New Approaches to Learning 291

Odiyan Mandala

Laying the Foundation 303
Learning How to Learn 313
Meeting the Challenge 323
Building the Odiyan Stupa 331
Creation of the Temple 337
Ornamenting the Mandala 345

Dynamic Action

First Year 361
Fifth Year 366
Tenth Year 379
Fifteenth Year 395
Summaries 417

Preface

Over nearly two decades, the Nyingma organizations in America have dedicated their efforts to preserving and sharing the Tibetan Buddhist tradition. We have been fortunate to have before us a vision that fills us with inspiration and purpose, and my students and friends and I have found enduring satisfaction in our work. Though we could not say all of the possibilities have been realized, our progress seems encouraging. Thinking that our ways of working might be of interest to others, I decided to compile a short history of our organizations.

Our various organizations have maintained records and archives about hundreds of different projects. I summarized these developments for Leslie Bradburn and made some of these records available to her. After several months of collecting project descriptions and memos, interviewing members, and reading accounts of their experiences at Nyingma, she reviewed various topics with me and put together an informal history. The staff of both Dharma Publishing and Press offered generous contributions of time and effort in preparing the manuscript for publication.

This short compilation touches upon some of our more important projects as well as describing the ways that we work, the reasons we work, and what our results have been. Though it is by no means a complete record, this volume does offer a description of the kinds of challenges we have faced, and examples of the learning process that our work has stimulated. In the course of accomplishing worthwhile projects, Nyingma students have gained practical skills of many kinds as well as deeper self-understanding. Our approach to work has brought us rich rewards, and we hope our story will encourage others to discover creative ways of work.

Introduction

Upon my arrival in America eighteen years ago, I established several organizations for the purpose of preserving the tradition of Tibetan Buddhism. The Buddhist traditions around the world have gradually declined in the face of modern political and social circumstances. The ancient knowledge traditions of Tibet seemed in special danger, and I hoped to make whatever small contribution I could to preserve this precious heritage for the future.

I also hoped to encourage Westerners' growing interest in the Dharma, for I am confident that the wealth of knowledge in the Tibetan Buddhist tradition could offer solutions to many of the problems besetting modern societies. My education had impressed upon me the importance of sharing whatever knowledge one had, and this was one reason I decided to come to America. The West knew so little about the Tibetan tradition; at least I might be able to stimulate more curiosity and encourage exploration of this spiritual way of life.

With these purposes in mind, I founded the Tibetan Nyingma Meditation Center in 1969 in Berkeley, California. By 1975, five sister organizations were in operation. TNMC especially focuses on preserving Tibetan sacred art, fostering ritual arts and crafts, and supporting the traditional culture here and abroad. Dharma Publishing and Dharma Press are devoted to the preservation of Buddhist texts and to publishing translations of Buddhist works and reproductions of sacred art. We have also published introductory study materials, which grew out of my informal talks and advice, eventually developing into various series of books. Though they are not traditional Buddhist presentations, these books seem helpful to Westerners new to the Dharma.

The Nyingma Institute was founded in 1972 for the purpose of introducing classical Buddhist teachings. To encourage the study of these teachings, the Institute also offers introductory seminars in simple relaxation techniques, meditation, and experiential programs that support the gradual growth of self-understanding and appreciation of the Dharma.

The Odiyan Country Center, established in 1975, provides an environment where Tibetan teachers will be able to continue practicing traditional teachings. Westerners interested in long-term studies and practice can pursue the traditional Buddhist education in addition to various approaches especially suited to introducing the Dharma in this culture.

Believing that these five organizations could accomplish something of merit, I have devoted time and energy over the last ten years more toward guiding our projects and less toward teaching classes — many worthwhile tasks beckon, but time is short. Implementing some aspects of the founding vision has required enormous efforts, demanding more sacrifices on everyone's part than I had expected. Simply maintaining the new organizations has sometimes proved difficult; working actively toward the accomplishment of our goals has brought us face to face with many challenging situations. Though it is difficult to predict the future, I see evidence of solid accomplishment—good results for the time and energy people have invested. I believe the merit of these efforts will continue to bring benefits to them, our societies, and the Dharma in the future.

Over the years our organizations have been staffed by students wishing to study the Buddhist teachings. Initially fascinated with the exotic or expecting largely personal benefits, Nyingma students have begun to appreciate that giving is more satisfying than receiving, and that self-centered goals in the long run limit creativity and enjoyment. Projects such as the publication of the Kanjur and Tanjur, the building of the Odiyan Stupa, and the creation of the temple have required willingness to work with difficulties, to learn new skills and concepts, and the ability and desire to take responsibility. It has been very rewarding to see abilities, strengths, and understanding develop with each new challenge. Though we are far from the ideal of the Bodhisattva, the possibility of working for others without recognition and without compensation has begun to inspire the lives of more individuals.

I hope all those who have worked with Nyingma will realize the value of what they have learned and what they have contributed. I offer my heartfelt gratitude for their efforts, which have been instrumental in bringing into being a vision I believe has great value. From the efforts of these five organizations a deeper appreciation for the range of human possibilities may emerge in the future. Our work has been one way to encourage recognition of the treasures within the Buddhist tradition and to provide fuller access to this precious human heritage.

More than a few decades may pass before the results of our endeavor are known. The work of all those dedicated to the Dharma—all the various centers, teachers, students, supporters, and contributors—will surely bear fruit, bringing the benefits of the Dharma into many lives in times when the Dharma will be greatly needed. The more progress modern technological societies make, the more urgent the need for spiritual balance to protect the high ideals of lasting satisfaction and individual freedom for all. With the blessings of the Nyingma lineage, may the Buddha Dharma become part of the enduring heritage of Western civilization.

Tarthang Tulku
August, 1987

Ways of Work

WORKING AT NYINGMA

Implementing A Vision

The first Nyingma organizations in America were founded by Tarthang Tulku, a Tibetan teacher trained in the traditions of Nyingma Tibetan Buddhism. After he left his homeland in 1959, he envisioned bringing these traditions to the West, where the ancient wisdom they transmitted could be safely preserved. Disruptions in Tibet and instability in other traditionally Buddhist lands made survival of this unique body of knowledge uncertain. Preserved and translated into Western languages, the collective wisdom of hundreds of generations of Buddhist masters might help resolve some of the more intractable problems facing modern societies, and open wider possibilities for the future.

Soon after arriving in California in spring of 1969, Tarthang Tulku began to share this vision with interested individuals and explore ways in which the wisdom preserved in the Nyingma tradition could contribute to the Western store of knowledge. He established the

Tarthang Tulku, Founder of Nyingma Centers

Tibetan Nyingma Meditation Center (TNMC) in Berkeley, where Americans could study the Buddhist teachings. Within six years, activities at TNMC had given rise to four additional organizations, each playing an essential role in unfolding the vision: a publishing company, a printing press, an educational institute, and a country center for study and practice.

In ancient societies, it was customary for those who devoted themselves to spiritual activities to retire from the world. Supported by devout laypeople, wealthy patrons, or by the ruling dynasty, they accomplished many worthwhile projects in relative solitude. In our society today no spiritual tradition has government favor. With religious freedom guaranteed, individuals are free to explore different traditions, but they cannot at first rely upon a broad base of support. In the beginning, they must find ways to be self-sufficient and to sponsor their own projects.

When we began to study at the new Meditation Center, we knew of no precedent for what we hoped to accomplish. What models could people in advanced technological societies follow in developing lifestyles suited to study and practice of ancient Buddhist teachings? How could we fulfill our purposes while practicing a spiritual way of life?

It is not possible to turn the clock back to earlier times or to completely remake the world we live in. However much we might wish to renounce money, position, and power to devote ourselves to spiritual practice, such a traditional approach does not seem possible for most individuals today. Our interest in the Buddhist tradition is new. Even if we have independent means of support, we have not developed the understanding and the resolve to go against the strong currents of modern ways of life. Like most Westerners interested in spiritual values, we were not yet prepared or inclined to retire from the world.

At the same time, it was evident that there was much to be done to promote a deeper appreciation of the Buddhist tradition. Thousands of texts awaited translation. Buddhist art was relatively unknown, and its value not well understood. Few people had any notion of the relevance of Buddhist teachings to modern life; even those interested in investigating them were limited by lack of materials to study.

If we hoped to implement the vision of preserving the Buddhist teachings and contributing to a stronger foundation for understanding, it seemed we had no choice but to work within the mainstream of modern society. To carry out the wide variety of necessary projects, we would need to build stable organizations and facilities. Creating them would engage us in the practical realms of business management, financial planning, and modern technology in fields ranging from art and publishing to construction.

As members of a modern society, could we find a way to use its advantages—its technical knowledge and tools—for spiritual purposes? Could we find a way to live and work in the world that is compatible with spiritual vision?

From a talk by Rinpoche, spring of 1987: "The inescapable truth is that our time and space are limited. We cannot extend our time or change our historical situation, but we might be able to extend our knowledge to make our time more meaningful. We cannot ignore modern conditions, but it is possible for individuals with a higher purpose to work within them to make substantial contributions of enduring value.

"If we are willing to ask what we can offer the world rather than what we can gain from it, we can find ways to put our skills, energy, and intelligence to finer uses. Spiritual vision can then complement and uplift modern knowledge, skills, and technology. Inspired by a deep and long-range vision and guided by sure knowledge, we can draw upon these advantages to accomplish meaningful purposes which transcend the limited self-centered values of power, wealth, and fame."

Human history shows that balancing the spiritual and material aspects of life has always been difficult. It seems especially challenging today, when the pressure and confusion of modern life can seriously weaken commitment to a higher purpose. We can easily be distracted by the excitement and controversies of today's fast-moving world, or drained by its demands. If we lose sight of our purpose, our efforts to work in the world will be shaped solely by materialistic values.

For anyone who aspires to accomplish a purpose, vision is the key to success. Vision is like a lamp in a dark forest—it helps to maintain a clear sense of direction, and sustain motivation, interest, and effort. Vision uplifts and protects the human heart from the confusion and dissatisfaction that so often characterize our lives, and leads us along a path of transformation.

From a talk by Rinpoche, spring, 1986: "Can you sense within your heart any purpose for your life besides your own benefit? Can you pick out some thread you would like to see carry on, some result you want to realize? What difference could you make in the world? Is there any gesture that would express this vision?

"If you do feel inspired by a vision of beauty and meaning, then ask yourself if you know how to bring it into being. Can you see a way to combine this higher purpose with the development of your own potential? Can you determine whether your success is limited because you need more knowledge or because you do not know how to implement the knowledge you have? If you consider these questions deeply and carefully, you will be able to open a larger vision and see the way toward enduring and meaningful accomplishment."

Over the past two decades, it has grown increasingly clear to those living and working within the Nyingma Centers that work in the world and spiritual education can be complementary. A spiritual tradition such as Buddhism offers profound insight into human nature and ways to realize the full potential of our bodies and minds. Touching humanity's deepest aspirations for meaning and value, it holds forth a compassionate vision of wisdom that benefits all people and enriches all cultural and spiritual traditions. In working toward preserving, studying, and sharing such knowledge, we can find joy and meaning in life that both satisfy and transcend personal interests.

Practical work guided by this deeper perspective on human nature sets up a continuing cycle of learning, creativity, and accomplishment. As we have grown in self-understanding, we have learned to work much more effectively; the longer we have worked together, the more we have learned about ourselves. Wherever we work, whatever our specific goals, sounder knowledge of our inner resources gives us a solid basis for skillful action. As this knowledge grows and is applied in the everyday world, it moves from theory to a direct and personal understanding that we can implement more effectively in our lives and our work.

When we are devoted to a purpose we care deeply about, we are more inclined to take complete responsibility for our actions to ensure good results. Working on Nyingma projects over the years, we have discovered that taking responsibility is the secret to increasing self-knowledge, self-motivation, and self-confidence.

Engaged in meaningful work, we learn how to develop awareness and other inner resources such as patience, determination, concentration, and open-mindedness. These positive qualities bring us greater control over our lives and allow us to persevere in the face of challenges. With a clear purpose in mind, we can find ways to develop whatever knowledge, skills, and personal qualities we need to succeed, and thus increase our ability to accomplish our purposes.

From a talk by Rinpoche, spring, 1987: "Because it is more comprehensive and more attuned to universal human aspirations, spiritual knowledge can operate in the practical world more successfully than ordinary understanding. Such clear-sighted knowledge can support our desires to derive deeper satisfaction from our work, to perfect abilities and skills, to defuse the pressures of the modern world, and to make a contribution."

Once set in motion, the dynamic of vision is self-generating. As initial goals are achieved, we can perceive their connection with a much larger vision. Discovering that we are able to accomplish something of value inspires us to undertake further challenges. As vision gains substance, it naturally begins to extend further into the future. The more far-ranging the vision, the more clearly priorities can be established, progress evaluated, and sound decisions reached.

When a long-range vision is imprinted on our minds, steady progress can be made in a single direction, and momentum can build; each goal accomplished becomes a signpost along the way, encouraging the next step. The clearer the path becomes, the more possibilities come into view, and the need for more knowledge becomes apparent. As we begin actively to invite knowledge into our lives, we gain greater flexibility and become capable of taking advantage of whatever circumstances arise.

As vision leads beyond self-centered interests, the path to enduring accomplishment unfolds. Motivated by a higher purpose, we can tap our deepest resources of energy and intelligence. Confident in our abilities and in the value of our goals, we can consistently support our finest aspirations, and work to bring into being all that we value for ourselves and our world.

From this perspective, an aspiration to realize a greater purpose is not contradictory to life in the world, but becomes a means to richer accomplishment and success. Work becomes a path of learning, a priceless education in human nature that allows us to make genuine contributions to the world. Guided by knowledge of the human heart and mind, efforts in the practical realm have long-lasting results that benefit individuals and society alike. We hope that our discoveries along this challenging path will suggest ways for others to balance their lives in modern society, tasting the joys of meaningful work.

Preserving and Sharing Knowledge

Tarthang Tulku was born in Golog in the far northeastern corner of the Tibetan plateau. He received a traditional Buddhist education beginning in early childhood, and then as a young man traveled widely throughout Tibet to study with prominent teachers.

Interview with Rinpoche, spring, 1986: "The course my life has taken has been far different from what I imagined as a youngster. After the early years of intensive training at my monastery, I spent several years traveling through parts of eastern and central Tibet. In 1958, I left Tibet for the small Buddhist kingdom of Bhutan, and from there I traveled to Sikkim. Due to the political situation, thousands of Tibetans were fleeing to India as refugees. For several years I traveled through India, visiting pilgrimage sites and Buddhist centers. In 1963, I was appointed by the head of the Nyingma school to a position at Sanskrit University in Benares. Holding a fellowship in Buddhist studies and research created by the Indian government, I worked with Indian Sanskrit scholars, teaching Nyingma subjects in particular. From time to time, I attended various conferences and gave lectures on Buddhism.

"The Tibetans in India found it extremely difficult to adjust to their new surroundings. The whole lifestyle was completely different, as well as the climate and diet. India is a very crowded land, far advanced on the path toward modernization. Tibet was a land of vast open spaces and few inhabitants, with a lifestyle that was still traditional. Added to this abrupt change was the sorrow of seeing our land and culture in distress, and the pain of realizing that we had lost our country. Since contact with Tibet had been cut off, we were faced with uncertainty about the fate of our families and friends—fewer than 100,000 Tibetans had escaped to India. Of that number a small minority were monks and lamas; as so many had passed away under these stressful conditions, we were deeply worried for the future of our cultural and religious traditions.

"In 1959 most of us thought Tibetan civilization as we had known it had come to an end, and it seemed imperative to preserve as much of our cultural heritage as possible. The survival of the Tibetan Buddhist tradition depends upon the knowledge preserved in thousands of texts, and so we gathered together the books we had been able to bring with us. Those few of us who were fortunate to have good health and energy sought to contribute in whatever way we could.

"We faced many challenges, not just because of our lack of technical knowledge, but also because support and encouragement for our efforts was limited at that time. No one outside our community knew what Tibetan Buddhism might have to contribute to the world. Now, many more individuals have become familiar with the teachings, but the cultural gap may not be closed; great benefits could result, but there could also be misunderstanding and confusion. Even today it is difficult to predict what the long-term effects of this interaction will be.

"In 1963 I set up a publishing and printing operation in India, naming it Dharma Mudranalaya after Tibet's largest, most famous printing house at Derge. Without knowing the language or the business practices of this new culture, and lacking the technical skills required for printing and publishing, my students and friends and I faced what seemed like an enormous task. But we learned from experience, and by 1968 had published over five hundred copies of more than twenty Tibetan texts. Our efforts inspired other lamas to publish works available to them. I have been very pleased to see how much my friends in India have published over the past fifteen years.

"During this period, a number of Tibetans felt that learning more about Western culture had distinct advantages. Some of my good friends devoted themselves to academic studies and went on to become professors. They urged me to do likewise, or at least to learn English so that I could be confident of having the skills necessary to survive. Some friends recommended I go to France where there appeared to be interest in Nyingma studies, rather than consider America.

"By 1968 I had been gone from Tibet for ten years, and I felt the time had come to make a decision about the course my life would take. Making this choice was not easy. Friends who knew me from the university thought that I would continue on in the academic world. Others knew of my early desire to give up worldly life and dedicate myself to practice in solitude, and were confident that this would be my decision. But life is short, and my time to accomplish might be short. The key question was how I, in my own limited way, could make a contribution. After much reflection, I chose the path of action in the world. Soon after, I left for America.

Since I came to the United States, I have been able to start several organizations, each of which in its own way has been able to accomplish something meaningful. Over the years, we have worked in a great variety of situations, both familiar and unfamiliar. I am grateful to have had such a wealth of opportunities, rich both in spiritual experience and in experiences of everyday life in the modern world.

"Working to preserve and share the Buddhist traditions is deeply satisfying, but it is an enormous task. Only a few teachers even reached India, and many were quite young. Of these only a few have come to the West. The body of knowledge preserved in Tibet for over 1,200 years has scarcely been tapped in modern times. To assure its full preservation is a work of many lifetimes; still, we can make an effort, doing what we can in our own small way.

"I do not claim that our efforts have actually transmitted the Dharma — I have no delusions about that. I believe our work is very preliminary. Our contribution is to preserve the knowledge transmitted in the tradition and to introduce background materials that encourage the growth of understanding. In the future, if people in the West grow interested in the Dharma, there will be something for them to work with.

"I cannot say for certain whether the results of my work in the West will ever prove to have lasting benefit. But if you wholeheartedly believe in the value of what you are doing, and if you work for results that benefit others, then you can say life has meaning and purpose. I am confident that our community has shown people how to work and how to choose what is worthwhile for their own lives. Even if some people work with us only a short time, to the extent that they have learned something of value, they have been able to make a contribution as well. If they look within their hearts, they will see also the benefit that remains with them.

"I hope to continue working for the preservation of what I hold most valuable. I firmly believe that while the Dharma is present, there will be light in the world, but if the Dharma should disappear, darkness will quickly descend upon us.

"Human beings everywhere have need of greater wisdom and compassion. The need is obvious here in the West where the speed and pressure of modern life promote dissatisfaction, and freedom from traditions of the past can also increase uncertainty and confusion. More and more, people are aware of the price societies pay for modern advances. With so much power and advanced technology in the hands of Western culture, it seems clear that broader vision and deeper understanding of human nature must develop as well. In this, the ancient knowledge traditions have much to offer the modern world.

"We have the opportunity today to pursue a new synthesis of the spiritual and practical approaches to life, to find a balance between these two apparent extremes. This would be a truly valuable contribution if we could foster the genius of human spirit together with the genius of modern technology. It seems to me that now is the time to try."

Seeds for Accomplishment

Tarthang Tulku arrived in Berkeley in February, 1969. The following month he leased a house on Webster Street, and soon afterwards applied for permanent residency status. Encouraged by the interest in the Buddhist tradition among educators, health workers, and psychologists, he participated in symposiums and seminars in the San Francisco area, and began offering classes at various institutes, in the homes of friends, and at Webster Street. In October, the residence at Webster Street became the first home of the newly incorporated Tibetan Nyingma Meditation Center (TNMC), established as a non-profit religious organization. At the time of its incorporation, TNMC had a membership of thirty-five individuals interested in studying the Buddhist teachings and practicing meditation.

While eager to learn meditation and explore what Buddhism might have to offer them individually, the early members of TNMC knew almost nothing about the

Buddhist traditions, their history, or the teachings they transmitted. Tarthang Tulku, addressed by his students as Rinpoche, a title of respect traditionally accorded distinguished teachers, was faced with the unfamiliar complexities of modern American culture. He devoted much of his time to acquainting himself with the backgrounds, interests, and expectations of the Americans who wished to become his students.

Rinpoche shared with us his perspective on how the knowledge transmitted in the Nyingma tradition could be offered to our culture. We would need to develop a center where we ourselves could study and grow in understanding. A separate educational facility would make it possible for many people to investigate the teachings, developing better understanding of the mind and emotions and experiencing the benefits of meditation practice. Through a publishing and printing company, we could preserve essential texts and art, and produce works in English that would introduce the teachings more widely. Eventually, if enough people became seriously interested in intensive study and practice, a large country center would be necessary.

In the beginning such a long-range vision seemed to us a far-off dream. We had little training in skills useful for such work and did not see how spiritual study could prepare us for carrying out such extensive plans. Primarily interested in focusing on our personal education, we were just beginning to sense that Buddhist teachings were relevant to our own lives. It was not clear how to combine spiritual development with practical work on the projects Rinpoche envisioned.

Without being fully certain of how best to begin, we were soon participating in activities that formed the seeds from which new organizations would develop. Establishing a place for study and practice involved making meditation cushions, robes, temple hangings, and small prayer flags. Over time, these activities grew into large-scale projects in ritual arts and crafts that supported traditional Tibetan religious practice.

TNMC students were invited to join in Rinpoche's efforts to provide assistance to the refugees in India, and began to collect clothing and arrange for shipping. The need to coordinate arrangements more efficiently led to the establishment of the Tibetan Aid Project (TAP), and later the Tibetan Relief Foundation, both of which were supervised by TNMC.

Students working with Rinpoche to make materials available for TNMC classes in basic Buddhist teachings, meditation, and Tibetan language were helping to lay the groundwork for a larger educational institute. The classes in philosophy and studies of Tibetan texts were becoming small translation projects to provide the community with study materials in English. Instruction in Buddhist iconography and art developed skills useful for creating other things that were needed, such as illustrations for brochures. Since there were few copies of Tibetan books or art available, we began to print line drawings and texts for student use. These activities led to the formation of Dharma Publishing and Dharma Press.

By the end of TNMC's first year, it had become apparent that larger facilities would be needed. The classes were growing in size, and a number of us wanted a place where we could study, practice, and work together on a full-time basis, instead of meeting only in the evenings and on weekends.

In September of 1971, we were able to make a down payment on an abandoned fraternity house close to the University of California campus. Sixty TNMC members worked on renovating the building and raising funds to help meet the monthly expenses. By November, Padma Ling, "Lotus Ground," became the new home of TNMC, Dharma Publishing, and Dharma Press.

Over the next four years, four distinct organizations took shape, coordinated and supervised by TNMC: Dharma Publishing, Dharma Press, the Nyingma Institute, and the Odiyan Center. In 1972 Dharma Press moved to a separate location and began to grow into a complete book-production facility, while Dharma Publishing remained at Padma Ling. In 1975, Dharma Press and Dharma Publishing were incorporated under the name Dharma Mudranalaya.

Padma Ling's public seminars and workshops, which by the end of 1972 were attracting large numbers of people, gave rise to the Nyingma Institute, founded in 1972. To house the new Institute, another large building was located and renovated. The new organization became the focus of formal educational activities; classes were soon offered in Buddhist philosophy, psychology, meditation, and human development. While regular classes were no longer offered at Padma Ling, the Nyingma Institute's administration and programs continued to be guided by TNMC.

In fall 1974, after years of planning and close attention to savings, land for the Odiyan Country Center was located, and construction began in the fall of 1975. Balancing all the requirements of each organization, Rinpoche gave time to long-term projects underway at Padma Ling, the Institute, and Publishing, while designing and coordinating details of Odiyan's construction. Over twelve years, volunteers developed skills as they worked. Members of all the centers contributed as much time, energy, and support as they could to bring the vision into reality. The Odiyan property has gradually been developed and now includes a temple, a stupa, and a complex of additional buildings on extensively landscaped grounds.

In 1976, the Nyingma Centers Corporation was established as an umbrella organization to assist in coordinating activities of the five Nyingma Centers: TNMC, Dharma Publishing, Dharma Press, the Nyingma Institute, and the Odiyan Center.

As work intensified and basic Dharma teachings were more available in translation and in Dharma Publishing books, students began to take greater responsibility for their study and practice. Some of us who had developed serious interests in philosophy, psychology, Tibetan language, and art were encouraged to share what we had learned through the Institute's new programs. Other Padma Ling residents were already working at Odiyan. After 1978, our time and energy were increasingly invested in a number of major projects underway at Padma Ling, Dharma Publishing, Dharma Press, the Nyingma Institute, and Odiyan.

It took time for many of us to adjust to working full-time on Nyingma projects. Some people had families to care for; others were involved in jobs and professional activities that they found themselves reluctant to give up. Those of us living at Padma Ling or the Institute sometimes felt constrained by the quiet, concentrated atmosphere or missed the social events and entertainments that play a significant role in most American lifestyles. While some people decided to return to a more conventional way of living, those of us who continued have found that the work we are doing supports a new kind of enjoyment. As we began to see the results of our efforts, we appreciated more deeply the value of our time and energy. In comparison to the opportunity for accomplishment, our accustomed entertainments became much less appealing.

From a talk by Rinpoche, spring, 1986: "There is a formal way to practice, with classes, ceremonies, and so forth. But our style embraces work as part of the process of self-perfection. The work itself is teacher, requiring that we practice the qualities that develop our potential: generosity, patience, discipline, effort, concentration, and higher understanding.

"In Tibet Nyingma has tremendous diversity, from scholars to siddhas. In America we can at least try to foster broad perspectives. We work at many different jobs, using a wide variety of skills, with perhaps ten projects going on at once at each center. We work for ourselves, for others, for the benefit of American culture and Tibetan culture. We work as much as possible!"

Lacking precedents for practicing the Dharma in the modern working world, we have not always known how to proceed. But following Rinpoche's guidance, we have gradually seen a vision of real accomplishment open before us, allowing our skills and knowledge to build in a coherent progression.

Almost everything needed to fulfill the founding purposes—equipment, skills, funds, and knowledge—has been developed out of the work itself and then "recycled" to support new activities. For example, making study materials for TNMC helped us gain book production and business skills essential for the success of Dharma Publishing and Press. Books we published were then available for the classes at the Institute, while TNMC students were ready to assist in teaching. As the Institute expanded, some of its students went to work at the Press or Odiyan. As the Press and the Institute began to flourish, they could provide funds to help support TNMC projects and Odiyan construction.

Each project offered opportunities to develop skills and knowledge that could be combined and recombined in complementary ways. Our projects fit together, supporting and contributing to one another, each a facet of a larger vision. This self-sufficiency, supported by a growing ability to work creatively, may be our main strength, as individuals and as an organization.

Seen from a distance, the history of our organizations reveals a slow but steady upward trend over more than eighteen years. Looking more closely at this curve, however, we see small variations. These ups and downs represent the meeting and overcoming of one challenge after another as we have learned how to benefit from spiritual teachings and to make good use of material resources and technologies.

Since we lacked precedents for our work and had no special practical or spiritual preparation, we faced several particular difficulties. Our greatest difficulty over the years has been our inability to maintain a sense of spiritual vision. Until we had a better appreciation of the Dharma, it was difficult to understand and to have confidence in the higher purposes for which Nyingma organizations were founded. In the practical realm, we faced daily challenges. No one had professional training in the technical skills needed for complex projects. In addition, many of these projects were unfamiliar to us; having just begun to study and appreciate the Buddhist tradition, we needed continual instruction and guidance from Rinpoche to accomplish projects relating to sacred art, religious literature, and other fields of Tibetan Buddhist culture.

Though we were interested and willing to work, we did not always accept Rinpoche's guidance intelligently. We wanted quick results and often assumed that we knew what we were doing before we comprehended the larger context of our activities.

It took time to develop bonds of mutual trust and understanding, and to recognize our need for greater patience, self-discipline, and self-understanding. These needs have slowed our learning process and made tremendous demands on Rinpoche's time. Until we became more skillful in dealing with the emotions evoked by challenging work, we could easily feel discouraged or confused. Periods of clear communication and productive work alternated with times of confusion, when we lost confidence in our abilities and misunderstood advice and direction.

There were times when what we were trying to accomplish seemed from our point of view nearly impossible, occasions when the lack of funds or technical problems appeared overwhelming. As we have slowly gained confidence and understanding, work has proceeded more smoothly, and good results have come consistently. Now, having worked with Rinpoche's approach over many years, we know that spiritual education and practical work in the world can support and even enhance one another — the synthesis is difficult, but possible, and deeply rewarding.

Students and friends often imagine Rinpoche as a kind of hero with extraordinary patience and abilities. We have seen how he combines knowledge, people, materials, and money in innovative ways to get results no one would have expected. But years of experience have proven to us that his way of working can indeed be learned, if we know how to develop and blend our visionary and practical capacities.

From a talk by Rinpoche, spring, 1987: "Vision belongs to no one individual — each of us can develop more far-reaching understanding and larger goals. But to implement that vision, we need open, independent intelligence and genuine willingness: to give time and energy, to take responsibility, and to practice dealing patiently and persistently with obstacles and challenges.

"To guide ourselves through challenging situations, we need to learn how to work with confusion, laziness, and fears of various kinds. We need good communication and flexibility, as well as the courage to stand for what we know is worthwhile. As we develop deeper appreciation for our efforts and those of others, the broader perspective we need for success will begin to open before us. Over time, these efforts will lead to more consistent motivation, stronger self-confidence, and more precise awareness. As they are tested and refined, these qualities will support our endeavors and link them to an even deeper vision."

To those of us who have persisted over the years, Rinpoche's advice to take work as our teacher has become very meaningful. Work affords us a way to generate a vision and contribute to its realization. At the same time, it gives us the opportunity to learn about ourselves by observing our thoughts, words, and actions. Work challenges us to develop the positive qualities necessary to accomplish our purpose; engaging this challenge refines our knowledge, which can broaden and deepen throughout our lives. In this way practical work is transformed into a means of spiritual growth, while spiritual vision inspires and guides successful work.

Looking back, we see that the original purposes of the Nyingma organizations have evolved, but have not changed. Seeing how much we have learned through our work, we are grateful for the opportunities to develop our spiritual practice and practical skills, while helping to create benefits for others. We offer the results of these years of growth in appreciation to our families and our friends, our culture, our teacher, and the Dharma.

Working with Challenges

Learning to implement a spiritual vision in the material world, we have faced continuing challenges in areas that prove problematic for most new organizations. While our unusual approach has created special difficulties, it has also helped us find creative solutions. In management, we have had to develop our own structures and procedures; we have found that ordinary business practices do not always provide the opportunities for individual growth we wish or the flexibility we need to work in innovative ways with our teacher. In the technical area, our projects have required a great many skills we did not possess. Our staff is small and self-trained; almost all skills have been learned on the job. In the realm of finances, we have undertaken expensive projects that required very careful managing of limited resources. We have had consistent help from many individuals interested in supporting the Dharma, though no wealthy patrons or foundation support. Each of these challenges offered a special opportunity for growth.

The first years were filled not only with Dharma studies, but also with establishing the appropriate legal structures for the new organizations, handling the administrative concerns, and settling Rinpoche's residency status. Besides overseeing these activities, Rinpoche spent much time offering guidelines for study and practice, giving seminars, and counseling students. For fifteen hours a day, month after month, this groundwork required his constant attention and energy.

Conversation with Rinpoche, spring of 1987: "A detailed description of my activities in these first years would be difficult to compile—many issues competed for my attention, each of which required careful consideration. I quickly had to familiarize myself with the way American society operates to guide the first steps of each newly formed organization."

The sheer complexity and wide scope of what the Nyingma Centers are working to accomplish have made both administration and management skills crucial, especially as projects expanded over the years. Each organization specializes in different types of work that need to be coordinated as part of a larger effort. It is difficult at first for individuals to understand how their work interrelates with other projects, and it may take years to develop the broad overview necessary for good management. In the beginning, each step needed to be guided and encouraged by Rinpoche. With increasing experience, students have become able to take responsibility for many tasks, but we still rely upon Rinpoche's inspiration and advice, and in critical areas, his direct guidance and supervision.

To be consistent with the vision behind the Nyingma organizations, our management style must foster individual responsibility and learning. It has not always been easy to combine the needs for both guidance and independence. What has emerged over the years is a basically democratic approach with "veto power" by Rinpoche. Within each organization he has delegated as much responsibility as possible—everything that can run smoothly and properly without his direct supervision is encouraged to proceed. This responsibility is then shared in various ways in our organizations so that one person's opinion rarely overrides another's, and many issues are decided by consensus.

Over the years, Rinpoche has tried to find the best balance of supervision and independence. Once we have developed the necessary skills and clearly understand the purpose of our work, he feels that it is important we take on full responsibility. Certain Nyingma projects may go several weeks or months without direct supervision, decisions being made by workers according to their best judgment. Such a project might come to Rinpoche's attention in its last stages for final review and approval. This process has worked successfully many times, especially as people gain in experience and confidence. Willingness to take responsibility, independent thinking, problem-solving, and creativity flourish under such an approach.

Many of our projects call for skills and knowledge of the tradition that we do not possess, and "creative variations" must be guarded against. Here undersupervision leads to mistakes and duplicated efforts when work must be redone. With the right degree of supervision, workers gain the feedback necessary to learn unfamiliar techniques or to develop the judgment to make sound decisions. On complex work where we do have some training, we do not always know whether we know enough. In such situations, we may be uncertain which decisions Rinpoche needs to make and which we can make independently. It has taken time and experience to know what each type of work requires.

It is sometimes hard for us as Americans to accept authority, but in the end, questions about supervision come down to varied degrees of vision, knowledge, and responsibility. The more we develop long-range vision, accurate knowledge, and the willingness to take responsibility, the more we can rely on our inner guidance.

From a talk by Rinpoche, spring, 1987: "It is difficult to convey the true value of long-range vision that has depth of purpose. Quick intelligence is commonly considered very valuable, but deep vision penetrates past quick interpretations and even beyond sharp intelligence. With patience, you can refine your intelligence toward a very subtle sensibility that sees to the roots of each situation — causes and effects, motivations, conditions, and consequences reveal themselves. When intelligence is devoted to deeper purposes and no longer confined within selfish patterns, new possibilities will open naturally."

One of our greatest challenges has been to develop a broad variety of skills ranging from editorial to heavy construction. We have made good use of books and manuals on technical and business matters, and have sought advice from experts and professionals; but in the long run, experience has been our teacher. For TNMC to flourish, for example, we needed effective community guidelines and attention to the day-to-day running of a large household and Rinpoche's offices. TNMC also coordinated much of the work in other centers, handling communications with the Institute and Odiyan. The Project Office was established for this purpose, as well as to facilitate the growing activities of the Tibetan Aid Project.

TNMC's projects have focused especially on preserving traditional Tibetan religious culture; in addition to printing thankas and creating artwork, TNMC has produced hundreds of prayer wheels and prayer flags and other ritual objects under Rinpoche's careful guidance. In the process, we developed an appreciation for the purposes of sacred art and associated crafts, while learning specific skills such as carpentry, embroidery, painting, silk screening, and sculpture.

Dharma Publishing projects, also centered at Padma Ling, include books in several series for which students needed writing, editorial, research, and translation skills. While none of Publishing's staff was professionally trained in any of these areas, we have gradually learned through experience, and from working with Rinpoche. Sales and distribution of Dharma Publishing books presented a major challenge for which none of us had any background.

The Press has been run by students who have learned book production skills by performing them. Each new type of work and new piece of equipment challenged our abilities. As the Press expanded into a full-scale operation, we had to learn typesetting, camera work, stripping, platemaking, printing, and binding; we needed to learn how to manage time, people, money, and material resources.

The Institute offered us another arena for work in a variety of different situations. Organizing Rinpoche's seminars, handling the publicity and budgeting, and researching the legal and adminstrative structures suitable for the new Institute were important early activities. Gradually, as Rinpoche trained students to be assistant teachers, a new challenge opened before us—learning to guide the learning of others as best we could, taking care not to misrepresent the teachings. Following Rinpoche's guidelines for core courses and working under his supervision, instructors have offered many types of classes that encourage the study of the Dharma and the growth of self-understanding.

Over the past twelve years, Odiyan has undergone several complex stages of development, requiring new skills to be developed at each step. The first stages of locating land, fundraising, and obtaining county approvals were followed by work on design and engineering. Building a rim structure of more than fifty rooms, a temple, a stupa, and several other large buildings required all phases of construction. Completing the ritual art and complex ornamentation that Rinpoche designed stimulated more refined crafts including sculpture, woodwork, tilework, cabinetry, and metal crafts, as well as plating and etching.

This kind of learning-by-doing inspires independent creative action and brings a deep sense of reward. Our beginner's approach has even allowed us to find innovative solutions. But working "from the ground up" does have disadvantages. Until we become proficient, we make many mistakes, which can be discouraging, time-consuming, and expensive.

Working our way through these difficulties, we have discovered that insight into how our minds and emotions operate has helped us learn how to learn. Most members of our organizations have studied meditation and psychology at the Institute or at Padma Ling at various times, and all of us have found useful guidelines for working with emotional difficulties in Dharma books. Over the years, Rinpoche has constantly offered advice and encouragement, urging us to implement whatever self-knowledge we have gained. We have found that this education has prepared us to persevere through discouragement, loss of confidence, and confusion. Study and meditation have helped maintain the clear and balanced attitude that underlies creative learning and fosters enjoyment of difficult work.

In addition to careful management and specialized skills of many kinds, our organizations have needed solid financial planning that is also in harmony with their founding purposes. In the unpredictable economic currents of the 1970s, small businesses and new organizations did not often survive; out of all the spiritual study centers that were established about the time of Nyingma Centers, relatively few continue today. From the very beginning, Rinpoche has urged us to manage our limited resources with great care. Our expenses are often high and call for constant fundraising; art materials and construction materials, for example, add up very quickly on large-scale projects.

While we must find ways to be self-sufficient, Rinpoche has impressed upon us that individuals must not profit financially from the Dharma; the income from Dharma books or art reproductions goes back into materials for more books and art. Finding ways to support our volunteer community while doing as much Dharma work as possible has been an ongoing challenge. Learning to work within tight budgets, to save money and conserve materials, to utilize both time and skills efficiently has been an important part of our education in responsibility, caring, and awareness.

The challenges in each of these areas—management, finances, and technical skills—have been intensified by the small size of our membership. Odiyan usually operates with no more than twenty-five people and sometimes with as few as fifteen. TNMC projects are handled by about ten people at any one time, though for special projects, workers are added from other organizations. Publishing also runs with a staff of about ten, while the Press requires about twenty-five. The Institute staff is usually no more than five full-time people, assisted by part-time faculty and volunteers.

Because of our relatively small membership, most of us have had to learn several different skills and adjust to doing different kinds of work time and again. Confronting work as a beginner can be stimulating and rewarding for some individuals, but others find the beginner's role frustrating and even demoralizing. To find the most effective ways of working, Rinpoche has urged us to develop two particular approaches: to learn to work at maximum capacity as individuals and to learn to work well together as a team. The self-understanding fostered by spiritual practice directly supports more effective work. By focusing on developing better concentration, more stable and consistent energy, and sharper awareness, each of us has increased our productivity and found greater satisfaction in our work. Likewise, teamwork improves as we gain knowledge of our bodies and minds. As we take greater responsibility for the effect our attitudes and moods have on others and on our work, we become more skilled at supporting and communicating with others.

Day after day in our work, we may not always be able to foster broader awareness, take fuller responsibility, and aim at a higher goal. It is all too easy to be influenced by the pull of money, power, and prestige, or by a desire for the more familiar lifestyles around us. Working in the midst of two worlds, however, we have become convinced that the growth in practical and spiritual understanding resulting from this unusual approach is deeply rooted and long-lasting.

Our ways of working bring a deeper self-confidence than those based on material success alone. With practice, we are able to view all experience as gateways to learning and as creative challenges. Once we know how to work skillfully with resistance, weaknesses, and obstacles, challenging ourselves to develop more skills, knowledge, and positive qualities becomes an interesting approach to life. Difficult work can transform into a demanding but fascinating game—we begin to enjoy testing our skills and teaching ourselves.

When we succeed in taking better advantage of challenging situations, we begin to feel new delight in finding room for improvement in our work. The more skilled we grow, the lighter and more playful we feel. In these moments it is difficult to say whether we are working for a goal or for the sheer joy of working. Creative work begins as goal-oriented and purposeful, but opens out into pure action and delight, the self-perfecting activity of human being, which is meaning enough unto itself. Yet the purpose is accomplished and the vision is brought into being: A wealth of knowledge is preserved and made available for others in the future.

A Precious Education for Life

When we look back now at our results, we can see accomplishments that are more than proportional to our resources. Odiyan is nearly complete, the texts of the entire Tibetan Buddhist Canon have been printed in a beautiful new edition, and hundreds of thankas have been reproduced. Many art and translation projects have been brought to successful completion; Institute programs have interested thousands of individuals in the riches of the Buddhist tradition and encouraged the growth of self-understanding.

In one way, it is difficult for us to comprehend how these results have come about, even though we have participated in all the projects. If any of us had been asked fifteen years ago whether such things could be accomplished, we surely would have said—impossible! But in another way, we have begun to realize that the rare education we have been receiving has allowed these accomplishments to come forth.

Realizing that individuals beginning with no special training can become truly innovative and creative workers, we can appreciate the great potential lying unused within our societies. Each of us has untapped talents to develop and unrecognized gifts to offer. If our schools could nurture this potential, they could bring increasing delight and satisfaction into many lives and great benefits to society as a whole. If large and small businesses could emphasize developing their workers' creativity as much as they emphasized success of the company, there might be unforeseen gains all around.

From a talk by Rinpoche, spring, 1987: "The human spirit, dulled by routine and mechanistic living, loves to explore freely and refine its possibilities. With greater encouragement and a comprehensive education in self-understanding, young people would readily become more independently creative. If they were prepared to learn by observing and evaluating their experience intelligently, and taught how to overcome or utilize inner and outer obstacles, they would not need to fear the unknown and the untried. This spirit of exploration and creativity is a precious human resource the modern world cannot afford to waste."

Advice from *Skillful Means*: "In the past, education played an important role in transmitting the knowledge needed to integrate learning and experience, to manifest our inner nature in a practical way. Today this vital knowledge is no longer passed on. Thus, our general understanding of work is limited, and we seldom realize the deep satisfaction that comes from working skillfully, with our total being."

Although traditional education prepares us for a particular role in life, and our careers may seem to lock us into certain patterns, determined individuals can find ways to develop a broader range of abilities and interests. One trained as a scientist may have a deep love of art or poetry; the construction worker may be drawn to the subtleties of the business world or the joys of music; the secretary may possess great talent for writing or a desire to work with people.

Moved by appreciation, we can bring together all that inspires and uplifts us, and find creativity and meaning in each activity. Whether we develop within our profession or move from one type of work to another, we can aim at bringing greater balance and richness into our lives. Out of this more comprehensive approach emerges a new pattern of living, a beautiful mosaic of many colors.

At first, we may feel we have no ability or talent in a new field; or perhaps we feel blocked by defined roles that limit our possibilities. Still, when we have a vision of what we wish for our lives, we can learn how to learn. Confident that questioning and challenging limitations will dissolve obstacles, we can sponsor our own talent and educate ourselves.

Any work situation offers a valuable place to begin a process of self-education. The work we perform reflects not only practical skills and technical knowledge, but also our attitudes, understanding, and emotional maturity: all our strengths and weaknesses. Boring routine challenges our patience and concentration; work that seems beyond our abilities and skills challenges self-confidence. Even these common working difficulties can become interesting learning opportunities if we focus on what they can teach us.

If we are willing to investigate problematic areas as we notice them, our awareness of frustration and dissatisfaction will help us improve our approach. Observing the effects of our actions and attitudes, we can see what supports results we value and what increases difficulties for ourselves and those around us. Once we see for ourselves how unproductive and unhealthy patterns are set up, and how we tend to perpetuate them, we can make better decisions and take more effective action.

With increasing insight into how our attitudes and actions affect the quality of our lives, we can appreciate the importance of taking responsibility for our situation. It may seem at first that full responsibility is too heavy to bear, especially if we are inexperienced at what we are doing. But if we practice determination and self-discipline, we may discover that responsibility rests more lightly on us that we had expected. When we honestly do the best we can in each moment, we create conditions for success in each following moment. Confidence and intelligence expand naturally, opening fresh opportunities for successful activity.

From a talk by Rinpoche, spring 1986: "If we look closely, we see our difficulties arise from three basic shortages: in confidence, in knowledge, and in motivation. To benefit from challenges, we must learn to deal with low levels of these essential human resources. If we begin by acknowledging that these shortages exist, and realize that there is no need to hide or fear them, then these weak spots can work to our advantage. They become the soil from which all the good qualities we desire will eventually grow."

Rinpoche's approach has shown us that even the most hidden side of our heart, our fears and weaknesses, can be gently revealed, appreciated, and uplifted. We become freer to devote ourselves to a larger vision that transcends self-protective instincts. When intelligence is no longer hemmed in by patterns of fear, ignorance, and confusion, our heart, mind, and body begin to refine themselves naturally. As the tangle of conflicting emotions and confusions is cleared away, creative activity freely emerges and expands.

From a talk by Rinpoche, spring, 1987: "When we begin to work for a good purpose that we care deeply about, we find much sharper intelligence and more consistent inspiration available to us. As our work grows more meaningful and enjoyable, and we begin to produce something of value, we can take real satisfaction in our activities. But within this satisfaction there is still a large measure of selfishness—a personal desire for more knowledge, more skills, for more pleasurable work, a desire for status or recognition, for power or money. These self-centered motives can exist side by side with our higher purpose for a while, spurring us on; but soon, we will run up against limits that only a selfless approach can transcend.

"A truly selfless approach appears to be less and less common today compared to the past. It can be very difficult to shift motivation from self-centered goals into a love of higher purposes. It is as though such a love spoke a language the self simply can not comprehend. Its call cannot be heard, its offers make no sense. Why should we give for the sake of giving—without getting wealth, fame, or pleasure in return? But if we aim at this kind of total devotion and open-hearted work, we will find a finer pleasure, a deeper joy than any self-oriented pursuit can provide. The more completely selfless our vision, the higher our achievement, the more dynamic our creativity, and the more perfect our results."

In moments when vision expands to include the benefit of others, we realize that we have a vast network of support that we can draw upon and offer to others. The aspirations and accomplishments of people who have worked throughout history to benefit mankind support our efforts in the present. Any small contribution we can make in our time builds upon past accomplishments and opens new opportunities for the future. Inspired by vision that appreciates this continuity, our actions have the power to benefit other people, and their effects spread in ever-widening circles.

TNMC student: "I do not know whether I have progressed very far toward enlightenment, but I have definitely learned things of great value. I know how to work. I know what is involved in accomplishing something; I have begun to appreciate the fact that I can make a contribution of some value. I do not always think of this in the middle of hard work, but the thought occurs to me more often. We *can* make a difference. Even a few people, if they know how to do something, can accomplish results that have lasting benefits."

TNMC student: "I think one of the most important things I have begun to understand is the quality of truly perfect work. It is like a beautiful bird that lands on a tree branch to sing, and then disappears, leaving behind nothing but the remembered sounds of its song. Or perhaps it is like a piece of wonderful music that brings enjoyment to the musician and the audience, or a fine painting that each art lover can appreciate in his own way, long after the artist is gone. There is something pure and enduring about good work. It leaves behind a good taste, a sweet fragrance. If I could learn to work so that my efforts were channeled directly into this rewarding realm, transforming every trace of the confusion that still underlies most of my work today, then I would be an artist of life."

From a talk by Rinpoche, winter, 1987: "When a true marriage of art and science, of beauty and knowledge takes place, then the whole process of work is transformed. Inspired by love and by joy, human action grows increasingly powerful and brilliant, like a diamond. It radiates sparkling colors and light like a rainbow. Inherently rich and refreshing, like a lovely garden, it also bears fruit for ourselves and others. Such beautiful and pure activity comes forth from love that is unconditioned; it yields immeasurable benefits that satisfy the deepest desires of the human heart."

TIBETAN NYINGMA MEDITATION CENTER

Approaching Unfamiliar Knowledge

The late nineteen sixties in America was a time of ferment, a time when many Americans were questioning traditions and exploring the values of other cultures. The people who turned to the East for inspiration were not only the young, but also educators, health workers, college professors, psychologists, and scientists looking for new understanding. Westerners made pilgrimages to the East in search of spiritual teachings; in America books on Eastern religions became popular, and hundreds of spiritual centers were established. Among the teachers available to the West were a few Tibetan lamas, displaced from their homeland.

The people attracted to Tarthang Tulku's center in 1969 were fairly representative of modern, middle-class Americans. Most had been to college; some were still students, while others had completed a professional training. Many had investigated other spiritual paths,

Padma Ling, TNMC Headquarters

and were interested in the Buddhist teachings personally and professionally.

Like other Americans exploring spiritual traditions, these people felt inspired with a vision of great meaning, but could not see clearly how to bring this ideal into practical, everyday living. Some were skeptical of the "work ethic" in traditional American culture and did not anticipate that work would be part of a spiritual education.

Looking back, it seems that we began blindly, almost accidentally, to study the Dharma. We had no first-hand experience of Buddhism or of the Nyingma teachings— only thoughts and feelings about human possibilities drawn in part from reading and hearing about the Buddhist tradition. We tended to separate spiritual teachings from everyday life, not fully realizing that the Buddhist teachings are about our own bodies and minds and their full range of possibilities. Like anyone who enters a completely new field, we found ourselves facing the unknown, not even knowing enough to ask useful kinds of questions.

Tarthang Tulku in *Crystal Mirror IV:* "Studying the Dharma means to look at ourselves honestly, with complete openness, not as we would like to be or think we should be, but just as we are. The Dharma is vast and subtle. It cannot be evaluated or appreciated without a willingness and openness to study; nor can it be approached from the outside. We need to investigate and internalize the meaning within our own lives.

"We are not trying to escape this world, but are thoroughly analyzing our participation in it. By understanding our own minds, we gain a knowledge no one can take away from us. With sincere study come clarity and certainty, a broad healthy point of view, and the solution to doubt and confusion.

"Over time, the effects and significance of Buddhist practices change and deepen as our minds and hearts become more open. Knowledge is infinite as the stars in the sky, yet the most valuable, the most useful, the most reliable knowledge is knowledge of our own mind. This is the lasting gift of the Dharma."

Rinpoche's approach seemed directly meaningful to us, immediately relevant to our lives. We began to study and practice, meeting at Webster Street for classes. Most of us continued our jobs or university studies, but a few worked full time to help establish the Center. Classes in meditation, philosophy, and art were held on Saturday mornings, while evening classes were devoted to language and Buddhist philosophy. Students also participated in religious ceremonies, and some began the traditional Nyingma preliminary practices.

Over the years, through study, practice, and work, we began to see how vast an undertaking the study of the Dharma actually is. The Buddhist tradition has an almost unimaginable wealth of knowledge to contribute to the modern world. Centuries of Dharma teachings cover a wide range of topics, from natural sciences and the arts to penetrating analyses of the human mind. Hundreds of commentaries by learned masters clarify subtle points of doctrine and offer guidelines for making the philosophy a living experience.

To begin to understand such a tradition, which is at least as complex as modern science, one might easily spend a whole lifetime. These teachings are new to our culture, and the need for a long-range approach to the Dharma is not yet clear to most of us in the West. Thus, we have difficulty cultivating the patience and persistence to investigate such an advanced and comprehensive collection of knowledge.

TNMC students found different aspects of the teachings more interesting or accessible than others. Some of us responded to the ideas and philosophical concepts; others were drawn to meditation. We did yet not understand how the many facets of this tradition fit together and were often inclined to pick and choose what we wished to study. Our initial approach was hardly long-range or systematic!

Though every year more books on the Dharma are available in the West, Western authors approaching the teachings from the outside can offer only outlines of basic principles or academic studies of specific topics for scholars. These do not offer the nonspecialist reader the materials to begin to educate himself in a balanced way. Gradually, as more suitable introductory materials are published, Westerners will have better opportunities to expand their appreciation for the Dharma and to comprehend what is involved in serious study and practice.

As Western interest in the Buddhist traditions has grown, Buddhist studies departments have been formed at a few universities, fostering translations and research. The study of Buddhist history and philosophy in academic environments, however, is very different from the classical approach.

From a talk by Rinpoche, summer, 1987: "To become knowledgeable in a tradition different from your own requires a great deal of time and experience. For example, though I have lived in the West nearly twenty years, I could not say I comprehended Western philosophy in all its complexity or was conversant with its more subtle terminology. Behind each idea or concept extends a whole history of usage. When it comes to Western science, no one would imagine that an individual from a different culture could simply learn English, read books, and thereby become qualified as an expert!

"Westerners who are interested in Buddhist traditions face these same difficulties. Language studies are only a beginning. Philosophical vocabulary in Buddhist texts includes myriads of specialized terms, which shift from subject to subject and from school to school. Even knowledge of Sanskrit is no guarantee of accuracy, for Buddhist Sanskrit differs from other applications of Sanskrit. Beginning in the eighth century, Tibetan translators worked extensively in collaboration with Sanskrit scholars to devise vocabulary to convey the inner meaning of the Dharma in Tibetan. A suitable vocabulary in Western languages will have to be created by Westerners with a sure grasp of the intricacies of their language as well as an understanding of the Dharma.

"To begin to appreciate the inner meaning of the teachings, meditative practice and deep devotion to the Dharma are also required. This kind of training is not considered a high priority among most Western scholars, and this places a limit on what can be successfully accomplished. Systematic study of Sutras and shastras would be very useful at this stage. The basic picture of

Buddhism in the West is still very vague and full of contradictions. Like the blind men who each grasped a different part of the elephant and reported conflicting 'facts,' Westerners have not yet obtained a broad enough perspective on the most basic topics: Who is the Buddha? What is the Dharma? Despite this lack of information, there is an inclination to draw quick conclusions about Mahayana and even Vajrayana.

"Only the most outer form of certain texts and materials can be studied without full participation in the tradition. Tantric studies require rigorous training to bring out the fuller meaning of initial intellectual understanding. The oral instructions and initiations from the teacher and the dedicated practice by the student are essential. Even when Western scholars work together with Buddhist teachers, it is uncertain how deep an understanding can be reached unless teacher and student are both willing to go through these traditional stages.

"The great eighth century master Buddhaguhya warned that intellectual studies without meditative practices cannot bring full understanding. If this is not clearly understood, the Tonpar Zhi (rTon-par-bzhi) are turned upside down, which means that one will be relying on the unreliable. Opinions will flourish and compete, obscuring the path to certain knowledge.

"There is only a limited amount of time and energy one can spend convincing people. At some point, it is important simply to work toward what one feels is meaningful. In my early training, I learned a saying I have often recalled as I work in the West: Log-pa'i lam-la mtha'-med-phyir/ Di-dag 'dir ni spro-mi-bya/ 'Because mistaken views are endless in number, it is not possible to deal with each and every one.' In America, there are many different views, all of which tend to be on an equal footing, for here we say: 'Everyone has a right to an opinion.' This attitude supports the tolerant, open climate necessary for exploration of new ideas, but it misses the difference between knowledge and opinion.

"In my personal opinion, it is wonderful that so many people are trying in their own way to understand the Dharma, but I also strongly encourage my friends and students to balance study and practice. My teachers called these the two wings of the bird, and I believe that for the depth of the Dharma to reveal itself, the intellectual and experiential facets must be united. This is a substantial task facing us today. I do not mean to discourage people, but we need to realize where we stand and what can be accomplished. If we compare our situation to former periods in the history of the Dharma, the modern attitude toward the Dharma is but a shadow of the deep devotion and dedication of those who came before us. But we can make efforts to lay the ground work for understanding. As appreciation deepens, so will devotion and dedication, opening a way to more comprehensive knowledge."

In earlier times in older, more traditional cultures, it was well understood that a spiritual education was best approached with great care and preparation. Aspiring students of wisdom prepared themselves as fully as possible, and considered their purpose seriously; recognizing the need for more knowledge, they would search out trustworthy teachers who could guide their study of human development. Rinpoche has described this traditional type of education as the study of both knower and knowledge itself; by bringing analysis and experiential understanding together, the objective and subjective approaches are unified and deepened.

In the West our understanding of education is very different—both in subject matter as well as in the style of teaching. Modern education focuses on career preparation, not on higher goals such as ethical and emotional training or the development of awareness. Our approach stresses learning based on exchange of information, facts, or techniques, while personal applications are left to the individual.

From a talk by Rinpoche, spring, 1986: "It is very important to study in the traditional way, but this is hard to implement in a culture where the Dharma is new and under the conditions of modern times. Today we are all students of the Dharma. There are no 'perfect masters' such as existed in the past. Those with more experience and training are taking the role of teacher, sharing their understanding and giving guidance to others as best they can.

"Spiritual training is a natural and genuine development, a process of unfolding that requires teacher, teachings, and transmission. People commonly speak of the lineage of transmission as if it were the external connection between teacher and student—who taught whom, and who studied with whom. But this external lineage may survive even when its inner light has disappeared. To assure that the transmission does not become superficial, lineage records note who obtained a full understanding, and who gained successful results. The real meaning of lineage is the continuity of such successful inner realization, the transmission of teachings that actually wake us up.

"In the traditional style of Buddhist practice, the path toward realization begins with taking refuge and receiving initiations. The significance of these activities must be very carefully and thoroughly communicated in a non-Buddhist culture; this requires both time and experience. The meaning must first be comprehended, then the teachings implemented, and results obtained. In Tibet where the Dharma had been deeply interwoven into the culture for centuries, people still spent their entire lives in full-time study and practice to go through these stages of understanding.

"In my experience, the Western way of life does not leave much time for Dharma studies. Daily obligations and activities consume the time and energy that are required to understand and practice. This makes great demands on both students and teachers. Teachers today do not always have time to teach in the traditional way, guiding the long preparation, the detailed study, and the rigorous practice of their students.

"Despite these difficult circumstances, the value of laying the basic foundation cannot be underestimated. Once a greater appreciation of the Buddha, the Dharma, and the Sangha has developed, then more traditional practices might be established. If people try to move beyond the basics without understanding and experiencing their value, good results cannot be guaranteed later. People may then lose confidence in themselves and in the Dharma, which is very unfortunate."

TNMC student: "For a number of years, I attended ceremonies and public teachings by different visiting teachers. The practices made me feel very good, very light and positive, and sometimes remarkable things happened. But then the teachers traveled on, and I could not sustain these experiences by myself. I did not know much about meditation, and I had just begun to read introductory books. I was interested in the Dharma, but I didn't really know what I was getting into. Eventually, I became greatly discouraged when I could not make lasting changes in my ordinary state of mind. I see now that I simply did not have enough background to understand what is involved."

TNMC student: "I initially became interested in the activities at TNMC because I had heard such phantasmagoric stories about the Tibetan tradition—magical empowerments and so forth. I must admit that I was disappointed because there were no esoteric miracles, just plain hard work, study, and basic meditation. I am rather surprised that I am still here. Many times I almost left for something more exciting. But my life began to feel healthier and more balanced, and my perspective slowly has changed. My idea is to gain a little more insight and control over my own mind. That would seem rather magical to me now!"

Because we lack experience of how the spiritual learning process evolves, it has taken us a long time to develop balance as we approach a wisdom tradition; many of us tended to vacillate between skepticism and blind faith in the beginning.

Our traditional education trains us to collect information, organize it, and examine it from the outside. But the level of the mind that performs these operations cannot fully grasp the significance of knowledge transmitted within a tradition such as Buddhism. Our facility with concepts and analytic methods, however, can convince us and others that we know what we are doing, and we may become skeptical of anything that does not fit with our opinions.

From this point of view, we observe each new idea through the filter of our personal understanding, accepting what appeals to us and ignoring or rejecting what makes us uncomfortable or what we do not understand. As we took advantage of the opportunities at TNMC to study and practice more thoroughly, our skeptical and argumentative attitudes began to shift. Tendencies toward self-doubt and close-mindedness have gradually been replaced by more patient and open inquiry.

At the other extreme is the attitude of naive acceptance. Sometimes new students were not inclined to undertake the careful inquiry that would strengthen real confidence and understanding, and support independent actions and decisions. With this attitude, it is easy to become involved in interesting ideas or activities without seriously questioning what we are doing. But in the longer run, this "acceptance" may not hold up.

Many of us were quite young when we began to study at TNMC, and had not fully realized the importance of carefully and independently investigating a course of action. Everyone had more or less idealistic fantasies about a "spiritual way of life" and very little realization of what hard, consistent work is required to increase self-understanding and learn how to change unhealthy patterns. Some students grew discouraged when they met with unexpected obstacles and difficulties, and found their commitment not strong and clear enough to enable them to persevere.

From a talk by Rinpoche, winter, 1986: "To make progress in any endeavor, in ordinary life or spiritual development, we need to consider our purposes and honestly assess our resources so that we do not meet with disappointment in the end. Even without complete understanding of our new undertaking, we can still determine to find out as much as possible, to clarify the value of our direction, and to assess our strengths and weaknesses. Then we can begin to see a path toward new possibilities unfold before us."

Our studies and practice at TNMC encouraged us to question the hidden rules that govern our views and decisions, to inquire into the basis we use for choosing a direction and evaluating progress. No matter how sophisticated our reasoning seems, often we find a simple rule at work. What accords with our expectations and makes us feel good is "good;" what challenges our attitudes and patterns of behavior and makes us feel uncomfortable is "not good."

To evaluate independently, we need to learn how to examine our own thoughts and feelings and sort out different layers of confusion. Each of us must consider for ourselves what brings us lasting satisfaction, what leads toward deeper knowledge, what touches our hearts, minds, and spirits.

If we can recognize which environments and friends support these aspirations, we can benefit by association with them. In the Buddhist tradition, there are sayings that express the importance of this choice. "Living among the mountains rich in gold, even the birds become golden. Growing within the sandalwood forest, even the ordinary tree becomes fragrant." Working together at TNMC over many years, we have begun to understand the value of the environment established by Rinpoche and the support of like-minded friends.

In the end, however, we are responsible to ourselves to make the most of our lives, no matter how confident we are that we are relying on someone or some teaching that is trustworthy. If we take responsibility in the beginning as best we can, our understanding will grow as we learn. The more we learn, the more effectively we can take responsibility. Again and again, we can reevaluate what we are doing, what our purposes are, and how successful our approach seems to be.

Our experience at TNMC has shown us that the ability to question and observe supports all our efforts to learn, from the most practical situations to the most sublime. Through open-hearted, intelligent questioning, we avoid the pitfalls of blind faith and skepticism, and trust ourselves to recognize what has lasting value for our lives. The learning process stimulated by such inquiry can lead to a more comprehensive understanding of ourselves and our world, and gradually mature into spiritual vision.

Tarthang Tulku in *Crystal Mirror VI:* "If we want to explore our situation as human beings, we need to commit ourselves to a truly probing thinking and questioning. Does our life really unfold the way we think? Are our options really so limited? Where do the rules of the game come from? Who makes them up? In asking questions, we do not necessarily have to find answers. The act of questioning itself stimulates something in our nature, and keeps us from falling into unthinking patterns that seem to characterize so much of our behavior.

"By taking advantage of the opportunity that questioning opens to us, we may transform the momentum of our lives; we may learn to harness the power of change, promoting what is healthy and counteracting what is unhealthy. Questioning lets us discover the value of our being on this earth; it encourages us to take responsibility for ourselves and for accomplishing something in the world. It suggests ways to use the vast wealth that this culture puts at our disposal and shows us how to live to the fullest. Our questioning can reach into every aspect of our lives, extending eventually to the global level.

"When we ask basic questions, we begin to turn away from our preoccupation with ourselves and our wants. At once we see things in a broader perspective, and a certain amount of pain, fear, and frustration slips away. We understand more completely the consequences of our actions, and the flow of events no longer catches us totally by surprise. Even if we never use the traditional categories of Buddhist thought, we are beginning to approach the Dharma."

We had come expecting knowledge to be handed to us. Now we discovered that the study of the Dharma begins with the study of ourselves. Over the next years, we would have many unexpected opportunities to increase this knowledge as we learned about ourselves through our work at Nyingma.

Preservation of Traditional Culture

The Tibetan Aid Project (TAP) was established by Tarthang Tulku in 1969 to offer Americans a way to become acquainted with Tibetans in India and to offer their support in a time of need. Under the Pen Friends Program, TAP provided names and addresses of refugees to interested individuals; for as little as $10.00 a month all the basic necessities for one refugee could be purchased in India. Each TNMC student took responsibility for sponsoring a pen friend, and many new friends of Nyingma were also glad to participate. Many hundreds of letters were exchanged over the years as Americans and Tibetans came to know one another personally. Such actions, though small individually, when joined together could make a tremendous difference, not only in the well-being of the Tibetan communities, but also in improving understanding between cultures.

In November 1974, TAP was reincorporated as the Tibetan Relief Foundation (TRF), making it possible to raise and dispense funds for direct relief. The board of directors, composed of TNMC and Institute staff, established a fundraising program through dinners, talks, and seminars. Such events became an important focus of TAP activities for several years. Proceeds from certain projects such as the children's books published in the Jataka Tales Series were also dedicated to relief efforts. TRF's wide range of goals included support for health clinics and agricultural programs, and distribution of food and supplies.

In the beginning, a few friends of TNMC helped administer TAP programs, with TNMC students participating on a part-time basis. Gradually, TNMC students took over the work of maintaining files, keeping track of donations, and coordinating with Indian, Nepalese, and Bhutanese agencies to handle the shipping and distribution of food, medical supplies, and clothing. Since most donations came as small amounts for specific individuals in the Pen Friend Program, it was also necessary to maintain detailed records. Each year, financial reports for the Tibetan Relief Foundation were prepared and printed in *Gesar Magazine*.

Through TAP, donations sponsored by the TNMC Head Lama have been made to monastic colleges and centers of all Tibetan schools. Religious ceremonies at twenty-seven Gelugpa, eleven Kagyu, nine Sakya, and forty-five Nyingma centers have been regularly supported. Over the years, hundreds of books have been donated, and over 60,000 thanka prints given to individual altars and offered to temples. The TNMC Head Lama also contributed assistance to Tibetan masters newly arrived in this country and made it possible for teachers of all the major Tibetan traditions to make nearly twenty different visits to America.

By 1979, the majority of the Tibetans in India had learned new skills and were reasonably self-sufficient. Monasteries and community facilities had been established, and lamas could continue their teaching. Knowing that most people were living in stable settlements, with sufficient food, clothing, and health facilities, we began to give higher priority to other large projects. Work on the new edition of the Buddhist Canon had begun, and Odiyan was entering a critical stage of development. Having offered as much support as we possibly could for many years, we expected the growing number of Dharma centers in the West would continue to support Tibetan Buddhist culture, encouraging and sponsoring the activities of all lineages. Through TAP, TNMC has continued to sponsor religious ceremonies on a regular basis each year and meet emergency needs to the best of its ability.

In 1984 Rinpoche began encouraging reconstruction at Tarthang monastery in Tibet. The previous year he had traveled to Asia together with a few members of the TNMC staff to visit Buddhist sites in Thailand, Japan, and China. Rinpoche located rare statues and paintings to add to the sacred art housed at TNMC and Odiyan, and the staff studied ancient monuments and temples. During this trip, Rinpoche also visited Tibet for the first time since 1959. While he was there, he spent many weeks at his old monastery, returning several years later for a second visit. Though conditions had greatly changed in many ways, people's faith was still strong, and monks at Tarthang had begun to rebuild the monastery complex.

Tarthang Tulku in *Gesar:* "Seeing my old monastery was very disturbing. I remembered Tarthang Monastery as one of the largest, most beautiful Nyingma monasteries in Eastern Tibet, a large complex that had housed more than five hundred lamas. I now saw that it had been completely destroyed; in its place stood only a few buildings, the start of a reconstruction project that will take many years to complete. Two temple compounds, one dedicated to the study of philosophy and art, and the other to practices, have been restored under the direction of my brother, Tulku Pega. Surrounding each temple are living quarters of one hundred units. Since my visit, TNMC has supported reconstruction, as well as rituals, ceremonies, prayers, and the forty-day summertime retreat."

To further encourage the study and preservation of Tibetan culture among both Tibetans and Westerners, Rinpoche began the Tibetan History Series as a gesture of appreciation for the land and people of Tibet. The first volume, devoted to research on ancient history, was published in 1986. Additional volumes on culture, art, and religion are planned.

For the West to continue to receive the teachings preserved in the East, the survival of some of the traditional centers in Asia must be assured. It would be hard to estimate the loss, not just for the West, but for all civilizations, if these ancient traditions disappear. As the problems of the modern world grow more persistent and complex, this precious collection of knowledge may prove to be essential for peace and harmony.

Interview with Rinpoche, 1984: "Modern philosophy has developed some very fine insights into the human situation, but it does not offer a very satisfying way of dealing with passion, aggression, and confusion. It still has no really comprehensive map of human consciousness and no generally accepted view on human destiny. Buddhism has powerful teachings that deal with all these subjects. Until now there has been so little work done with the tradition, so few translations compared to the wealth available, that the West is still in the dark as to the scope of the teachings. The Dharma is truly all-encompassing."

Sacred art, with its power to touch the heart and senses directly, has always been an important complement to the written teachings. Necessary for the powerful visualization practices of Tibetan meditation, art is particularly vital to the Tibetan Buddhist traditions; for twelve hundred years, it has supported the transmission of enlightened knowledge in Tibet. As the Dharma develops in the West, the presence of this art as an inspiration and support for religious practice is essential. Because of its sophisticated perspective and its compellingly beautiful forms, Tibetan art may eventually have profound effects on Western art and psychology.

Today this precious tradition is endangered. It is uncertain how many statues and thankas, some dating back to the eighth century or even earlier, have survived the disruptions Tibet experienced earlier in this century. Few living artists have the training and background to create fully accurate representations, while thankas of the finest periods of Tibetan painting are dispersed in museums and private collections throughout the world, inaccessible to most Tibetan artists and practitioners.

The first sustained contact many of us had with Tibetan art was in 1970, when TNMC began to organize art exhibitions in the Bay Area. Most of the artwork displayed was brought to America by Rinpoche or contributed by friends who supported this project. Since the 1970 art exhibit at the California College of Arts and Crafts was well attended, additional exhibitions were held at Lone Mountain College in 1972–1973, in Berkeley in 1972, and at Grace Cathedral in San Francisco in 1974. These exhibits inspired a film on religious art, produced by a San Francisco filmmaker and directed by Rinpoche. The catalogue for these exhibitions, which included an essay on the principles and purposes of Tibetan art, was Dharma Publishing's first book-length publication, *Sacred Art of Tibet.*

TNMC student: "After the excitement of the opening day, some of us who worked on the art exhibition felt a sense of loss. Surely much more was needed to help preserve this ancient art and to communicate its value within our society. Although color printing was far more complex and expensive than ordinary book printing, Rinpoche felt that it was important to preserve thankas through publication. After working on the art exhibits, we began to better appreciate this need."

Using the small, single-color Harris press acquired in 1974, we produced several large thankas and a portfolio of twenty 8″ × 11″ color prints within the year. Preparing and printing thankas was a major undertaking—to reproduce the different colors, each thanka required as many as seven passes through the press. Each pass demanded tight control by both platemakers and printers, since each new color had to register precisely with all the previously printed colors.

Early in 1978, Rinpoche began to share with us some of his specific plans for publishing a new edition of the Tibetan Buddhist Canon. To complement the texts and preserve fine examples of Buddhist art, he hoped to locate especially beautiful Tibetan thankas. TNMC began a project to research thankas available in museums and private collections; eventually, Rinpoche selected more than two hundred for reproduction in the new edition. In all, this one special project, which involved museums and private collectors in America, Europe, and India, took about two years to complete, while technical preparation and printing spanned nearly a year in itself. Though at the outset we did not realize how much work the project would entail, bringing together the texts of the Buddhist Canon and the sacred art of the tradition was deeply satisfying.

In 1985, when the purchase of a new Heidelberg press gave us the capacity to print high-quality full-color work, Dharma Publishing began another publication and preservation project. The primary purpose of this project was to provide monasteries and private practitioners with reproductions of iconographically accurate thankas painted within the outstanding schools of Tibetan art.

This new project had unforeseen complications. Obtaining permission to reproduce thankas in Dharma Publishing books took time, but presented few difficulties, since such requests are relatively routine for Western museums. But when we sought to reproduce over one hundred thankas as full-size art prints, we began to encounter a surprising amount of resistance, which baffled us at first.

Although some museums recognized that we shared their interest in preserving cultural treasures, and supported our wish to make them available to Buddhist practitioners, others were reluctant to grant permission or charged extremely high fees. These policies raised important questions about rights of ownership related to sacred art. To whom does sacred art belong? Does a tradition lose access to art and ritual objects essential for religious practice if these items pass out of its control under adverse conditions? These issues arise in working with art dealers as well. Rare Tibetan Buddhist temple pieces are frequently sold to individuals with little understanding of their significance rather than to those who would deeply appreciate their purpose and meaning, but have fewer funds.

It may have appeared to museums that we should pay for the right to publish their art works, particularly when the reproductions would closely resemble the originals. From a business point of view, they may have felt that we stood to profit and could well afford the fees they were asking. But large, full-color art prints are very time-consuming, technically difficult, and costly to prepare for publication. We rarely recover expenses; it is usually necessary to subsidize thanka reproduction from other resources.

Out of respect for the value of sacred images, we use the highest quality paper and inks; this care makes the reproductions as useful for meditation purposes as the original thankas. Since we print at most two thousand copies of each thanka, we cannot keep costs down through volume. Eighty percent of what we produce is donated to support study and practice; the prints we make available for sale are priced at little more than cost. While we may seem hopelessly naive by modern business standards, our purpose is achieved: to preserve the thankas and make them available to the spiritual traditions that produced them. From our perspective, each thanka printed is one more treasure preserved.

Publishing staff: "When Rinpoche urged me to persevere, I felt caught between two cultures. On the one hand, I knew this project was important. On the other, I felt obligated to respect the museums' points of view and tried to explain their position to Rinpoche. When Rinpoche asked me, 'Isn't this important?' the question woke me up. Our efforts appeared in a new light: the long years of preparation and sacrifice to develop resources to print sacred art; the cost of collecting prints for the new edition of the Canon; the research to locate specific artwork. I could comprehend the reasons for Rinpoche's pleasure when we could print even a few thankas and share them with others who valued them.

"I began to negotiate more clearly and strongly with museums, querying policies and helping to remove barriers to mutually beneficial arrangements. Several museums cooperated readily, seeing how our work furthered preservation and education—their purposes as well—and were very pleased with the results. In the process, I feel I learned something very important: Accomplishment and skilled communication come from a solid connection with inner knowledge and vision, not from manipulative skills."

Between the fall of 1985 and the summer of 1987 we published fine art prints of more than one hundred thankas, including images of the Buddha, a beautiful series of thankas depicting the Sixteen Great Arhats, and a rare set of thankas portraying the Manifestations of Padmasambhava and Eighty-Eight Great Siddhas. By 1987, eight different thanka portfolios, each containing fifteen plates in full color, and an introductory booklet on sacred art were also in distribution.

Dharma Publishing currently has a total of over 200 thankas in print, in addition to 360 reproductions included in our books, and 120 in portfolios. About 60,000 prints have been donated to monasteries and practitioners in India and Tibet, where they may help inspire a new generation of artists to continue the tradition of sacred art.

It is obvious that so much more could be done if all those who have valuable collections of thankas could promote the publication of sacred art themselves or make their thankas available to those willing to undertake the effort and expense. Unfortunately, appreciation of Tibetan sacred art is still rare in our culture. Because the complexity of the forms requires extensive education to understand, most people can approach this art only as decoration, leaving the deeper level of symbol or blessing untouched. In the future, we hope to continue efforts to preserve sacred art and help make its value more widely known in the West.

Ritual Arts and Traditional Crafts

The Tibetan tradition has developed a sophisticated science of working with subtle energies in nature. Prayer wheels, prayer flags, tsa tsas, and stupas interact with natural energies, promoting balance and harmony; they both stimulate positive energy and protect against natural catastrophes. The centuries-old traditions that passed from India into Tibet and other Asian lands have attested to the power of special shapes and colors, and the efficacy of such prayers.

Prayer wheels were developed some two thousand years ago in India by the Buddhist master Nagarjuna. According to the Tibetan tradition, they are an especially powerful way of offering prayers, bringing balance to nature and benefits to human beings. Within the prayer wheel mantras (sacred syllables) written or printed on paper or film are wrapped around a central axis. As the wheel rotates, the blessings of the mantras are activated and sent forth into the world.

Our first prayer wheels, built in 1970 for the center on Webster Street, were designed to run on electrical power so that they would rotate continuously. In succeeding years, Rinpoche asked us to produce prayer wheels in larger numbers and sizes, and to develop more efficient designs. The first sets of wheels were 35″ in circumference, but within a few years we were constructing much larger ones. In 1973 a 6′ × 2½′ wheel was built at Padma Ling. A 4′ × 7′ wheel was built for the Nyingma Institute in 1974, and a five-and-a-half-ton wheel was installed in the Institute's garden in 1976. By that time, construction on a much larger ten-ton wheel for Odiyan was underway. Within seven years, we rolled 170 three-hundred-pound prayer wheels for the Institute, Odiyan, and Padma Ling, as well as 1,008 hand prayer wheels encased in hammered, gold-plated copper and fitted with carved rosewood handles. The speed of modern printing made it feasible to produce wheels in volume as well as in large sizes.

In planning each new series of prayer wheels, Rinpoche selects prayers and mantras from traditional collections, often including mantras that have the power to protect against earthquakes, particularly important in California. The mantras are printed on press paper 3½′ × 5½′ long, with specially prepared ink mixed with precious substances.

For mantras and prayers to be effective within a prayer wheel, the words must be placed on one continuous horizontal line. Many separate sheets of paper may be required to hold the string of words for an entire prayer, with all sheets being attached end to end and precisely aligned. The pages are then taped together and rolled up on a steel shaft. Modern photographic techniques have allowed us to reduce the size of the printed prayers so that more prayers can be contained in each wheel, thereby increasing the blessings generated by the turning of the wheel.

Working out efficient combinations of bearings and drive systems for the wheels has been an ongoing activity for ten years. A few early workers with training in physics and engineering designed systems, but they were not always successful. Later we obtained the help of experts for creating some of the larger wheels, but their designs did not always work properly either.

Prayer wheels are time-consuming to design and build; they are also expensive. When we are making sets of sixty or more at one time, costly parts become a consideration. By 1977 expenditures for prayer wheels had run into thousands of dollars for mechanical parts, paper, and other materials.

Prayer wheel crew: "Engineers know how to create good bearing systems for all kinds of situations, but you have to be able to describe the system and give them the numbers. For prayer wheels there were many uncertain factors because much of the work is done by hand — we are not dealing with precision-tooled aircraft parts. When we roll that much paper onto a shaft, the load itself is bound to be somewhat uneven, no matter how carefully we do it, because we are doing it by hand. Then there are the difficulties that arise when we are not careful enough. Once, we miscalculated the weight, and the shafts of that whole set of prayer wheels bent slightly. All of this means that the bearings are going to suffer a lot of wear and tear. Over many years, we have collected various bits of advice, considered it in light of our experience, and learned by trial and error. Our first wheels broke down continually and took long hours to repair. The wheels we create now are much longer lasting and more efficient than our original designs."

Since prayer wheels are not part of our culture, it has taken us time and experience to appreciate their value. Prayer wheels are like generators of healing energy that dispels negativity and darkness. Rinpoche has explained that the amount of power they convey depends on the mantras moving like an electrical current in one continuous unbroken line. This was why we had to be so careful in preparing mantras for printing, in aligning them precisely, and wrapping them as evenly as possible. Even if we could not understand how or why they worked, if we took care to prepare them in the traditional way, we could bring their benefits to our land.

Institute student: "When I was first exposed to the prayer wheels at the Institute, I sensed something different immediately, even though there was no way I could rationally understand it. The prayer wheels seem to be surrounded by an atmosphere or energy field that is light and invigorating. I am convinced that everyone experiences these effects whether they notice them or not. These effects might be compared to changes in the weather, which have profound impact on our moods. When I am near the wheels, I can feel physical heaviness diminish, and energy, clarity, and joy increase."

TNMC student: "Pasting strips of paper together for three months, ten hours a day, I found it hard to see what I was learning or who would benefit. Accustomed to more intellectual work, my mind was restless, my hands hurt, and before long, I began to feel resentment and self-pity. Since Rinpoche asked that we chant a short mantra when we do this kind of work, I put all that emotional energy into the mantra. Soon I found myself going faster and faster without discomfort.

"As the paper strips grew into long rolls, it seemed they were linking my efforts to the past and the future. I could imagine people in Tibet doing this kind of work, offering their time and energy for the benefit of the world. I had always thought of prayer as reaching out and pulling something toward me; but this outward-moving, offering quality was much more powerful. It began to occur to me that the value of this work was precisely that it has no value for me personally. At the same time, something was coming back to me as well. Maybe this is what the Buddhist tradition means by meritorious action."

Another unusual craft introduced by Rinpoche was the traditional Tibetan practice of making tsa tsas, small clay Buddha images. These miniature statues are stamped out of clay with a die, kiln-dried, and finished in various paints or metallic leafs. Like prayer wheels, tsa tsas promote natural balance and bring blessings into the environment. Buried in the ground they help balance the energies of the earth.

When we began making tsa tsas in 1976, Rinpoche asked us to produce a set of 100,000. Even though the forms are small, that seemed to be a very large order. We soon found that production was affected by several variables: room temperature, consistency of the clay, the different work patterns as the crew size changed.

The first day, twelve hours of work yielded only 350 images. After several months of persistent effort, the crew found they could average 800 tsa tsas per day. As the working rhythm improved, we produced more than a thousand forms per day.

A set of eight small stupas was also created for the temple at Padma Ling. According to the Buddhist tradition, stupas in any size represent the enlightened mind of the Buddha. The special proportions are symbolically related to different levels of the human body, speech, and mind, to the stages of the path, and to different teachings. Even on the simple sensory level, the shape evokes balance and clarity, and many people who view stupas find themselves naturally attracted to them. The set of eight stupas made for Padma Ling is particularly connected with eight events in the life of the Buddha.

In 1986, we began a project to create over one thousand small stupas. This time we used modern materials such as latex molds and polyester resins for casting.

Blending Eastern and Western knowledge is innovative and satisfying work. It preserves an ancient tradition while bringing a new kind of knowledge into our culture. Over time, we have begun to appreciate the special power of these unusual forms of prayer. Unfamiliar with the principles of ritual objects in the beginning, we did not know why it was important to do things one way rather than another way that seemed to us faster and more efficient. In our impatience, we could easily make mistakes. As we began to comprehend the real value of making stupas, prayer wheels or tsa tsas, much stronger motivation supported us.

Prayer wheel crew: "According to the traditional understanding, once prayer wheels are set in motion, they should never stop. They are like the electricity to a hospital. If it is cut off, the darkness takes over, and disease becomes stronger. To accept this view involves being willing to get up at any time of night, in any weather, to repair a prayer wheel that has stopped. This discomfort isn't a test of one's faith in prayer wheels. It is more a test of one's level of caring about the world."

Art projects at TNMC included not only traditional thankas and drawings, but also sewing projects to create thanka frames, temple banners, and many other types of fabric art. From one-person crews and small projects, large-scale operations gradually developed.

By 1976 we had learned to make traditional altar and ceiling hangings for the Padma Ling temple, as well as welcome banners, an Avalokiteshvara banner, and decorative prayer wheel covers called yolwas. Soon we learned how to frame thanka prints and to create long, cylindrical banners of chevrons. The full-time TNMC seamstresses numbered only three or four and were not professional, except for one who knew design; the rest had learned to sew for personal and practical reasons and had no special training. But by trial and error we learned to produce unusual forms.

Rinpoche shared with us the methods used in Tibet for designing with fabric and creating patterns. Adopting a new approach to sewing was initially confusing, but with practice and encouragement, the sewing crew began to speed up, producing large volumes of precisely sewn flags and banners. After 1974, many new designs were created especially for Odiyan.

Sewing crew: "Rinpoche did not create a pattern the way any of us would. We would have to draw out the design, transfer it to heavy paper to make the sewing pattern, lay it on the fabric smoothly, cut it, and then begin to sew. Rinpoche's approach skipped all the steps! He just gathered up the fabric in his hands, arranged it, pulled at it, studied it, arranged it some more. 'Cut here, sew there!' He has also shown us how to sew based on squares, circles, and rectangles so no fabric is wasted. Very little material needs to be cut if the shapes are properly combined. Trying to follow this more direct approach, we have begun to see that much of what we felt was necessary, careful planning turned out to be unnecessary after all."

Another traditional Buddhist craft that Rinpoche wished to develop in America was making prayer flags. Printed with prayers and sacred images, surrounded with special borders and decorated with chevrons, flags were a common sight on Tibetan hills and rooftops. Flying in the wind, the flags offer continual prayers for the benefit of all beings and touch elemental energies that operate on a subtle level. The first prayer flags were made at Padma Ling in 1970.

The design of a flag is carefully considered, for colors and shapes, like prayers, have specific meanings and purposes. Rinpoche selects prayers and images, and lays out the design for each flag. Types of flags produced in any one year will reflect particular needs. For example, one year when earthquakes were of especially great concern, we created many flags for protection against natural disasters.

Our first flags, printed with water soluble inks on yellow cotton, did not last very long, considering the time and energy we expended in making them. So we began to do research to find more durable materials. When we discovered that certain fabrics and dyes interact with ultraviolet light to break down the materials, we located weather-resistant inks and began using special nylon designed for boat flags and sails.

Sewing crew: "At first we didn't really understand what we were working with. The sewing seemed simple enough, but it requires great sensitivity and complete concentration. With experience you begin to realize that sewing the borders on a flag is like adjusting a precision machine. Everything must match up exactly; nothing can overlap the wrong way. This is quite a feat if you are moving fast to produce large numbers of flags. Because of mistakes, we had to redo flags quite often for years.

"Making frames for thankas also requires special concentration. The different images have very distinct qualities that affect your consciousness, so you have to be careful. We have found it very easy to argue, for example, if we work without enough sensitivity on very powerful thankas. It is a little like listening to dynamic music while you work. You must tune into it the right way, or it will just agitate your mind.

"Even the simplest sewing creates special objects that people have used and appreciated for thousands of years. Sometimes, I can imagine a whole array of people back through time, working on flags like these. The very patterns and designs then seem packed with knowledge.

The rational mind can't follow this, but human beings do have other resources, other ways of knowing, and these objects speak to those parts of the human mind."

Beginning in 1978, sewing projects began to expand. As concentration and skills improved, we began to see more creative possibilities. Even as the products became more beautiful and complex, the volume of our production was increasing. For example, in 1977 we had sewn eight appliqué banners and an entry gate banner for Odiyan. In 1983 we made frames for over one hundred thankas, more than twenty-five temple hangings, four large victory banners, and more than two hundred meditation cushions. We also learned to make better altar cloths, door covers, book covers, and prayer wheel covers.

The number of flags produced also increased yearly. In 1979 and 1980 we made 150 to 200 flags per year; by 1982 we made almost ten times that many. By 1984 we had made a total of 3,800 flags. In 1986, we began making a new kind of flag, reproduced from the victory banners etched in copper for Odiyan. These flags, imprinted with special texts and mantras, were 6′ × 7′, four times as large as any made previously. In all, we produced over five hundred victory banner flags. We also made two hundred special half-tone flags and six hundred flags 3′ square. Many flags were sent to India and even into Tibet.

The large flags were much more difficult to produce. The material had to be silkscreened by hand, and the printing quality had to be unusually good because the prayers must be clear and readable. Although professional silkscreeners had told us that it is impossible to hand-print such large pieces of cloth successfully, we found that it can be done.

Sewing crew: "We discovered that if we reinforced the stitching, the flags would endure weather of all kinds, including winds that can whip the end of a flag at fifty miles per hour. Now our flags last almost two years; the life of a boat banner made of similar material is three to six months."

The complexity of the work also increased dramatically as the sewing team adapted Western embroidery techniques to traditional forms. Special hangings for the temple entryways, for example, were created with an intricate combination of appliqué and machine embroidery, which took a long time to evolve.

Sewing crew: "Our appliqué designs are very subtle and complex, using flowing shapes such as flying birds, curling hair, delicate flowers. You have to learn how to 'paint' with the sewing machine. The whole process for making just one twelve-inch appliqué emblem takes about a week. When the design is final, then the fabrics are prepared with special backing. The shapes are cut, and the actual sewing begins. Since we are creating flowing lines using tiny, close stitches, it takes tremendous concentration and sensitivity. Each fabric, each kind of thread has a different feel, a different amount of tension and movement that it will bear. This is what requires experience."

Sewing crew: "As our teamwork improves, our products have improved too. We have learned by experience how to create what Rinpoche envisions. Some of us are not good with fabric but can draw, others know color and fabric very well now. We have found ways to combine our skills to produce real beauty."

As sewing skills increased, we began using materials of the highest quality. Rinpoche has searched out fabrics from India, China, Japan, and Hong Kong, as well as from America. This care and attention creates a beautiful form that helps convey the preciousness of the Dharma. Even people who do not know much about Buddhism can sense its beauty and richness in vivid colors, fine fabrics, and exquisite designs.

Sewing worker: "Working around these beautiful objects is deeply satisfying. I could sew and sew for many years to come and never grow tired of it. The beauty sinks into your mind."

The Study of Tibetan Art

Since 1969, Rinpoche has guided artists and craftspeople within the Nyingma Centers in expressing traditional art forms in a wide variety of materials. Artists attracted to work at TNMC and Dharma Publishing encountered a new view of the creative process, one that has challenged their patience and flexibility, as well as their artistic skills.

The Tibetan approach to art is very different from that of the West, which values individual expression and a strong personal style. Unlike decorative art or art that conveys a personal message, sacred art expresses the nature of human consciousness through proportion, color, and symbolism. These forms serve as a map that reveals the "terrain" of the mind, promoting understanding of emotions, thoughts, and mental imagery, and leading toward a more enlightened view. Thus, Buddhist art follows exacting iconographical rules, first stated in the Buddha's teachings. To master such rules requires many years of apprenticeship even for traditional artists. Because they are unfamiliar with the principles of sacred art, Western artists face greater difficulties in learning this discipline.

Working without any Tibetan assistants in a foreign culture, and with many projects at hand, Rinpoche has had to make difficult decisions about quality and accuracy in art production. While the Dharma may not in any way be distorted, it is also important to create forms that speak to Westerners as directly as possible. Since certain aspects of Tibetan art are culturally conditioned and do not need to be duplicated exactly, there is some degree of flexibility, although from the point of view of traditional Tibetan artists, such art might not be considered precisely accurate.

While Rinpoche is deeply interested in iconography and art, his knowledge of the subject is not comprehensive; at the same time, our ability to follow and understand directions puts limits on how much can be usefully explained. Some subjects are of such complexity that many years of study and explanation would be required before a Western artist could begin to work. We often lack the patience and the openness to study in depth, and these attitudes are reflected in our results, even when we spend long hours on a project.

Art projects meeting with Rinpoche, winter, 1987: "It is difficult to determine what the best approach to certain art projects would be, and there are several factors that must be carefully considered. Anyone beginning something new knows results will not be perfect right from the start. Most observers say our work is very careful, even overdone; there are, however, aspects that

I know we could improve with more time and effort. At the same time, making additional efforts might not help people appreciate the art any more deeply. If our work leads to the Dharma or in some way supports and inspires people in the West, then it is worthwhile, even if not completely perfect."

Artists at TNMC began by tracing traditional forms from woodblock prints, gaining familiarity with the images in the process of training both hand and eye. Rinpoche worked with them, sharing his knowledge of the artistic tradition and guiding their hands as they prepared borders and ornamental designs for ritual objects and books, or attempted simple line drawings of Buddhas and Bodhisattvas.

Some artists have worked on long-term projects that required sustained concentration and consistent efforts. Between 1979 and 1980, students worked intensively with Rinpoche to produce the 282 line drawings for the new edition of the Tibetan Canon. Artists have begun to paint thankas, using traditional thankas as models. More recently, TNMC students have learned to cast and sculpt images from metals, plaster, concrete, and resins.

Through the years, artists have worked in a great variety of mediums, implementing Rinpoche's designs for stained glass windows, silkscreen printing, copper work, and fabric creations, often projects connected with the Odiyan temple. Some people have become familiar with graphic arts and have helped reproduce the ornate letters of the Lantsa script that are printed on the backs of thankas and in Dharma Publishing books.

In 1983, seven $3\frac{1}{2}' \times 8'$ murals of the life of the Buddha and another of guru Padmasambhava and the masters of the Nyingma lineage were painted for the Odiyan temple. Recently, seventeen thankas painted by TNMC artists have been made available by Dharma Publishing, including seven thankas illustrating the Twelve Acts of the Buddha and a set of nine thankas portraying the various manifestations of Padmasambhava. Another series of TNMC paintings is now in progress.

Artwork at TNMC is a good example of the kind of project that Rinpoche guides step by step. He follows day-to-day progress, making corrections and adjustments until the product is satisfactory.

TNMC artist: "Rinpoche has a vast appreciation and understanding of the art of his culture, and he conveys images with great clarity. In a matter of minutes, he can present his ideas for a project that will keep us busy for months. Then we begin the process of doing sketches and having them reviewed and revised.

"This revision process depends on the type of artwork, for each type requires different qualities. For example, decorative art for a chapter opening is to be done quickly with little revision. Images of Buddhist deities may have many rounds of corrections before they are appropriate. At first I felt frustrated with making small changes, but I usually had to admit that even these subtle changes made a significant improvement in the quality. Eventually I could see this difference clearly."

Working directly with Rinpoche on traditional projects is an experience for which nothing in our background has prepared us. Though he has been in America nearly twenty years, he does not seem to have an "American mind." Perhaps because he has lived in three different cultures and because of his training, his style of working and communicating does not always match the approach that feels comfortable to us.

TNMC craftsperson: "Rinpoche sometimes works so fast, it seems impossible to keep up with him. I imagine he has hundreds of projects in the back of his mind. I have seen him give the actual outlines for several large projects in one afternoon. We just cannot move quickly enough to facilitate everything. If we do move faster, he does too! So it can be very tempting to shy away from working intensively with him."

TNMC artist: "Dharma Publishing art work has to be approached in a very consistent way. It is not something that waits for an individual to be inspired. Often, though, I found myself questioning why it was so important to accomplish so much so fast. I would be reluctant to push myself. But at the same time, I could see that the quality of my work was improving, and my confidence was increasing."

TNMC craftsperson: "From time to time, I have felt that Rinpoche is very demanding or impatient because he wants things finished so quickly. He urges us on as though everything were long overdue. Usually we do not understand the urgency—how much could be accomplished and how important it is. At other times, I realize how remarkably patient he is because he persists in working with us, even though we are untrained and do not fully understand the value of this work. He has to explain things over and over, find ways to correct our mistakes, encourage and inspire us, and rescue one project after another. At those times, I really wonder why he hasn't just given up."

Because Rinpoche's approach does not always fit our logical pattern of thinking, we may misunderstand his directions, or feel we need longer explanations. But many details are hard to convey to inexperienced workers. With so many projects under his care, Rinpoche will often give us a rapid outline of essentials to get our work started, and then fill in the details later as we begin to understand the task better. When both the type of work and the style of instruction are unfamiliar, our preconceptions can easily get in the way of clear communications. Sometimes, we have found that the mind just balks at a large, unfamiliar task.

TNMC craftsperson: "At the beginning, Rinpoche may sketch an outline of valuable guidelines, but we miss part of it because of confusion and a kind of resistance. Once the mind senses how big or how hard the job is, it can easily tune out or start to think up all the reasons why this unusual approach won't work. Part of the mind seems almost to prefer this confusion because then we do not have to take any action. Later we may say that we just did not understand, but it is difficult to know whether that is really true."

Even if we feel we understand instructions, we may take certain recommendations very literally without thinking for ourselves. This mindless approach rarely leads to good results.

TNMC craftsperson: "When we follow mechanically what we have been told, it almost always leads to trouble. We screen out our own ability to think and just follow rules. Then we come back to the 'boss' and say, 'You told me to do it this way!' The open space that invites participating in a creative, spontaneous process becomes instead room to be confused. On the other hand, something may need to be done according to exact instructions, even if it seems like a mistake to our eye—we just do not know enough on some kinds of work to be able to judge. To know which is the case takes experience. We have to understand when we need guidance and when we need to take the initiative."

Though this work requires more patience, openness, and intelligence than we sometimes feel we possess, it is well worth the effort. While contributing to preservation of sacred art, TNMC students have been able to learn both artistic skills and a new way of working.

TNMC artist: "From giving consistent efforts on a long-term basis on a project of such vast scope as the *Nyingma Edition* of the Canon, I came to appreciate the results that could be achieved by making stronger effort. Many aspects of this work required learning new processes, which meant ventures into the unknown. If I was willing to move forward quickly with the knowledge and skills I had, if I was willing to attempt the unfamiliar, then I could greatly expand what I was able to accomplish."

TNMC craftsperson: "The practice of awareness in work is simple and at the same time complex. It is a learned ability to watch one's own thoughts and actions as they arise. The more you watch, the more you see and learn about yourself and others. But there will be a point beyond which everyone refuses to look alone. Then the energy and concentration of awareness are dispersed to thoughts, emotions, and activities. These points in time where we lose the focus of awareness are hard to catch because of deeply ingrained patterns of avoidance.

"Working at TNMC has offered me countless opportunities to see this avoidance in varying situations; my concentration fragments, and then the power of my energy and momentum dissipates. When resistance comes up it shifts my concentration, and I miss a timely conclusion. I eventually conclude the task, but by the time I get around to it my own way, it has lost a sense of vitality and growth. It becomes only a completed job with no memorable quality. What could have been uplifting and satisfying becomes only finished.

"If I can maintain awareness of this simple but devastating weakness, I will become a very powerful and success-filled individual. I will reach a reliable, consistent source of energy and ability. Two decades of practice have made me aware of this power. Perhaps two more decades of practice will teach me how to use it for the good of mankind."

Developing Business Sense

Though our work is quite different from that of a traditional American business, to support our many projects we have had to develop solid "business sense." We need to keep track of how well our limited resources are being used so that funds and materials are available as necessary for each project; we also need to follow specific procedures for records and meetings in connection with the bylaws of our organizations; and we must be able to provide for the basic needs of our members, who are all volunteers.

Our living expenses are moderate, for no one has adopted a luxurious lifestyle, but the costs of running a large house and supplying even the simple needs of our workers in Berkeley and at Odiyan add up over time. We need to have funds, for example, to cover emergency needs, health insurance, auto insurance, and other types of financial plans essential for living in the modern world. Through both TNMC and the Nyingma Centers, an umbrella organization that oversees activities at all the centers, we have established general student self-sufficiency funds and projects to meet expenses. One project, Dharmart Designs, was set up within Dharma Publishing to develop a line of greeting cards, notebooks, and calendars. Its growing sales have provided some additional student support. Learning to invest our savings has also helped us obtain the best return on our limited funds.

Our project expenses, however, have increased year by year, and have required constant attention. Working within a limited budget has been a continuing challenge. Our most expensive projects such as text and art preservation rarely pay for themselves. Odiyan creates no income, while requiring large outlays of funds for building and maintenance. In the last decade, ongoing expenses for projects supervised by TNMC have run into many thousands of dollars each month. Funds to meet these expenses are derived from the sale of Dharma Publishing books, small donations, Institute classes, and typesetting and printing work at the Press.

In the beginning, most of us were not at all interested in business, which we tended to separate from spiritual concerns. How remarkable that Rinpoche arrives in the capitalist center of the world and finds himself urging young Americans to learn good business practices! Most of our members were unaware of how to make up a complex budget or keep good business accounts. At the start, Rinpoche was asked daily to approve one expense or another because we did not make long-range plans. As our projects expanded, this lack of business sense became an obstacle we had to surmount.

Over the years, Rinpoche has especially stressed accounting and budgeting and has laid down several useful guidelines for our organizations, such as over-all assessments at yearly meetings, annual budgets, detailed accounting and requisitioning, and comparative shopping for all large purchases. After getting approval for general operating procedures, the Institute and the Press have generally run their own internal financial affairs.

At TNMC Rinpoche established specific procedures for projects sponsored by the TNMC Head Lama and directly overseen by him: ongoing TNMC, Publishing, and Odiyan projects such as the printing of Dharma books, the reproduction of art, text preservation, and the construction of buildings at Odiyan.

After a particular project was initiated, it would go through a period of design and planning. When preliminary plans seemed acceptable, "take-offs" listing all the required materials would be written up by at least two different people. The project's purchasing agent would then work out costs on all the items, calling at least three different vendors to get the best prices and writing up a complete project requisition. Sometimes take-offs would be written up for several designs, and each of these priced out as well. Requisitions would be presented at a monthly financial planning meeting where Rinpoche oversaw the decisions. Each manager would be asked many questions on requisitions and take-offs, and sometimes hours of discussion were needed before a budget could be approved. Rinpoche stressed considering the alternatives, so the managers learned to gather additional information and to make comparisons and evaluations.

At this same monthly meeting, each project manager would also present the bills for accounts due from the previous month, which could be matched up with that month's requisitions. In this way, the purpose of each dollar spent could be clearly seen. This complicated and time-consuming procedure taught us to keep very careful monthly budgets that could be checked and evaluated at different points.

TNMC student: "If a bill was not accounted for by requisition, then no check could be signed to pay it. After each project coordinator had to pay a bill or two like this out of his own pocket, we learned pretty fast! At first people really resisted this tight control because we did not know how to keep good records. Some people do not seem to have much aptitude for bookkeeping; others are just not interested. But anyone in charge of a project has had to learn at least basic procedures and take overall responsibility."

After years of this carefully controlled approach, one financial manager was appointed to present all of the project requisitions at the monthly meeting. This manager now had to check the budgets and plans carefully before presenting them, which saved Rinpoche's time and gave us a broader overview necessary for long-range financial planning. In recent years, we have not used the formal monthly meeting, but the lessons were learned well: project coordinators keep careful records and work out monthly budgets. Details of many of our budgets are available in *Gesar* (TAP), *Copper Mountain Mandala* (Odiyan), and *Nyingma Annals* (Publishing, TNMC Art Projects).

Once the budget is approved, there follows another round of checking as materials are purchased and delivered. Inventories are painstakingly carried out, for we cannot afford to waste. If our estimates are not accurate enough, oversupplying ties up any extra cash, while undersupplying holds up schedules.

Dharma Publishing for example, has to handle cash flow very carefully. We want our books to be reasonably priced so that anyone interested in the Buddhist tradition can afford them, but they are very high quality books, and expensive to produce. Therefore, the money made on a given title will not always fully cover the costs of production; our books are not "best seller" types, and our market is basically very small, so we cannot make up the difference in volume. Because of the small return, cash may not be available for purchasing supplies such as paper in larger quantities, even though this might sometimes be cheaper. So we must time the steps in production accurately to make sure that materials are available at the right moment, but no sooner.

On big projects, such as the *Nyingma Edition* of the Buddhist Canon, our expenses are tremendous and are not at all covered by sales. We may borrow funds from other Nyingma centers if they can afford to help us. This gives us added flexibility and self-sufficiency, but also requires very careful planning and balancing of priorities within our different organizations.

Publishing staff: "As editors, we were not usually thinking in terms of money. It can be quite a shock to find out how many thousands of dollars it costs to produce Dharma books. When people first begin to realize this, there is often a lot of resistance and ignoring. I think it is partly because none of us is trained in business; but we also resist seeing this larger picture because we start to realize this is an actual business, and we are responsible: Our mistakes cost real money."

TNMC student: "The more we see of this larger picture, which includes the funds, the coordination, the administration, and all the other messy details of ordinary life, the more fully we can appreciate the scope of what Nyingma is trying to accomplish, and what is required to succeed at worthwhile, challenging work. To me, our approach has a very American feeling to it —hard working, practical, and sort of pioneering."

It has been very important for our staff to learn sales and distribution so that our books and art reach those interested in the Dharma. Over the years we have built a distribution system and developed a mailing list. Our salespeople had to learn how to market our books and find ways of presenting them to dealers who usually had little knowledge of the subjects we published.

Much effort has gone into developing catalogues that present our books and thankas accurately and reflect an attitude of respect toward the Dharma. Since our catalogues serve an educational purpose, we preface them with introductory surveys of the Buddhist tradition and information on our founding principles, development, and future plans.

Gradually we expanded our contacts as we gained experience. By 1978 we had sent sales representatives to almost every state and reached markets in Canada, Mexico, and Europe. Not long afterward, we began receiving requests from foreign publishers for permission to translate the Nyingma Psychology Series books. Translated into as many as five languages, our books have now reached most areas of the world. On a recent trip to Europe, our sales representative was welcomed by dealers familiar with Dharma Publishing books in each of the ten countries she visited.

Promoting and distributing books has given us interesting opportunities to work within the business world. Challenging their inexperience, Publishing salespeople have learned how to accomplish results by experimenting, observing, and persisting through difficulties.

Sales representative: "On a personal level, I had to learn how to plan, organize, move quickly, and break through my own resistance. The most frightening situations are actually disguised opportunities. Faced with a new job that might expose my inadequacies, I feel fear raise its head. When I examine carefully what I fear and who within me is afraid, I can find a way to let go of the fear. I will never know what I am capable of if I only do what I already know how to do. This has helped me understand how to open up other people's resistance as well. 'That kind of book doesn't sell well here' sometimes translates into 'I don't know much about that, and I'd rather not deal with it.' I found that when I made the right effort, I could open new possibilities for other people. This has made my work truly satisfying."

Using work as a learning opportunity, we have discovered that the positive qualities developed by a spiritual approach can be effectively applied in the everyday world of business: a strong sense of responsibility, clear thinking, patience and determination, combined with insight into the effects of our actions. It has been very important to take individual responsibility for not wasting our human resources—our own and others' time, effort, and knowledge.

TNMC student: "I'm not sure that my view is exactly in line with the Dharma, but I am seeing my life more in terms of investments—what is worth my time and energy, what will repay me in the longer run? Material satisfaction just does not last that long, so why devote all my resources to that?"

Advice from *Skillful Means:* "As you plan your day, looking ahead to what your work will require, let your mind travel from external irrelevant distractions to an internal immediate concern with the work itself. Shifting from a scattered mind to a focused careful attention will allow you to bring full concentration to each task, and to complete it before starting the next. This way of working dispels the sense that there is too much to do, and never enough time in which to do it. By planning well and directing your energy into your work, you will accomplish far more than you expected.

"You can also review your progress at the end of the day by looking at how much attention and concentration you applied to your work, and how much you accomplished. When you have worked efficiently and well, with all your energy, your mind will feel clear and refreshed, and your body vigorous. Even if you have not accomplished all your goals, your energy will have actually increased, making it possible for you to accomplish even more in the future."

From a talk by Rinpoche, spring 1987: "One of the secrets to accomplishment is comprehending the full meaning of responsibility. Taking more responsibility commits our energy and intelligence to the work, inspiring real discipline and involvement. Our senses sharpen, awareness expands, and we begin to call upon and implement our knowledge. In this way, we discover what is truly possible. We become independent, stable, and self-reliant, and our experience becomes helpful to others. Taking responsibility opens our most precious resources, bringing us genuine knowledge, power, and authority. Since these grow from within, they will support us far better than the power and authority that come from position alone."

TNMC student: "Sometimes it is hard to take full responsibility, especially when it involves admitting our contribution to a problem. If someone just pulls up the carpet, everything underneath comes into plain view — things we put off, little mistakes that add up, a lack of attention here, a bit of laziness there. At each point along the way, we could have made a different, better decision, but we tend to let little things accumulate, and then end up with a crisis on our hands. Once we are caught inside this dilemma, feelings of embarrassment and guilt easily take over. Everyone seems to go through this, like a drama we have to play out again and again until we catch on to the pattern and change it."

Dharma Mudranalaya meeting with Rinpoche, in the spring, 1987: "If we do not begin a job with wholehearted energy and intelligence, we will not get good results. Since we will know that we did not really do our best, we can easily feel guilty. We either blame someone else, or we blame ourselves. While it is crucial to recognize our mistakes, there is no need for guilt, which only damages the spirit. Understanding and educating ourselves do not in any way require guilt. What is required is that we take responsibility for improvement.

"When we find ourselves giving excuses, blaming, or feeling guilty, we should take these as signals that our energy and commitment need to be stronger and purer. With practice, we can respond openly and more effectively to whatever situation arises."

Creating Art for Odiyan

Over the last several years, the efforts of TNMC craftspeople have been directed more fully toward Odiyan projects. Beginning about 1982 the work at Odiyan has gradually shifted from heavy construction toward the creation of ornamentation, religious art, ritual objects, and decorative landscaping.

In recent years, several new series of prayer wheels have been created at TNMC especially for Odiyan. In 1982, 112 three-hundred-pound wheels were built for the temple as well as 112 smaller wheels containing microfilm mantras. In 1984–1985, 364 exterior wheels and 120 interior wheels were constructed. These contained entire Sutras, as well as mantras and prayers. The total number of prayer wheels constructed for all the Nyingma Centers now reached 886; together, they generate over twenty billion mantras per minute, offering prayers for worldwide peace and harmony. In 1987 Rinpoche initiated another large-scale project to add two rings of prayer wheels and two covered walkways around the outside of the stupa.

Nearly five hundred decorated windows for Odiyan have now been produced according to designs and images selected by Rinpoche. Figures of sixty-four Buddhas and Bodhisattvas were sandblasted onto clear glass, while a similar number were silkscreened in gold onto blue glass. More than fifty windows were created with silkscreened images of important lamas, and designs for ninety entryway windows were sandblasted onto glass. Over one hundred cabinet panels and library bookcase panels were etched using sandblasting techniques, as well as seventy-seven flashed amber and colored glass windows for the temple. The images on glass will endure for centuries, casting beautiful reflections in the temple as sunlight passes through the windows.

Because religious art requires the use of the best available resources, TNMC students have been fortunate to have access to a wide variety of fine materials. Only the most experienced craftspeople would usually have the opportunity to work in fine metal or the most expensive synthetics. For example, we use specially ordered mineral pigments, which are hand-ground for paint; wood, metal, plaster, and plastic resins are used in carving and casting; materials such as copper, silver, gold, precious and semi-precious stones are used in plating and ornamental art.

TNMC craftsperson: "Working with such beautiful and precious materials is very satisfying, but it is also a tremendous responsibility, for a small mistake can cost thousands of dollars. The possibility of mistakes is increased because we are continually expanding our knowledge, learning new skills and applying them right away. There is no time for apprenticeship, and no one to learn from but ourselves. Though we do extensive research and obtain the best advice we can on each new project, in the end our own work and its inevitable mistakes are our teacher."

Extensive use of rare metals often makes Americans uncomfortable. In our culture, only the very wealthy or the ostentatious would surround themselves with gold, silver, and precious stones. Why should we use such materials when we have so few funds? Creating the most beautiful product we can is a labor of love and appreciation.

TNMC craftsperson: "At first I really didn't understand the value of what I was working with. I knew it was gold, but I was amazed to see Rinpoche picking little fragments off the ground, saving every scrap. Over time, through working with this material, I began to sense its deep value. Gold has an enduring significance for human beings. It comes from the depths of the earth, a golden shining creation of nature. The more it is tested and refined, the more beautiful it grows—like knowledge. It seems appropriate that we are using this natural wonder to preserve the most precious and wonderful human knowledge—bringing the best to the best.

"Theoretically I understood all of this, but not until I worked with gold every day did I actually feel its value. My mistakes frightened me at first, but they taught me to be careful. Transforming gold salts into beautiful art is a genuine alchemical process. I could sense this shifting and deepening of my appreciation as a corollary, the transformation of an inexperienced worker into a skilled artisan with real appreciation for both the material and the purpose of the work."

In the summer of 1985, Rinpoche initiated a project to create seventy-five life-sized statues of Buddhas, Bodhisattvas, and other deities for the Odiyan temple. The grounds at Padma Ling were converted into a huge outdoor workshop, where a crew of six to ten people worked ten months under Rinpoche's daily guidance. Though a few workers were trained artists, no one had previous experience with sculpture. Our crew was made up of Dharma Publishing staff, TNMC craftspeople, and a few Odiyan construction workers.

Since crafts such as sculpture are no longer very common in our modern culture, we were not sure how to begin learning the necessary skills. We started studying photographs, drawings, and thankas, relying constantly on Rinpoche's advice and inspiration. In addition to developing some understanding of iconography, traditional sculpture techniques, and anatomy, workers researched new materials that might be of use. The goal was to create long-lasting statues in lightweight materials that could be finished in a variety of ways.

In less than two months, nine original statues were sculpted, each requiring two to five hundred pounds of oil-based clay. Molds were made from various rubber compounds, and both plaster and resin forms were cast, with arms and small parts molded and cast separately for each type of statue. Each cast form was then assembled, sanded, and finished into a unique statue in a process that required about six months for all seventy-five. After sealing and priming with special coatings, the statues were goldleafed and ornamented with hundreds of pieces of copper jewelry and ritual objects, also handmade by TNMC craftspeople.

The value of such art was well understood in traditional cultures. As the Buddhist teachings first entered Tibet, for example, the Dharma Kings spared no effort to acquire statues and other symbolic forms that could inspire their people. Though the purpose of sacred art is not easily understood in modern culture, working with these forms gave us the opportunity to sense their power to uplift, inspire, and transmit knowledge. Working closely with Rinpoche, students who knew little of sculpture or Buddhist iconography have gradually learned new ways of seeing and working.

Sculpture crew: "The way we learned to do sculpture is hard to explain, but it was essentially very simple. Even though none of us knew anything, we just started. Rinpoche was carving clay, and he had several of us watch for a while. Then he handed us tools, and we learned as we went along. What we did was not so good at first, but he encouraged us each time we got a little closer to the right form. We would watch him shape an arm, and then we would try the other arm. Rinpoche would comment and point out imbalances, and we would try again. Each time, we could see a little better, and so our effort was more successful."

Sculpture crew: "Working long hours every day with the beautiful faces and postures, we started to sense the real value of what we were doing. Rinpoche gave us talks on iconography, and we could glimpse the meaning of the forms. But after a while, our inexperience and the hard physical work of sculpture drained our energy. The project was going slower and slower and felt like it might come to a stop at any moment. But with Rinpoche's encouragement, we could renew our energy by thinking of the possibility that even our beginner's efforts could truly be of benefit."

Sculpture crew: "While others listened intently as Rinpoche talked about iconography, I found myself far away from my editorial desk, sitting in an enclosed tent with a compressed-air helmet over my head, using a large drill to ream out the inside of some solid plaster statues. By some coincidence, two of the three of us drilling were women, and none of us had used such a tool before. If the tool slipped, I could ruin a statue. How did I end up with *this* job? But as I continued working there in a cloud of white dust, unable to see the end of the drill, I found no room for anger. All my attention had to be focused to avoid damaging the statue. It was a beautiful meditation. Months later when the statues were nearly done, it seemed incredible that Rinpoche could take the energy of ten people like me and transform it into the shapes of Buddhas. Through these statues our energy was becoming a very special gift to American culture."

Speaking directly to the heart, art can transcend language barriers and close gaps between cultures. On a simple level, the image of the Buddha radiates qualities that many individuals can recognize as the finest development of humanity. On a deeper level, a properly created and empowered statue or thanka conveys the energy of enlightenment and the blessings of Buddhas and Bodhisattvas.

Motivated by a growing understanding of the deeper value of our work, we can learn difficult skills more quickly than we would ever have imagined. As our skills increase, the positive results stimulate energy, creativity, more appreciation, and the desire to refine our skills even further. TNMC workers have seen this cycle of creativity begin when we give energy freely and trust that results will come with effort. Appreciating the value of our work for ourselves and for others is a catalyst that dissolves limitations and stimulates a joyful creativity.

Over the last eighteen years, TNMC students have had rare opportunities to work and study with a Dharma teacher, and to begin to appreciate the art and religious traditions of Tibet. Knowing our goals are worthwhile is a great encouragement in a world where meaning and value are often in short supply. When we are able to take this longer view, each small accomplishment brings satisfaction and renews confidence that we are not wasting our time and effort. The results show the value of what has been learned as well.

TNMC student: "I have lived and worked at the Nyingma Centers for ten years and am now fifty years old. Many people my age are peaking in their careers and will soon retire. How will they feel as their energy ebbs and their work is finished? I have learned that work is not something to be picked up and put down at particular times or periods of life. Work inspired by a large vision is a creative and beneficial action; it links us to those who came before us and is our gift to those who come after us in the future."

One organization or one teacher can only accomplish so much, while the need in the West for a deeper understanding of the Dharma seems to be very great. TNMC's contribution is difficult for us to evaluate, but with each passing year, we have seen positive results. Because of Rinpoche's willingness to work with us consistently over a long period of time, slow but steady progress can be made.

TNMC student: "It is almost impossible for us to realize how much time and effort and love Rinpoche has given to these many projects: coordinating all the tasks at different centers, watching the finances, guiding the complex work, and encouraging the students. All day every day he 'troubleshoots.' He picks up the energy wherever it slows down, catches mistakes, and solves problem after problem. Even when he delegates responsibility and tells us to go ahead, we still come back to him for more advice and more suggestions because his vision is so much larger than ours. Each of us gets involved in our particular projects and rarely sees the greater vision that he is implementing."

TNMC student: "I would say that the people here are very talented, and everyone works very hard, but where is the vision and inspiration coming from? All the skills and talent in the world won't accomplish much of significance without an overarching vision. We each need to ask ourselves what we would be doing today if we had not come to work at Nyingma. I'd probably be in a laboratory, doing something useful for science, but would it have the long-term effect of what I am doing today? I sincerely doubt it."

TNMC student: "Caught up in the daily work, we forget the real significance of what we are doing, or how we have learned so much. We forget the beginning, and we forget the process, as if it were almost embarrassing to acknowledge how much we have gained. When I came here I knew next to nothing about the Dharma and sacred art. Now there are days when I feel the satisfaction of real craftsmanship. And my understanding of mind, emotions, and human nature is much deeper and more effective than it was ten years ago. How do you go from concepts and images about human potential to real action and real results? Certainly each one of us can credit our own individual efforts, good intentions, and natural abilities. But there is something else at work here, a greater knowledge that is very powerful, reliable, and true."

The more fully we dedicate our efforts, the more confident we can be that our results will be valuable and enduring. Though some aspects of the founding vision have not yet manifested clearly, and some goals have not been reached or even approached, the roots of real accomplishment are present and growing stronger.

DHARMA

PUBLISHING

The First Publications

In Tibet books were considered extremely precious, not only because of their sacred contents but also because of their rarity. Publishing a book was an exacting and time-consuming process. A wealthy patron sponsored the publication of a chosen manuscript by arranging for it to be sent to one of the two major printing houses, Derge in the east or Narthang in central Tibet. There, a skilled craftsman drew mirror images of letters to be printed onto blocks of wood, and apprentices laboriously carved out the intervening spaces. One by one, oblong sheets of handmade paper were pressed onto the inked blocks and set aside to dry. The dry leaves were stacked in order, the edges painted, and the text wrapped in cloth. Carved blocks were then stored for future reprints.

Only a few copies of a given text were generally produced at one time and distributed according to the wishes of the patron to monasteries, libraries, or friends.

Dharma Publishing Nyingma Edition

For centuries, publishing sacred texts was a way of making an offering to the Dharma and an important means of preserving and spreading the teachings.

Shortly after Tarthang Tulku's arrival in Berkeley, the new Meditation Center made its first attempts at publishing and printing. To reproduce the Vajra Guru Mantra and a small drawing of Avalokiteshvara, the Bodhisattva of compassion, students sought out local companies interested in donating equipment or services. With the donation of a small hand letterpress, TNMC students began to produce brochures, flyers, and additional mantras and images.

To make Tibetan texts, English translations, art, and introductory material on the Tibetan Buddhist tradition more widely available, professional equipment and skills would be needed. Because letterpress printing was painstakingly slow, two students began to learn offset printing. Within a few months, arrangements had been made to use a press at a local shop during the evenings. Full-color reproductions of Padmasambhava thankas were printed in this shop in 1970–1971, the first full-size Tibetan thanka prints ever made in this country, and the first of our art preservation projects.

Publishing and printing activities were soon established in the name of Dharma Publishing and Dharma Press, under the directorship of TNMC. For a time, Publishing and Press functioned as one organization, sharing overlapping staffs. As Dharma Press acquired equipment and staff gained technical skills, activities became more specialized, but the two organizations have always worked in concert. Most publishers do not have such close association with printing companies;

developing both capacities has made us unusually self-sufficient. When Dharma Press moved into a separate location in 1972, editorial functions remained centered at TNMC. In the years that followed, close ties were maintained with TNMC. Staff members of both organizations continued to live at Padma Ling, and the older students helped coordinate publishing, compositing, and printing activities.

Dharma Publishing was the first Buddhist publishing house in America. When operations began, few Westerners, including the TNMC students of Dharma Publishing's staff, knew much about the Tibetan tradition or the vast collections of texts it preserves — works translated from Sanskrit and other languages, as well as thousands of contributions by Tibetan masters. Only a few translations were available, known mainly within a limited academic circle.

TNMC student: "During the late 1960s there were a number of popular books about Buddhism available. I eagerly read all of them and came away with conflicting impressions of the teachings. The Tibetan tradition seemed the most mysterious and the most controversial. I had no sure sense of what was fact or fiction."

In its more than two thousand years of history, Buddhism has developed a variety of approaches to enlightened knowledge, and this wealth of teachings is now beginning to find its way into English. Without a background in the essential views, purposes, and history of Buddhism, new Dharma students encounter many different types of material at once and have no way of knowing where to start their studies. While translations are a high priority, there is a clear need for works that accurately introduce the Tibetan tradition and convey basic Buddhist views and teachings in a meaningful and non-technical manner.

TNMC student: "I had read books about Buddhism for several years, but after studying at the Institute, I realized that I had been very selective. I read only what interested me. I had no sense of Buddhist history, no interest whatsoever in the lives of great masters or even the Buddha. I was intrigued by the philosophy, and that is what I read about, trying to fit it together with ideas from Western philosophy."

Students working with Rinpoche shared the same lack of knowledge as other Westerners exploring the possibilities of meditation and Buddhist philosophy. Initially, each article we edited and prepared for publication had to be carefully reviewed, corrected, and clarified by Rinpoche. Gradually, we learned how to present basic views and history in a helpful way. For student editors and production workers alike, each publication became a training ground for the next.

From a talk by Rinpoche, spring, 1987: "It is very difficult for people to develop balance as they study. They either 'know nothing' and lack all confidence, or they 'know everything' and become arrogant about their small gains in understanding. In the very beginning, people may not be interested in serious study; then gradually they grow eager, but their approach is not grounded in humility—they are still 'deer hunters,' intent on obtaining the musk and indifferent to the deer itself. The true mark of progress in understanding is the growth of humility and devotion to the Dharma."

Publishing staff: "It was very easy—and still is—for us to misinterpret what we work on, or in some way distort or change it. Once we learn a little bit of something 'special,' the mind begins to grow arrogant. Now *we* are special or important. We know something others do not know. This is really sad to see with spiritual teachings, but it happens all the time. This attitude starts to affect our judgment, and we make assumptions about our work, thinking that we know what we are doing. Rinpoche reminds us constantly to watch how the mind twists the truth."

Publishing staff: "It would be wonderful if instead of us Rinpoche had well-qualified, knowledgeable individuals to work with, people trained in the tradition and deeply respectful of it. But in this culture there are not yet people with this complete background. In the meantime, it seems we have to start somewhere."

In 1971 TNMC published the first issue of its new journal, *Crystal Mirror*. This volume described the activities of TNMC and began to relate the history of the Buddhist tradition, the Nyingma tradition in particular, and Tarthang Tulku's lineage. Fundamental Buddhist ideas were discussed by Rinpoche from both theoretical and experiential points of view, providing detailed information that was rare in the early seventies. Some of it is still not available in English anywhere else. We also began to publish texts Rinpoche had brought with him from Tibet, but had not already published in India.

The second volume of *Crystal Mirror* emphasized the importance of an established lineage for transmitting the heritage of the Nyingma tradition, a subject about which most Westerners were completely uninformed. *Crystal Mirror III,* published in 1973, offered readers basic materials on Buddhist philosophy, psychology, and meditation. Translations were made of some traditional teachings from the writings of recent Nyingma masters, and talks by Rinpoche encouraging self-understanding were included. A brief description of the major acts of the Buddha introduced readers to the enlightened guide whose teachings form the heart of all Buddhist traditions. Later, Dharma Publishing would bring out full-length biographies of important teachers, but from the very beginning, Rinpoche emphasized studying biographies of great masters.

TNMC student: "I had been interested in Tibetan Buddhism for many years before I ever read anything about the Buddha. I wanted to study what I thought of as the serious things, psychology and meditation — not history, which seemed like legends and folktales to me."

TNMC student: "When we read the biographies of great individuals, we are usually inspired by their life's strengths and message. But a sense of uneasiness may follow as we try to discern the differences between ourselves and them. It takes a great deal of honesty to face all the things that make us different from those we admire. But reading such works encourages us to begin to examine ourselves in a new light."

Crystal Mirror IV, published in 1975, focused on the early history of the Dharma in Tibet, and included a translation from the works of the fourteenth century Nyingma master Longchenpa, and an informal survey of Tibetan life and culture. An excerpt from a text under translation introduced Padmasambhava, the powerful teacher instrumental in transmitting the Dharma to Tibet, and his twenty-five principal Tibetan disciples, who established the roots of the Nyingma tradition.

Crystal Mirror V, published in 1977, is an integrated book-length survey of Buddhist teachings and history from the time of Gautama Buddha to the decline of the Dharma in India. It includes a summary of the philosophical, psychological, and meditation teachings transmitted to Tibet, as well as short biographical accounts of masters of the Nyingma lineage, compiled from traditional texts and from information based on Rinpoche's studies in Tibet.

Although this more detailed volume took a long time to prepare and proved very difficult for student editors, it provided TNMC students with a valuable overview and served as a foundation for some of the Buddhist studies courses at the Nyingma Institute.

In working on *Crystal Mirror*, we began to realize that efforts to preserve and transmit these teachings extended back many centuries in a history that most of us had never encountered in our university educations. The spread of Buddhism involved the contributions of hundreds of great masters and disciples, the translation of thousands of texts, and the establishment of innumerable centers across all of Asia.

As our view expanded, we understood the vision behind the Nyingma organizations in a new light. While our efforts seemed much smaller in this larger perspective, they took on far greater meaning and significance within the continuum of enlightened knowledge. More aware of our lack of knowledge and the importance of preserving the tradition, we began to sense the depth of commitment required of those who aspire to participate in making the Dharma available in a new land.

The first book-length translations, published in 1973, clarified basic meditation and offered insights into traditional Tibetan practices. *Calm and Clear*, an introduction to analytic meditation by the nineteenth century master Lama Mipham, guides the beginner's study of the human condition. *The Legend of the Great Stupa* presents a narrative by Padmasambhava that demonstrates the power of devotion and the beneficial results of meritorious action. Included in this volume is a simply expressed but deeply symbolic account of the Dharma transmission to Tibet, centering upon the activities of Padmasambhava and his principal disciples. That same year we published *Elegant Sayings*, short poetical expressions of Buddhist insights by the masters Nagarjuna and Sakya Pandita.

Reader: "I do not think people in America knew much about Padmasambhava until Rinpoche published these books. There were one or two important translations available, and perhaps scholars found them useful. But to me they seemed so strange and esoteric, I couldn't relate to them at all. I also believe it was Rinpoche who first began to teach Padmasambhava's mantra. At least I had never heard of it before."

With the founding of the Nyingma Institute in 1972, TNMC's contacts began to include an ever-widening circle of individuals interested in the Buddhist teachings. To inform friends of our activities, TNMC, in cooperation with Dharma Publishing and the Nyingma Institute, began publishing *Gesar News*.

Gesar takes its name from the epic hero of Tibet, the legendary ruler of the kingdom of Ling. A symbol of courage and freedom, Gesar embodies the direct, responsive energy of the spiritual warrior, focused on overcoming inner and outer obstacles that arise on the path to enlightenment. In its first issue, *Gesar News* featured the opening episode of one of the Gesar epics, which continued to unfold in each subsequent issue.

The simple format of the early issues gave student editors practice in type design and layout. *Gesar* and other smaller projects such as the Institute catalogue helped us learn to plan production schedules and meet publication deadlines. The shortcomings in one issue could also be analyzed, and improvements developed for the next. What was learned here, on a small scale, could be applied to production of full-length books in the coming years.

After the first three issues, *Gesar's* scope expanded, and its format changed from a news bulletin into a magazine. The quality of the design was improved by using a clearer typeface, more photographs and line drawings, better quality paper for clearer pictures, and a heavier coated paper for more colorful covers.

Gesar articles edited from talks by Rinpoche conveyed the value of meditation in daily life, addressing questions raised by participants in seminars and classes. Interviews with visiting Buddhist teachers brought their insights on traditional and current topics to *Gesar*'s growing readership. Adaptations of passages of Tibetan texts helped make available the advice of numerous Tibetan masters previously unknown in the West, while motivating students of Tibetan to develop translation skills. To researchers in the future, *Gesar* could serve as a valuable resource for studying the increasing interest in the Dharma in America.

Reader: "I looked forward eagerly to each issue of *Gesar*. It was like my lifeline to the Institute because I lived far away and could only come to classes once a week. I found many helpful ideas in the articles because they were written by people engaged with the Dharma, people trying to find points of contact in their own lives. Participants in the Institute's programs—philosophers, health professionals, psychologists, and artists—often wrote essays relating their own experience. I was very interested to read staff members' descriptions of living and working at the Centers. I wondered what it would be like if I got more involved at Nyingma, and these articles gave me some idea."

As *Gesar* expanded, its small staff, usually only a single editor and a part-time assistant, had to work especially hard at bringing balance to the contents, collecting articles on subjects both useful and interesting to subscribers. This involved encouraging those knowledgeable in such subjects to contribute articles, arranging for photography and artwork, checking facts, and editing final copy. The staff was also responsible for coordinating production with Dharma Press and developing and maintaining subscription records.

Gesar staff: "In the beginning I truly knew nothing about editing. Rinpoche guided my efforts closely for several years, giving me feedback on my work each week. I learned a lot by doing things wrong. When I had given an article what I thought was my best effort, I would present it to Rinpoche. He would often advise me to reduce it by half. Sometimes I am sure that I took out the wrong half. But gradually I saw for myself unnecessary repetitions and unclear ideas."

Now in its tenth volume, *Gesar Magazine* has presented well over three hundred feature articles, including translations excerpted from traditional texts and more than thirty Gesar episodes, as well as articles on Dharma teachings and history, on meditation and relaxation practices, psychology, and fine arts. *Gesar* now reaches subscribers in every state and in more than fifteen foreign countries.

In order to evaluate our progress through the years, Rinpoche urged Dharma Publishing to document the history of the Nyingma Centers and to offer a record of the process of establishing a Buddhist center in the West. The first volume of historical documents, the *Nyingma Annals,* was published in 1975; the second volume followed in 1977, and the third in 1985. These records describe our various activities—classes, publications, art projects, and Odiyan's development—with photographs and detailed summaries. Rinpoche's introductions provide a perspective for evaluating progress and planning toward the future.

Tarthang Tulku in *Annals I*: "It is probable that within twenty years, this [influence of the Dharma on Western culture] will have become so complex and pervasive as to defy analysis, unless we undertake now to provide the material required for future students of the developing trends within psychology, philosophy, religion and society at large."

Our early efforts at publication brought us the great benefit of increasing our understanding of the Dharma. At the same time, we were gaining valuable experience that would support the growth of Dharma Publishing and Press. Learning to work on Publishing projects with Rinpoche was a rewarding but demanding task.

Publishing staff: "We each have had many experiences of presenting an article or chapter we think is edited and finished to Rinpoche for approval, only to find we have made mistakes or wrong assumptions. Then the work must be redone, schedules are delayed, and Rinpoche has to explain again what is needed. The mistakes come partly from inexperience, it is true, but they are perpetuated by our pride or fear. These prevent us from asking for the guidance we need to do the work. It is hard to acknowledge that our problem is self-created. Faced with our mistakes, we grow resentful and defensive or else confused and defeated. These emotional dramas undermine the project, but they can become part of the learning process. Very slowly, we begin to see how self-centered attitudes operate. This work is a very direct, personal education."

Reaching A Wider Audience

In 1975 Dharma Publishing and Dharma Press were incorporated as a non-profit organization under the name Dharma Mudranalaya, which means Dharma Publishing in Sanskrit. This name linked Dharma Publishing in America to Tarthang Tulku's publication efforts in India, and established a symbolic connection with the ancient printing house in Derge. From its inception under TNMC, Dharma Publishing has served two major purposes: to preserve the knowledge transmitted within the Tibetan traditions, and to communicate this knowledge to the West.

Understanding and appreciation for the Buddhist tradition began to deepen as we took advantage of the opportunities Rinpoche offered for studying and practicing the basic teachings. Writing and editing skills were improving as we worked on articles for TNMC's journal, *Crystal Mirror*, and *Gesar Magazine*. Through classes at Padma Ling, we acquired enough knowledge of Tibetan to work with Rinpoche on short translations. By the end of 1974, Dharma Press's acquisition of a modern printing press offered us full book production capabilities. Once students had gained a little experience, making Dharma books available seemed less a distant dream and more a real possibility.

The need for such books was growing more apparent every year. As Tibetan Buddhism entered Western culture, people interested in the Dharma sometimes grew discouraged because the books available to them gave the impression that the teachings were mysterious and esoteric or involved sacrifices modern people could hardly make. How such teachings might become helpful in a society traditionally oriented toward the Judeo-Christian outlook was not yet apparent. Literature, history, translations, and introductory teachings were needed so that people interested in practicing and studying would have reliable information and instructions to guide their aspirations. Though people are often more attracted to meditation than to study, Rinpoche strongly recommends study of Dharma texts to deepen meditation toward genuine insight.

By 1975 – 1976 Rinpoche had created several distinctive series of books to introduce basic teachings to people of various interests and backgrounds, including scholars, philosophers, mental health professionals, scientists, and business people.

Several scholars, responding to Rinpoche's encouragement to translate important Tibetan texts useful for new students, completed translations: Longchenpa's trilogy, *Kindly Bent to Ease Us*, Yeshe Gyaltsan's *Mind in Buddhist Psychology,* and *Golden Zephyr*, by Lama Mipham and Nagarjuna. All were published between 1975 and 1976 in the Tibetan Translation Series.

Oriented toward a general audience, *Golden Zephyr* is a compassionate and accessible teaching on the benefits of virtue and responsible action. *Kindly Bent to Ease Us* is an introduction to Dzog Chen, the Great Perfection teachings preserved in the Nyingma tradition. Beginning with basic insights into the value of a human existence, *Kindly Bent to Ease Us* unfolds the stages of the spiritual path and evokes a deeper understanding of the joyful creativity of enlightened awareness. *Mind in Buddhist Psychology*, a concise analysis of the teachings on mental development, gives Dharma students and psychologists alike a new perspective on the nature of mind, as well as a systematic way to ease stress and develop clarity. Both books became foundation texts for the new Nyingma Institute courses. Recently, *Kindly Bent to Ease Us* has become the basis of year-long programs and special retreats at the Institute.

In preparing and producing books in the Tibetan Translation Series, we watched Rinpoche carefully combine art with the texts in appropriate ways: color plates of thankas as frontispieces in translations; line drawings to conclude sacred texts. The staff began to sense the Nyingma tradition's high regard for books as channels of enlightened knowledge.

The exacting nature of Buddhist scholarship and the range of its philosophical concerns became more apparent as Dharma Publishing prepared a collection of commemorative volumes and anthologies of articles by scholars. *Revelations in Indian Thought, Buddhist Thought and Asian Civilization*, and *Tibetan Buddhism in Western Perspective*, published between 1976 and 1977, offered readers a wealth of new ideas.

During this period of time, Dharma Publishing published works by traditionally trained Buddhist teachers: Dr. Thien-an's *Zen Philosophy, Zen Practice*, and Lama Govinda's *Psychocosmic Symbolism of the Buddhist Stupa*, the first authoritative discussion of the meaning and history of Buddhist monuments. In 1979 *Tibet in Pictures*, a two-volume photo essay by Li Gotami Govinda, was published to document traditional Tibetan art in its original homeland. In preparing these books for publication, the staff gained greater familiarity with traditional terminology, important concepts in Buddhist thought and culture, and the scope of the Dharma teachings.

Simultaneously, editorial staff and artists were collaborating on the Jataka Tales Series, colorful books for children. To demonstrate the teaching of karma and the power of compassion, the Buddha related accounts of his previous lives to his disciples. Known as the Jatakas, or Birth Stories, these tales convey the ethical and moral basis of Buddhism in a lively, forthright manner that people everywhere have readily understood. Many of these stories portray heroic animal characters, whose caring, considerate actions are especially inspiring to young children.

To produce the Jataka Tales, we had to develop more expertise in color printing; artists accustomed to painting now had to work within unfamiliar technical constraints. Editorial and artistic cooperation was unusually important to integrate the story with the illustrations, while production required more preparation and plates than an ordinary book. Between 1986 and 1987, we produced a second set of six books.

In 1975 Rinpoche created the Nyingma Psychology Series to introduce the benefits of meditation and new perspectives on everyday life to a wide audience. Ever since his arrival, he had been exploring the Western traditions of psychology, philosophy, science, and religion for concepts and terminology that would convey the meaning of the Dharma to people of diverse interests and backgrounds. Seminars and classes, daily life situations, and business interactions were all opportunities to discover the attitudes and concerns of Westerners. This exploration of common ground was continued in the Human Development classes, held first at Padma Ling and later at the Nyingma Institute, and attended by professionals in psychology, education, and religion.

Essays contributed by participants in one of these programs were collected for *Reflections of Mind.* One of the earliest publications to explore the meeting ground between Buddhist and Western psychology, *Reflections of Mind* helped introduce a new understanding of the different aspects of human consciousness. Published in 1975, *Reflections of Mind* was the first book of the Nyingma Psychology Series. Between 1977 and 1978, four more volumes in this series appeared: *Gesture of Balance, Openness Mind, Kum Nye Relaxation,* and *Skillful Means.*

Books in the Nyingma Psychology Series appealed to professional psychologists and educators, as well as to people with no special training in these fields who appreciated and readily understood a psychologically oriented approach to human development. *Gesture of Balance* addresses the quest for self-understanding in clear and direct fashion, offering basic meditation practices that build confidence and inner strength. *Openness Mind* helps the reader to work with emotions such as anxiety, fear, and frustration, and introduces meditation practices that channel energy into awareness and deepening insight. *Kum Nye Relaxation* presents physical exercises that integrate the energies of body and mind, promoting clarity, balance and a sense of renewed well-being. *Skillful Means* grew out of Rinpoche's interactions with students and staff of our organizations. It describes the attitudes that deprive work of meaning and supports a positive approach toward work as a key to lasting satisfaction and success in all aspects of life.

Gesture of Balance and *Openness Mind* were valuable resources for faculty and participants in the Institute's meditation classes, while *Kum Nye Relaxation* and *Skillful Means* gave rise to training programs that systematically develop self-healing skills and creative attitudes toward work. By making these books available, Dharma Publishing conveyed the practical benefits of broader self-understanding to many thousands of Westerners who did not have the opportunity to study at the Institute or the Center.

Reader: "With complete confidence I can say that *Gesture of Balance* marked a turning point in my life. I changed my major in college to Humanities and took courses in Buddhism. The teachings seemed to answer basic questions that I had always had. When I realized that a friend was working with Nyingma in Arizona, I began studying in Mesa and Tuscon. Then I worked at Odiyan, and later at Dharma Press. Now I myself was participating in making these books available."

Publishing staff: "When I make follow-up calls to individuals who have ordered our catalogue, I find that many readers sincerely appreciate Rinpoche's books. Maybe they have only read *Gesture of Balance* or *Kum Nye*, but they feel they have gained something of real value, something trustworthy and helpful. When I tell them about our other projects, such as Odiyan or new translations, they often want to make a contribution. People do seem to understand that behind these very basic introductory books is much deeper knowledge that could benefit our culture."

In 1977, Rinpoche presented a new vision of the interrelationship of reality and human awareness in *Time, Space, and Knowledge: A New Vision of Reality*. Discussions of philosophic and scientific ideas were combined with exercises that linked the creative imagination with direct experience. This approach enabled the reader to extend familiar perceptions of space, time, and knowledge into a profound understanding of new principles.

The original manuscript took shape over a two-year period in which more than three thousand pages of Rinpoche's oral presentation were transcribed and then edited. Rinpoche worked closely, first with one student editor and then with several, monitoring the editing process, which proceeded with careful attention to organization and terminology.

Prior to publication, Rinpoche introduced the ideas of TSK in seminars and in a summer program at the

Nyingma Institute. There participants had the opportunity to practice the exercises, which were then further refined. Early responses indicated the value of this penetrating methodology. When the book was published in 1977, one reviewer called it "the most sophisticated cosmology to emerge in years." TSK stimulated requests for intensive programs, which were developed and offered at the Nyingma Institute beginning in 1978.

TSK student: "The discussions are always directed to what is reality—not as abstract theory, but as the underlying truth that arises through one's own investigation. The deeper one goes, the more open everything becomes. No idea, no concept, no assumption is sacrosanct. Everything is examined. This is the knowledge I had always wanted."

Professors of psychology and philosophy were especially interested in the new ideas presented in TSK. Some applied what they found to their own disciplines, noting connections with their own interests. Some wrote about their experiences with TSK in academic classes, experimental group situations, and their own personal investigations. Their essays, together with articles written by participants in the TSK programs at the Institute, formed the basis of *Dimensions of Thought*, published in two volumes in 1980.

Psychology professor: "I would like to share the light that TSK has shed on my study of phenomenology and to show some of the ways in which its methods and insights can radically alter phenomenology, at the same time that they illuminate it."

Philosophy professor: ". . . Tarthang Tulku's teaching is unitary, there being no room in it for conflict among science, philosophy, and religion. I am mainly concerned with calling attention to the fundamental difference between Tarthang Tulku's approach to time, space, and knowledge and those of others . . . it is experiential and experimental through and through, just as any science worthy of the title ought to be."

From 1979 until 1983, Publishing's efforts were directed almost exclusively to the *Nyingma Edition of the Tibetan Buddhist Canon*. During 1984 Rinpoche began writing a new book for the Psychology Series, *Knowledge of Freedom: Time to Change*. This work offers an overview of human experience, inviting us to reflect on how we apply what we know in our lives. Written in a clear, direct style, *Knowledge of Freedom* takes first a historical, then a psychological perspective. In urging readers to assess and develop their own intelligence and abilities, this book encourages a quest for a more comprehensive and satisfying knowledge to address difficulties we face in modern society.

Grounded in insights arising from Rinpoche's years of interacting with people of all backgrounds and interests, the essays in *Knowledge of Freedom* developed out of several years of discussions with Dharma Publishing staff. This book covers a broad range of topics especially timely today, topics that encourage a search for meaning and point to broader possibilities for human freedom. Readers who have had difficulty in comprehending TSK have found *Knowledge of Freedom* a helpful introduction. For the editors, the book became an exercise in responsiveness to a deeper perspective.

Publishing staff: "The manuscript for *Knowledge of Freedom* kept expanding; more chapters were added continually. The text was reorganized in its entirety as Rinpoche shaped its final form and presented more difficult materials. We often encounter our limits in editing Rinpoche's books. Rinpoche will work with us patiently, clarifying meanings and suggesting helpful ways to express them. He gives a remarkable amount of his time and energy to this process. If the finished book is 350 pages, you can be sure Rinpoche gave 600 pages of original material and spent well over 600 hours on it, maybe two intense hours a day for a year. And some books take two or three times that much effort."

Soon after *Knowledge of Freedom* was published, Rinpoche provided Center students with a worksheet of suggestions for study. The book inspired several intensive programs held at Odiyan and the Nyingma Institute. Participants have remarked that *Knowledge of Freedom* offered them a creative approach to self-understanding that was completely free of dogma and encouraged a deeper sense of responsibility for their lives.

Over the years, we have come to appreciate that these books have made a difference not only in our lives, but in the lives of many readers; we have begun to value more deeply the opportunity to participate in preparing them. Contributing to efforts to bring more knowledge into our culture gives us deep satisfaction, for we know our time and energy is not lost, but will continue to have results in the years to come.

Opportunities for Learning

In the early years, our editorial staff seldom exceeded four people, whose only editorial experience was the previous Dharma Publishing book they had worked on. Shifts in staff necessitated an ongoing process of training new editors, which took place in the course of work on brochures, catalogues, and manuscripts for books.

Our biggest challenge was our lack of understanding of the Dharma. Rinpoche has stressed the importance of developing the open and appreciative attitude that allows real learning to take place. Very gradually, with continuing study and Rinpoche's guidance, we have begun to appreciate the basic teachings. The more we glimpsed the deeper dimensions of the Dharma teachings, the more we realized our own need for knowledge. Often we did not even recognize that we might be making mistakes, for everything was unfamiliar — the concepts, the images, the whole approach to knowledge. Our work, however, gave us a special opportunity to study, and year by year we have learned more about the Dharma and more about ourselves.

From a talk by Rinpoche, spring of 1987: "The Buddhist teachings of enlightenment are much more comprehensive than what most Westerners think of as 'knowledge.' Extensive preparation is necessary to approach such teachings, and to say it is easy or effortless is misleading. At the same time, to discourage people with the difficulty of the task is not helpful. In America, people say 'You get what you pay for.' That seems true for the Dharma as well. As much effort and intelligence as you invest, that much knowledge comes back to you."

Dharma Mudranalaya meeting with Rinpoche, spring of 1986: "The work of each individual becomes a study process. To do editing here, for example, you have to study the Dharma teachings. To accomplish your projects you must also practice the Six Perfections: generosity, discipline, patience, effort, concentration, and wisdom. Gradually, this learning process produces results within the world and within yourself."

Staff members soon found that expressing unfamiliar technical concepts called for an openness of mind that proved difficult to achieve. Buddhist concepts may be translated into English terminology that seems familiar, but the implications of these concepts are not often the same. Publishing staff had to become sensitive to new meanings and learn to question the connotations and nuances of English words much more closely. The style, too, had to be carefully developed to convey thoughts clearly to readers of differing backgrounds. Rinpoche gave us twenty-eight guidelines for writing and editing.

Later, these guidelines were integrated into a preliminary style manual.

In more recent years, most of the Dharma Publishing staff have been women. Though Western cultural tradition assigns intellectual work to the province of men, Dharma Publishing has found that women have no more difficulty than men in learning research and editorial skills. A good editor must be sharp and penetrating, yet receptive to and supportive of the contributions of others. In this way, the unique strengths of each editor can support areas in which others are weak, bringing balance and perspective to the work as a whole. Developing an ability to be sharp, flexible, and open-minded seems equally difficult for men and women.

In preparing one of Rinpoche's books for publication, the principal editor works closely with the author to shape a rough draft into a more finished manuscript. When the book seems to be drawing to a conclusion, another editor or perhaps a whole team of editors may be asked to review the manuscript. At this point new material might be given, or styles of expression modified. Though this process is time-consuming, the result can be a richly textured presentation free of personal interpretations and editorial idiosyncracies.

Publishing staff: "Before I began to work with Dharma Publishing books, I had never done any editing, although I had a good background in English, and my teachers had always been pleased by my interpretive abilities. But this interpretive faculty caused difficulties. In editing, I felt compelled to establish connections between statements that had personal and profound meanings for me, and I tended to incorporate my own conclusions. This tendency soon became a great burden, slowing the work and causing confusion for myself and for others. When I was able to see the arrogance and selfishness in doing this, not to mention the danger of distortion, work became easier and more successful."

Working in a group shows up personal resistances and gives us an excellent opportunity to develop the qualities known in the Buddhist tradition as the Six Perfections. In the beginning, none of us could see our own weaknesses and strengths clearly. Lack of self-understanding has added unnecessary difficulties to the work: emotional conflicts, confusions, time wasted in poor communication.

Publishing staff: "My critical faculties make me a good editor, but when these were joined to my temper and my impatience, the result was very destructive. This has taken years for me to see, years of being put into positions that would show me both the negative and positive aspects of a critical mind."

Publishing staff: "I felt I was a good editor because I was flexible and could see different points of view. When I worked in a team, I found that some of this flexibility was actually uncertainty. Faced with this same pattern over and over again, I saw that a lack of concentration was undermining my ability to penetrate more deeply into the material. As my concentration improved, I had much clearer perception."

Over time, editors have seen how their own attitudes directly affect the outcome of the work. Possessiveness or opinionatedness block good editing; negativity has an immediate effect, preventing the appreciation of the material essential for working carefully and sensitively.

Publishing staff: "Appreciating the real value of the manuscript is perhaps the most important thing. When that awareness is present, then the work energy becomes dynamic, and people keep working for the sheer joy of seeing the result. Knowing that what you are doing matters is deeply satisfying. You keep thinking that maybe this book will make a difference to someone, really help someone. What could be more satisfying?"

Dharma Publishing projects require cooperation and good communication among editors, pasteup, and production people at the Press. Working together, we have noticed interactions that masquerade as real cooperation. For example, "cooperating" or "being friendly" may actually be a way of promoting one another or generating an air of excitement that stirs up energy, but does not create anything very useful. This "positive energy" can be fascinating until we see that it is not based on anything stable. Emotional factors that impel us toward "mutual support"—loneliness, uncertainty, lack of confidence, various fears—can in the next moment turn us into competitors or even enemies.

Publishing staff: "We 'work well' with people we feel most comfortable with, ones we can control or influence. This is what we usually mean by cooperating! When difficulties arise, however, you can observe how readily people will undermine each other and blame each other. Working in a group has been a real education for me. I had no idea how much we secretly enjoy others' faults and weaknesses, and even support them. There is a part of each of us that does not want the other person to improve. Their weaknesses make us feel more secure, and they give us a scapegoat—I couldn't finish because *he* forgot something."

As each individual has developed more awareness and willingness to take on responsibility, we have been able to work together more effectively. Rinpoche has often reminded us that teamwork depends on good communciation, and communication with others depends on how well we understand ourselves.

Guidelines from Rinpoche, 1986: "Try to recognize the situations co-workers are in and sense how they feel. When we are able to appreciate our own positive qualities while clearly seeing our weaker side, then we can view others in this same balanced and friendly way. With this bond we can cooperate readily and openly, moving toward a common goal. Concentrating on the quality of the work instead of competing with one another, everyone can contribute their best work and support a truly creative process.

"At the same time, each individual needs to develop strong, independent self-confidence. This also fosters better cooperation, for we are not interacting on the basis of weakness and defensiveness, which only creates hidden emotional undercurrents. If each person can combine cooperation and self-confidence, then actions become both flexible and very clear-cut, like a dancer's precise moves that mesh perfectly in time and space with his partner's every step."

Publishing staff: "To complete the preparation of a huge four-volume translation, Rinpoche added three extra editors and four additional pasteup people to the project for a short period of time. We worked together in one large room for several weeks, moving material as fast and accurately as we could through the stages of paging and corrections. To complete all the cycles and keep material flowing, we just kept trading typesetting, editing, and pasteup functions among us, according to who was available and what needed to be done. Because the energy was so high, people were glad to stay on into the evenings, completing work others would need in the morning. If we make the right overlaps in scheduling, we can save many days of 'lag time.' Even a few years ago, we could not have worked so well together."

The more skillfully we can work together as a team, the more possibilities expand before us. With more energy, skills, and knowledge available, vision can naturally unfold. Teamwork brings the joy of working toward a common purpose with like-minded people; our appreciation for the efforts of others grows, and our perspective widens. We recognize how our efforts are being supported by the work of the whole group and by all of the work in the Nyingma Centers.

Those of us who have worked together a number of years have begun to grasp the larger context of our work: Rinpoche's gift of knowledge, time, and energy; the original ideas, the planning and coordination he provides; the resources and opportunities he makes available; the efforts of our co-workers to support our work. All these contributions have been required to sustain Dharma Publishing. Though our focus often narrows down to the daily difficulties we are facing in our particular projects, remembering the larger context changes our perspective. We feel the desire to offer something of value in return, as gestures of appreciation and ways of sharing with others what we have learned.

Now that our books are fairly well known, we receive applications from people searching for editorial positions, and we find ourselves trying to convey to others the value of what we are doing.

Publishing staff: "Answering some of these applicants' letters, I at first felt apologetic mentioning the kinds of projects we work on. I knew they would probably not understand why we do not offer people substantial salaries to do complex work such as editing and writing on difficult subjects, projects with foreign languages involving typesetting, proofreading and sometimes pasteup. My discomfort made me reflect on the way we work and what it offers.

"Where else would an editor have such opportunities? How much would I have to pay to receive this kind of education? How long would I work as a beginner in each aspect of the work I do now, before receiving any real responsibilities? How far could I progress before my opportunities were confined? Where would I find an employer willing to push me beyond my limits and work patiently with my lack of knowledge? Where could I work on books that have so much value for people's lives? Where else would I get to write and rewrite material that expresses enlightened knowlege until some of the real significance begins to sink in? This is more of a whole life education than a job."

The Nyingma Edition of the Tibetan Canon

In 1979, Dharma Publishing began research and preparation for publishing the *Nyingma Edition of the Tibetan Buddhist Canon*. The Canon, an entire library in itself, is the most comprehensive collection of Mahayana Buddhist texts in existence, translated into Tibetan from Sanskrit, but also from other languages.

In addition to the direct teachings of the Buddha (the Kanjur), the Canon includes texts composed by more than seven hundred masters of the Buddhist tradition (the Tanjur). It is also a repository of treatises on ancient arts and sciences, many of which are found nowhere else in the world today. This collection, which preserves about five thousand texts, spans more than three hundred volumes in Tibetan and represents the combined efforts of nearly five hundred Indian panditas and more than four hundred Tibetan translators. While a large number of these works were brought into Tibet and translated during the eighth century, translations and revisions continued until the fourteenth century, when the texts were compiled into the Tibetan Canon.

From one perspective, undertaking such a monumental task was extremely impractical for our small organization. While we could draw upon modern technology, we had no experience with large-scale production; the expense of such a project was far beyond our means, and we had no source of outside funding. Traditionally, printing an edition of the Canon has required the patronage of rulers or wealthy laymen, as well as the sponsorship of outstanding religious leaders, the participation of scholars, and the skills of hundreds of woodcarvers. With such support, most editions have still taken many years to produce. Even photographically reproducing one edition thirty years ago required three years of work for one Buddhist foundation. The *Nyingma Edition* was envisioned as much more complex—a new presentation in a modern format.

While living in India, Rinpoche had seen the need to preserve the canonical texts in a format which would withstand the passage of time and provide a basis for translation into modern Western languages. By 1979, it was even clearer that the survival of the Canon was endangered. The condition of editions remaining in Tibet was uncertain, and few copies of the Canon existed outside of Tibet. Scholarly research and translation were hindered; students learning translation often had difficulty gaining access to the texts. With so few copies extant, the texts were vulnerable to loss or destruction.

Initially, Rinpoche gave us a broad overview of the purpose and value of publishing the *Nyingma Edition*, as well as the research and production stages involved.

Press production managers were asked to review what equipment would be needed and to determine the best methods to accomplish each phase of the work. A large-scale research project was quickly set in motion. Under Rinpoche's direction, Dharma Publishing located and acquired copies of all available canonical editions. Important Tibetan resources such as catalogues, indexes, and lineage records were made available to the staff. Rinpoche shared his knowledge of the texts and repeatedly described the kinds of information needed for the *Nyingma Edition*. To begin, we researched several major library collections and collected all the Western resources available, including catalogues of the Canon and extant Sanskrit manuscripts.

Publishing staff: "Before joining the work on the Kanjur and Tanjur, I had no knowledge of the Buddhist Canon. Besides hundreds of Sutras and thousands of tantric texts, there were more than twenty other categories of texts and elaborate networks of commentaries and subcommentaries. I was amazed at the work of the early translators, who seemed to have produced more in one lifetime than whole universities do today."

While staff familiar with Tibetan began studying the Tibetan resources, others were assigned to look into the Western materials and began more extensive library research for useful bibliographic and historical information. Since Sanskrit texts were the basis of the Tibetan Canon, we were encouraged to find out what Sanskrit manuscripts of canonical texts still existed and where they were located. If we could provide this information, as well as information on translations into major

Western languages, our publication would be even more useful for scholars and translators.

In addition, we were asked to collect and study a wide range of resources, even if their value to the project was not immediately apparent. Faced with large quantities of unfamiliar materials, we learned how to sort through a mass of information, review it, organize the results, and present them for evaluation as quickly and carefully as we could.

Research soon evolved into a dynamic educational process. In daily meetings with the staff, Rinpoche reviewed the collected findings, explored the connection of each aspect of research to the overall plan, and indicated where additional information was needed. As new possibilities emerged, priorities were reexamined and new goals established.

Publishing staff: "This was a huge project — the largest publishing endeavor ever undertaken in this country. Few people outside the Nyingma Centers even thought we could do it. We didn't have the money or the manpower, let alone the scholarship. Time after time, I was asked to do things I considered myself incapable of doing. For example, over the years, I had resisted learning much Buddhist philosophy, but now study became my work. Another example was creating charts cross-referencing all editions of the texts — a logistical nightmare to me. But it grew clear that if Rinpoche thought something could be done, it could in fact be done."

Once basic research procedures were established, Rinpoche requested more detailed information on texts, Dharma history, linguistics, scripts, and archaeological discoveries. Soon we were compiling a bibliography for each text with lists of editions and translations in thirty-five languages; information on the classifications for Buddhist texts; data on the history of all the canon compilations; and historical outlines of Dharma transmission throughout Asia over fifteen centuries.

Often authorities in specialized fields were contacted to clarify unfamiliar subjects and identify controversial issues. In this way, much valuable information on little-known languages, manuscript holdings, and specific editions and translations came to our attention.

Publishing staff: "Rinpoche emphasized that he was not a scholar, and that we would have to work very hard if we were to achieve results that we could publish. But he certainly knew how to ask questions! I sometimes tried to take shortcuts — there was just so much to do, I couldn't cover every area. But he could find the places where I was uncertain, and he continually encouraged me to go further. Even when I felt confident that I had done all I could, a few questions could open up another whole area that we could explore. The more receptive the staff became, the more we could participate constructively in this dialogue, and the more we could expand all areas of research. I had never worked harder, or learned so quickly, before."

As research began, a team of eight to ten people began to prepare the texts for reprinting. Over 200,000 folios of Tibetan texts were checked for missing pages, photographed, trimmed, and set into new frames, while the original blockprint art was carefully cleaned and retouched. Since the pages were unusually wide, all pasteup elements such as running heads and folio numbers had to be placed individually by hand. This process, which continued a little over a year, produced more than 50,000 pages of Tibetan texts. Printing of the text pages was completed on Padmasambhava's birthday in July, 1980. In honor of that auspicious occasion, we published the *Guide to the Nyingma Edition,* a preliminary mini-catalogue. The experience of producing the *Guide*, which listed every text in Tibetan script and in Sanskrit, together with authors and translators, was invaluable practice for the exacting work ahead.

About this time, Rinpoche met with the staff in a series of planning and evaluation sessions to create a total design concept for the *Nyingma Edition*. Introductions, title pages, ornamental scripts for Tibetan, Sanskrit, and Chinese, charts, lists, maps, and timelines were carefully designed to present a wide variety of information. We wanted to include Tibetan and Sanskrit titles, authors and translators, as well as text information such as chapter and commentary listings, comparative data, and historical information. The recent completion of thanka collection and line drawing projects allowed us to include many reproductions of fine thankas. The bibliographical information was to be reserved for the *Research Catalogue,* which would be prepared as soon as time permitted.

Every element was designed with great care—from charts and title pages to protective parchments for the art, endpapers, and cover designs, even the material for slipcases. Only materials of the highest quality were used. Cost considerations, technical limitations, and time-saving short-cuts were overruled time and again in favor of materials and designs that would insure both beauty and durability over several centuries.

Publishing staff: "It is difficult even for those of us on the staff to comprehend how one person could conceive of and implement such a complex design. Even though decisions on specific elements evolved over time, Rinpoche seemed to know just what result he was aiming toward—the most useful and beautiful edition we could produce. His approach gave new meaning to the idea of 'doing your best.' We usually take this to mean pushing ourselves enough that we just begin to reach our limits; anything more is 'impossible.' What Rinpoche means is doing everything you can think of, everything you have energy and knowledge and time to do, and then some."

We soon began assembling, proofreading, and checking at every stage of production—an incredibly painstaking process that involved all of our staff. Cooperation, organization, and flexibility were essential. The sheer volume of the material magnified every oversight, error, or lapse in communicaion into a problem of major proportions. At times, staff members became frustrated and lost patience with what seemed an ongoing test of human endurance; personality conflicts could surface abruptly, slowing the work and creating confusion. For more than two intense years, producing the *Nyingma Edition* was a rigorous daily practice in awareness, patience, and determination for the staff of Dharma Publishing and Dharma Press.

Publishing staff: "To work well on the Kanjur and Tanjur required being open and cooperative, willing to give and receive help, and to offer time and energy without thought of personal gain. These attitudes were not just appropriate to working on religious materials; these attitudes were prerequisites for getting any work done at all on this gigantic project."

Publishing staff: "While working on the *Nyingma Edition*, I began to see that this may be the kind of effort we read about in the Sutras and shastras. I am grateful to have seen it in action, even if it did feel like being caught in a hurricane at times. I realized my own idea of effort is to work within schedules that seem reasonable to me, to take three days if three days are available; I work at my own pace and resent having my schedule speeded up. Pushing myself to finish quickly so that my time is available to do other work just did not occur to me as a serious possibility, although Rinpoche had been asking me to do this for at least five years. Left to myself I would be satisfied, even proud, of accomplishing far less. Maybe that is why we have difficulty in valuing the work we do. Some of our projects require capabilities we do not even imagine possessing, and thus we cannot really believe we participated in them."

Pasteup artist: "In my earlier experiences with pasteup at the Press, the proofreading cycle was a relatively painless correction of a few minor mistakes. But once the *Nyingma Edition* pages entered the proofreading circuit, they seemed impossible to retrieve. When they finally surfaced, they were covered with hundreds of tags indicating errors, queries, changes, inconsistencies, possible misspellings, items to check or recheck. The continued handling was wearing out the pages and making it easy for the pasteup to move around. Weather conditions were also causing trouble. What seemed straight one day was definitely crooked the next. We had to hurry or else we might be destined to redo our work again and again, never finishing."

Even the more experienced people in leadership positions had never done coordination or organization on this scale. Our staff was so small that we had to let go of one job to perform another to keep the work moving. With people juggling several different tasks at one time, we sometimes made scheduling mistakes and lost the momentum we were trying to maintain. We gained very useful experience in developing flexibility and determination, but it was often an uncomfortable way to learn.

Pasteup artist: "In the beginning I was asked to perform pasteup, which I knew quite well. Everything was prepared for me and I did my job. But soon I was asked to substitute for the coordinator for a few weeks. There was more to do than I imagined, but I could cope for a short time. When the coordinator returned but did not resume this job, I realized it was mine. I had a lot of trouble being in this leadership position, since I confusedly equated it with an ego-trip. My feminine upbringing had taught me to be passive and a follower. Now I had to manifest assertiveness and strength. Frankly, I had no choice. The job called for these qualities, and I had to manifest them."

Completed in 1981, the *Nyingma Edition of the Tibetan Buddhist Canon* encompassed 120 separate volumes. In addition to the reprint of the entire Derge edition, this edition included nearly six hundred texts drawn from two other Tibetan editions, nine major works preserved only in Chinese, and a special edition of the Bhadrakalpika Sutra.

Publishing's efforts now focused on completing the *Research Catalogue* and preparing a revised and expanded edition of the *Guide*. The *Catalogue* was envisioned as a compilation of canonical information that would be a useful resource for researchers, translators, and bibliographers responsible for building library collections of Buddhist texts and translations.

After the prolonged effort to complete the *Nyingma Edition*, the staff had mixed feelings about resuming the demanding work. Having sustained high energy efforts for months of production, we found it difficult to engage the new work wholeheartedly. As workers felt the momentum building for completing the *Catalogue*, some could see their working patterns more clearly.

Publishing staff: "I was now accountable for results once again, and I started to get very uncomfortable. My usual approach has been to work hard, impress my superiors, and then coast on the image I have established. When I saw this familiar pattern emerging, I realized how much it undermined work I truly felt was important, and how often I had settled for far less than I was capable of doing. Surely I could let go of this habit in order to capitalize on past results and reinvest the energy of accomplishment more effectively."

As of the spring of 1983, the *Research Catalogue/ Bibliography* spanned eight large volumes, a total of 4,200 pages with more than seven thousand entries. Basic information, such as listings of chapters and commentaries, was reproduced from the *Nyingma Edition*. Charts listed locations of the texts in all Tibetan canonical editions, as well as in the Mongolian Canon. Text bibliographies included existing Sanskrit manuscripts and editions in some fifteen canonical languages and translations into modern Western languages. A unique numbering system was devised for the bibliography, in anticipation of entering this information into a data base and updating it periodically.

A comprehensive reference text to all editions of the Tibetan Canon, the *Catalogue/Bibliography* contains supplementary information as well: comparative charts cross-referencing all editions of the Tibetan Canon and two editions of the Chinese Canon, extensive listings of Sanskrit Buddhist manuscripts, a separate bibliography of the Pali Canon and the major Pali commentaries, and a selected bibliography of research tools such as bibliographies of Buddhist materials, canonical studies, manuscript catalogues, and indexes.

Because of unusual efforts necessary to complete the *Nyingma Edition* and *Catalogue,* our small staff had deepened their understanding of the tradition and had gained invaluable lessons about work, while making a substantial contribution to the Dharma in the West. No one who worked on this project could ever again fully believe that inner voice that says "I can't."

One hundred and eight sets of the *Nyingma Edition* were produced and distributed to selected major libraries and research centers in the United States, Europe, Asia, Australia, Tibet, Mongolia, China, and Japan. This wide distribution of the canonical texts will ensure their survival for many generations to come.

While the significance of this publication was not always fully understood by the public, its sheer size and complexity, the beauty of the art, the quality of the materials, and the unique completeness of the edition were soon recognized. "Publisher brings out monumental work on Buddhist teachings" (*Chicago Tribune*); "120 Volumes on Buddhism coming out" (*The New York Times*); "Sacred writing of Tibetan Buddhism published in 120 volumes, 65,000 pages" (*Los Angeles Times*); "A major breakthrough in preserving a vast source of knowledge" (*Toronto Star*); "A magnificent tour de force of the printer's art"(*The Japan Times*); and "Milestone in Buddhist history" (*San Francisco Examiner*).

Creating Beauty for the Dharma

A finely crafted book can reflect the qualities of the Dharma through its beauty, durability, and lasting value. Though such craftsmanship is rare today, a fine book holds universal appeal and inspires a natural respect for its contents.

From the beginning, Rinpoche stressed the importance of creating beautiful Dharma books, preparing them with the greatest care, and using only the highest quality materials in their construction; ideally, the contents and design complement and enhance one another. Drawing upon the artistic heritage of the Tibetan tradition, Rinpoche developed the design elements that now characterize Dharma Publishing books.

Over the years, Dharma Publishing editors, artists, and production staff have participated in the creative process of book design: the selection of typeface, the placement of type on the opening pages, the color plates or line drawings, and the format of contents pages and chapter openings. By his example, Rinpoche taught us to take into consideration every detail of design and production including the grade of paper, the cover material, and the binding method.

Pasteup artist: "At first my attempts at designs are not completely satisfactory, but it is important to have something to begin with. Then Rinpoche can guide the design from there, and I can see how to improve. Especially when we are working with traditional images and designs, we rarely know the best way to present the material because we do not know the meanings of many elements. But these mistakes are an important teacher, for they reveal the path to appropriate action."

Clarity of design has evolved simultaneously with clarity of content. Publishing staff are encouraged to take full responsibility for manuscript preparation, to the extent of proofreading manuscripts seven times in various stages of production.

Publishing editors try to work as closely as possible with pasteup artists, who usually prepare the actual layout of the book. Another cycle of revisions is often done to fit the typeset copy onto pages to obtain a pleasing, balanced page or to end chapters with special illustrations or ornamentations. The final pages are usually proofread once again both by editors and by Dharma Press proofreaders. These expensive and time-consuming steps are reduced or eliminated altogether by commercial publishers. But in light of the importance of Dharma books, and our intention to keep them in print indefinitely, the staff has learned to appreciate the value of extra effort, even if it means experimenting with new approaches and redoing difficult work several times.

Publishing staff: "Since Dharma Publishing editors and pasteup staff work closely with each other, as well as with typesetting and camera personnel at the Press, we can be very flexible. To test a design, we can process a sample page or chapter overnight. If there is a better way to do something for a Dharma book, we will usually try to do it, even if it involves extra work.

"This flexibility, however, can create confusion and delay if we do not use it properly. Since we are open to changes long after a commercial company would have frozen the material and sent it off to printing, we can let certain procedures wait 'until later,' or we can hesitate in finalizing aspects of design and doing the final rounds of proofreading."

In the long run, our unorthodox approach creates very fine products. Our books are considered "impossibly labor intensive" or "overdone" by industry standards, but we have no completely fixed guidelines that define what is possible. More consistently, our books manifest the creativity and caring that appropriately ornament Dharma books.

Since 1978, the volumes published in the Tibetan Translation Series have reflected this care in design. *The Life and Liberation of Padmasambhava* contains reproductions of fifty-eight full-color thankas and hundreds of original drawings prepared by staff artists under Rinpoche's supervision.

Because the thankas are historically and spiritually important, parchment overlays were prepared that outline each figure on the thanka, enabling readers to easily identify the numerous images in each thanka. Printing the full-color thanka reproductions, aligning them precisely with the parchment overlays, and inserting them properly into the books required more sophisticated technical skills than had any previous publication. Prepared in two gold-stamped, clothbound volumes, with endpapers imprinted with mantras and large type well spaced on the page, this publication set a high standard for future volumes in the translation series.

In implementing the designs for the many elements of the *Nyingma Edition*, Dharma Publishing and Press staff greatly increased technical skills; case-binding, gold-stamping, and gilding equipment acquired for the *Nyingma Edition* have made it possible for us to consistently produce Dharma books of even higher quality. Translations are now published in fine editions with gold-stamped covers, gilded edges, numerous parchment-protected full-color plates, and graceful ornamental art. Two-color line drawings of protective figures and stupas appear at the end of each book, accompanied by mantras in the ornate Lantsa script.

Dharma Publishing designs and formats have begun appearing in other books, a true compliment to our work. It is satisfying to see our efforts beginning to inspire other publishers; at the same time, we would hope to encourage others to make their own individual efforts, for the creative process is deeply rewarding in itself, and many different beautiful books could result.

In 1985, we published a beautiful and comprehensive volume entitled *Copper Mountain Mandala: Mystic Land of Odiyan* to document the history of Odiyan. This very special book explains the Odiyan legacy from the perspective of the significance of the mandala. It traces the background of Odiyan's founder, describes the efforts necessary to build Odiyan, and explores various possibilities for the future. Illustrated with hundreds of photographs, beautiful full-color art of many kinds, and extensive archival summary charts, this huge volume is the most elaborate book we have yet created.

Copper Mountain Mandala had its genesis in the summer of 1983 after the temple was constructed and the mandala of Odiyan was nearly completed. At this point a small collection of photographs was assembled for a press release. Rinpoche began adding to the material, assembling documents, and composing a narrative.

Pasteup artist: "This was a remarkable book to work on because of its length, its great beauty, and its complex design. It took about eight hours to lay out each of the five hundred pages, and several rounds of typesetting to fit copy around illustrations. There were charts and graphs, maps and diagrams, line drawings, colored designs, halftones, tints, color photos, black and white photos, polaroid shots, instamatic prints — a veritable scrapbook of material collected over many years of work at Odiyan.

"The challenge was to present all these kinds of materials in a meaningful and harmonious way. A book with some five hundred photos requires a delicate balance between text and art. Each page was unique. The editor was rewriting materials to fit the photo pages, while pasteup was changing sizes and shapes of photos to fit text. This process took over a year and a half to complete. The end result offers people much more than a document. The beauty of the book manifests appreciation and giving, which I know will be transmitted to the readers."

Since the book was printed in 1985, a series of art and landscaping projects have brought added beauty to Odiyan's physical and spiritual environment. As they form an important part of Odiyan's history, we plan to incorporate materials documenting these projects also. Distribution of *Copper Mountain Mandala*, planned for 1985, has been deferred until projects now underway are completed. In its final form, *Copper Mountain Mandala*, a record of one effort to bring new knowledge into this culture, will serve two purposes: For those who have contributed to Odiyan's growth, it will commemorate the lasting value of their work and support; for future generations, it will serve as a record of the beauty and meaning that can be created when efforts are guided by deep purpose and far-sighted vision.

Translations and Research Projects

Although translations from Tibetan texts were appearing more frequently by the late 1970s, progress was slow in light of the vast quantity of valuable works preserved in Tibetan. In addition to encouraging qualified scholars, Rinpoche had supported students' early efforts at translation, and considered the feasibility of preparing English versions of translations made into other Western languages. The biography of Padmasambhava, one of the most important Terma or "Treasure Texts" preserved in the Nyingma tradition, existed in a French translation that expressed the literal meaning of this profound account well enough to be useful for beginning students of the Tibetan traditions. Translated by two professors of French who had participated in programs at the Nyingma Institute, *The Life and Liberation of Padmasambhava* encouraged Dharma Publishing to undertake another such project. Work began immediately on the next volume of the Tibetan Translation Series, *The Voice of the Buddha*.

The Voice of the Buddha: The Beauty of Compassion, the first complete English translation of the Lalitavistara Sutra, was based on the French translation and compared with the Tibetan translation as preserved in the Tibetan Canon. Though the translation from French was begun in 1976, editorial work had to be delayed until after the completion of the *Nyingma Edition*. Since the Lalitavistara Sutra is as important to the Buddhist traditions as the Bible is to Western religions, an English translation seemed particularly essential for new Western Dharma students.

In describing the Buddha's life and early teachings, the Lalitavistara Sutra conveys the insights, attitudes, and resolve that insure success on the spiritual path. This authoritative work, spoken by the Buddha himself, expresses the nature of a fully enlightened being in a way that integrates the explanations of all the Buddhist traditions. For Western students, it dispels the confusion arising from modern interpretations emphasizing historical and psychological aspects of the Buddha.

To introduce the Buddha more completely to modern Western readers, it was decided to review an early English translation of the Jatakamala, a collection of twenty-eight episodes of the Buddha's previous lives assembled by the great master and poet Aryashura. This translation, checked against the Tibetan text, then rephrased in a more modern English style, became the basis for *The Marvelous Companion*, published a few months after *The Voice of the Buddha*. The Jatakas clarify the Buddhist meaning of compassion, which far transcends our ordinary concept, and communicates a profound understanding of karma by revealing the ever-widening range of benefits created by enlightened actions and compassionate intentions.

With these works in progress, it was decided to bring out another biography, *Mother of Knowledge: The Enlightenment of Ye-shes mTsho-rgyal*. This work is especially important for Western students of the Tibetan traditions. In describing the training, development, and achievements of one of Padmasambhava's principal female disciples, it demonstrates the pure dedication to enlightenment needed to benefit from the Vajrayana practices. The manuscript, compiled by a student from Rinpoche's oral translation years before, had also been set aside during work on the *Nyingma Edition*. In 1983, it was again reviewed with the Tibetan original, edited, and prepared for publication.

In the process of preparing these manuscripts, Publishing staff who aspired to develop translation skills began to appreciate the challenge of translating from Buddhist languages. Seeing the difficulty of comprehending (let alone expressing) views and concepts for which English has no satisfactory equivalents, we began to understand the extent of the communication gap between Eastern and Western traditions. We listened to Rinpoche's explanations and worked with extreme care, revising and checking material again and again as we consulted with him and gained more understanding.

Publishing staff: "I must admit I had not realized that Western attempts at translation are still so incomplete. Rinpoche pointed out that texts such as Yeshe Tsogyal's biography have many levels of richly symbolic meaning embedded in the narrative; it seems almost impossible for a translation to present all of them, even assuming we could understand them. I began to realize how complex the terminology was, and how our efforts would only touch the surface of this profound work."

Work on these books led to preparing a new translation of the Dhammapada. A concise anthology of Buddha's teachings on spiritual practice and everyday living, the Dhammapada is beloved by all Buddhist traditions. First noticed by Westerners in the eighteenth century, this text has often been translated as an exercise in learning Buddhist languages. As the basis of our publication, we chose a Tibetan translation prepared by the twentieth century Tibetan scholar, Gedun Choephel. To encourage readers interested in translation, we included the Tibetan text, a wordlist, and a trilingual glossary of important Abhidharma terms that we had found useful. Published in 1985, the *Dhammapada* offers students of Buddhist thought and Tibetan a rewarding text for study and translation.

The knowledge and confidence we were gaining in editing and translating enabled us to undertake the first English translation of the Bhadrakalpika Sutra, a teaching that demonstrates the qualities of fully enlightened beings and the Perfections that develop the potential for enlightenment. This Sutra offers descriptions of the thousand Buddhas predicted to appear in this aeon, revealing an expansive vision of human possibilities.

Entitled *The Fortunate Aeon*, the Bhadrakalpika Sutra was published in 1986 in a four-volume edition after more than three years of preparation. Begun as a translation project in a Tibetan class, the rough draft of the translation was finished in 1984 and refined many times over the next two years. While this process of refinement could have been continued, considering the value of the text, it seemed best to offer it as a preliminary translation. To facilitate further study, the complete Tibetan text was printed facing the English.

Publishing staff: "Working with Dharma Publishing books, I have learned to respect the power of language in a new way. Rinpoche's sense of English is excellent: He has a fine grasp of the subtleties of English expression. When we read something back to him, he will pick out any words and phrases that are slightly 'off.' I began to get a sense of the care that must have characterized the ancient translators' efforts. Though they translated thousands of texts, they chose each word thoughtfully, creating beautiful and deeply meaningful expressions. Perhaps one day in the future, the Western world will have the Tibetan Buddhist Canon in a fine English translation."

To encourage the development of translation and Buddhist research on a wider scale, Dharma Publishing, together with TNMC and the Nyingma Institute, co-sponsors the Yeshe De Project, established in 1983. Under its auspices, scholars will have the opportunity to work at Odiyan on projects connected with Buddhist studies research and translation, assisted by a trained research staff and supported by the facilities of Dharma Publishing.

Since the Yeshe De Project is closely linked to the development of Odiyan, full-scale projects will begin as the necessary publishing and research facilities are expanded and plans are made for specific projects. In the meantime, we have continued to develop research skills gained during work on the *Nyingma Edition*, and have offered results of some of our preliminary research in several types of publications.

A substantial amount of background information on Buddhist subjects was offered to readers in volumes VI and VII of *Crystal Mirror*, both of which were published in 1984. Volume VI, based on Rinpoche's recollections of his education in Tibet, provides serious students a more comprehensive perspective on the meanings of Buddha, Dharma, and Sangha, as well as an overview of Dharma transmission through Asia, surveys of the four major and eight minor Tibetan schools, and short biographies of 132 outstanding Buddhist masters and translators, each illustrated with a line drawing reprinted from the *Nyingma Edition*.

Crystal Mirror VII places the development of the Dharma in a broader historical perspective, using study aids first developed for the *Nyingma Edition*. Each chapter's information is summarized using two-color maps, augmented with timelines that compare the chronologies of major events in the East and the West. Sections covering the history of the Buddhist Canons and the prospects for Dharma transmission in the West are supplemented by an extensive bibliography and a guide to reading the Tibetan script.

Tarthang Tulku in *Crystal Mirror VII:* "Investigating the Buddhist written tradition lets us begin to appreciate the enormous wealth of knowledge that the Buddha has made available to humanity, and helps us prepare for deeper study. Tracing the evolution of Buddhism through different countries and cultures, recognizing how often people from every way of life have dedicated themselves to the Dharma, we can renew our confidence in the value of the Buddha's teachings."

Publishing staff: "Working on *Crystal Mirror* was like a crash course in world civilization. I had studied Buddhist philosophy and history at the Institute and had learned a great deal. Doing the research myself, however, on such a wide range of topics, I began to sense relationships between ideas and history, between cultures and philosophies. Developing an accurate compilation of detailed information is an important aspect of good research, but a sound overview is needed too. The volume and scope of what we try to accomplish is always pushing us toward a wide perspective."

In the last several years, the Yeshe De Project has maintained the focus on translations and historical research. In 1986 and 1987, it sponsored publication of *The Fortunate Aeon*, as well as two translations prepared by Western scholars: *Master of Wisdom*, a collection of translations of seven works by Nagarjuna, the founder of the shastra tradition, and *Joy for the World*, a delightful play by Candragomin, the seventh-century Buddhist master.

Under the auspices of the Yeshe De Project, we began the Tibetan History Series, devoted to research in areas related to Tibetan literature, history, and civilization. In 1986 we published *Ancient Tibet*, a collection of research materials on Tibetan history. Focusing on the land, the people, and the ancient empire, this book provides a solid background for anyone interested in the study of Tibetan culture. Drawing together data from Tibetan, Chinese, and Western sources, it is a valuable introduction to ancient Tibetan history, complete with maps, timelines, and a lengthy list of materials for further study. Volumes on religious history and traditional culture are planned for the future.

Although we would like to spend much more time on research, we find it difficult to balance all our priorities. Yeshe De and Dharma Publishing often share staff, and as we undertake one project, we are compelled to set another aside. While it is possible for some individuals to work on several projects at once, this does not always give good results. On the other hand, interrupting a project breaks the continuity and momentum, making it difficult to resume six months or a year later.

While the various aspects of the Yeshe De Project are at different stages of development, it is best envisioned as a large-scale and long-range undertaking. In the near future, if the opportunity arises, we hope to be able to preserve additional Nyingma publications. Although such an undertaking would require more work than the *Nyingma Edition* project, preserving the precious texts in the lineage of the Nyingma Canon would be a significant contribution to the future of the Dharma.

Working at Dharma Publishing has given us a rare opportunity to grow in understanding while we help preserve Buddhist teachings and make them available to modern culture. Combining these aims creates a most unusual kind of education that synthesizes study, work, and practice, while creating results that benefit others as well as ourselves.

Publishing staff: "Through the years my attitude toward serious study has gone through different stages.

In the beginning I thought I really understood something about Buddhism because I had read a lot of books. When I began to study at the Institute, I realized I did not know very much. Then I started to work at Publishing, and I could not believe how fortunate I was to work on the Kanjur and Tanjur project. But after a while, I began to take this opportunity for granted; I started learning a few things, and again I was 'knowledgeable.' I even began to resent it if I did not get to work on certain interesting manuscripts. After years of research projects, I have a better sense of the scope of the Dharma, which helped me realize how little I understand. I am sure everyone working at Publishing has come to some similar sense of their own limitations.

"But there remains an underlying possessiveness toward knowledge that shows through in subtle ways all the time and causes tension and difficulties among the staff. Whose opinion is right? Who knows more? We even compete with Rinpoche! Once we put time and effort into a project, we think it is *ours*, as though we had the ideas and the knowledge all by ourselves. This arrogance makes it very hard for Rinpoche to work with us. We become so full of our own opinions that we can not receive anything.

"Rinpoche has often reminded us that the more someone studies, the more humble he or she must become. But this attitude is not exactly natural to our way of thinking and takes constant practice. I am beginning to see that in the long run that is the only way to learn."

Advice from *Skillful Means:* "Humility is an experience of the commonality of all human beings. It leads to a balanced outlook on human nature that takes into account all the strengths and failings each of us is subject to. Pride is actually a sign of our lack of self-confidence and self-respect. Because we cannot accept our own shortcomings, we maintain a false view of ourselves. We compete with those around us, point out others' faults, and ignore their abilities. But such comparisons and judgments only expose our lack of self-knowledge and widen the gulf that stands between us and our genuine humanity.

"Participating with others in a mutual sharing of knowledge and experience generates the wisdom to fulfill all needs and to live in harmony. This expression of true humility is one of the most valuable insights that we as human beings can attain."

Publishing staff: "I have found it hard to appreciate how much I have learned over the years. If I think back to what I understood about the Dharma when I first started working here ten years ago, I realize that my understanding has changed in unexpected ways. I have actually forgotten some of the Tibetan terms and philosophical concepts I had studied so hard, but I have learned something else that more than replaces such 'book learning.' Working on Nyingma projects, we have the opportunity to see the truth of fundamental teachings in ourselves: how ego manifests, how we hold onto suffering and confusion, how we undermine ourselves and our best aspirations.

"Working with Rinpoche is like standing before a mirror, watching ourselves go through our various acts. Eventually we can hardly help but see the games we are playing. This seeing is not always pleasant, because we have believed for so long in the games. I think this is why it is so hard to acknowledge that we have actually learned something. The kind of knowledge we gain is not at all what we expected to get."

Publishing staff: "I think Dharma Publishing has accomplished a great deal in a short time, but it can be difficult for us to recognize that. We understand so little of the Dharma that we can hardly appreciate what Rinpoche is trying to do. We sincerely feel we value the teachings, but we actually do not know how to measure the value. If an art student were given a rare treatise on nuclear physics, he might turn the pages and notice the illustrations. He might be impressed with the knowledgeable 'look' of the text, but he would not be able to appreciate the quality of the knowledge. If the book were lost or destroyed, he might be disturbed at the loss of knowledge *in the abstract*. But he would not *feel* the loss for humanity or himself.

"I think we are all a lot like that art student. And so when Rinpoche urges us to finish a project or tries to impress upon us the need for more care, we do not feel the urgency. Eventually, I believe Americans will grow to appreciate these teachings as more people study them. But judging by myself, it is a long, slow process."

The Dharma is rich beyond all imagining; innumerable treasures await translation, study, and research. Though in light of this vast wealth, our efforts seem very small, if our contributions help foster a strong and balanced foundation for the future, our time and energy will have been well spent. Though we cannot measure the Dharma, we have glimpsed the benefits of Dharma work, for ourselves and for others.

DHARMA PRESS

Setting Up the Press

In 1963, while living in India, Tarthang Tulku established Dharma Mudranalaya, a small printing operation, to reproduce the texts he had brought with him from Tibet. In Tibet, texts were printed from blocks carved in a painstakingly intricate process. Since woodblocks of Tibetan texts were not available in India, Rinpoche had to learn how to set moveable type and acquire the necessary equipment. As one of the first Tibetans to engage in this kind of printing, he had no precedents to follow, nor even any ready-made type. He began at the beginning, learning each step necessary and then showing his friends and students who wished to help publish texts.

To understand how modern presses were operated, Rinpoche journeyed to Bombay, Calcutta, and New Delhi. Using the proceeds from his research position at Sanskrit University, he rented a small garage and began to set up operations. Everything had to be done from scratch. Before work could even begin, the roof needed thatching because the rainy season was approaching; he and his friends located a grassy plot twenty miles away where they cut sheaves of thatch and hauled it back in a wooden cart to make a new roof.

The first texts printed were reproduced through a lithographic process. Chosen texts were photographed, and the film images transferred to metal plates by chemical etching. The plates were then used to make multiple copies of the texts.

While a Tibetan typeface had been created for small news bulletins printed in Darjeeling, Kalimpong, and Dharamsala, it seemed unsuitable for printing Dharma texts. Rinpoche and his friends designed a new typeface and purchased several hundred kilos of lead. After dies were prepared for more than eight hundred combinations of characters, the new type was cast in lead. Unfortunately, the first complete set of dies was stolen and had to be replaced before printing could begin. Undeterred, Rinpoche and his associates began again and found the work went faster and smoother the second time. Over the next six years, Dharma Mudranalaya published hundreds of copies of some twenty volumes of valuable texts. The reproduction of the Seven Treasures of Longchenpa was begun, and some of Lama Mipham's commentaries were brought out.

Soon after his arrival in the United States, Rinpoche founded Dharma Press and continued the work begun by Dharma Mudranalaya. The new Press had three founding purposes: to preserve the Buddhist teachings and make them available for the West; to provide a testing ground for patterns of conduct inspired by the

Dharma and suited to the modern workplace; and to generate resources to enable Nyingma students to work full time on Dharma Publishing and other projects that unfold the meaning and value of the Buddhist tradition.

When we began to work on our earliest projects at Padma Ling, the machinery, the materials, and the technical knowledge necessary to fulfill the purposes of the Press seemed a distant dream. Our assets consisted of an antique letterpress and a handful of enthusiastic but inexperienced people. Rinpoche shared with us his knowledge of printing from his work in India, and encouraged us to learn more.

A few of us began working at borrowed facilities at night to learn technical book production skills such as typesetting, layout, and printing. Gradually during 1972 we were able to acquire light tables, a process camera, vacuum frames, a cutter, and a binder. With each purchase, we felt a growing excitement as we watched the new business become a reality.

The major need was for a press. In spite of a shortage of funds, Rinpoche began to search for an old press to rent or purchase. At one shop in San Francisco, he found two huge 65-inch two-color Harris presses built in 1936, one of which was no longer being used. When the owner agreed to donate the unused press to help support Dharma Publishing and Press, we were amazed at our good fortune. Such a large press would make it possible to print Tibetan texts and TNMC publications much more efficiently. A Tibetan book of two-hundred-fifty folios, for example, would now require only four large sheets of paper instead of sixty-three sheets on the small press. But it was to take more than five years of frustrating work to learn how to use the huge press.

Press worker: "I remember in 1972 when we first acquired the Big Press, as it came to be called. We had rented a warehouse in Emeryville to house it. There it stood on the pressroom floor . . . its size, its age, its hundreds of complex moving parts totally overwhelmed us. Two years of apprenticeship are generally required to master basic printing skills, but we had only a few weeks to observe experienced pressmen run the sister press in San Francisco, and no opportunity to work with them. There was no money for training or hiring experts, so we had to teach ourselves.

"A few of us started tinkering with the Big Press, trying to repair it. It would roar into life, vibrating the whole building, only to slow to a full stop for reasons no one could understand. Hour after hour we climbed around among the gears and rollers, trying to pinpoint the problem, but it was pretty much hit-and-miss. If we had not had constant encouragement and troubleshooting from Rinpoche, we would have given up in despair. But he insisted this challenge was a priceless opportunity to learn about printing and about ourselves."

To cover our rental of warehouse space and to reimburse volunteers for their living expenses, we contracted for a small amount of work from local businesses while printing announcements and brochures for TNMC. But with our limited skills and complex equipment, it could take weeks to print even a simple job, and we could not control the quality of our printing on the Big Press. Since printing mistakes are expensive, we could lose more money than we made. It was a hard way to learn, but we were gaining printing skills.

At the same time, we were trying to learn typesetting through a time-sharing arrangement with a San Francisco firm. This was how we typeset *Crystal Mirror II* in 1972. In 1973, we took on a major responsibility in purchasing a Harris fototronic TxT typesetter and type fonts.

Now we had equipment to pay for, accounts and contracts to handle; production was complex and demanded careful coordination, while purchasing required advance planning and accurate estimating. Supervision was necessary for scheduling and quality control. There were books to be kept, sales to generate, customer relations to maintain. Where did we start?

We shared the same difficulties as other TNMC students, some of whom were attempting to establish small businesses to raise funds for a country center. Almost all of us were in our twenties; besides being inexperienced at book production, no one had any basic business skills or even knew how to keep accounts.

Press worker: "There were only eight of us then. We worked long hours, twelve to fifteen hours a day, seven days a week. Our food and living expenses were covered at first by people's personal savings. But we were young, energetic, and excited by the challenge of developing a business that involved technical skills. Every month we felt we had succeeded if we could pay the rent and the phone bill, and keep up with the payments that were due on the TxT."

A few people kept attempting to operate the ancient Harris press effectively enough to build a reliable printing operation. But every few weeks there was another breakdown. The pressmen came to believe that only with new equipment could they build a successful printing business. Running or not, the press's huge black shape dominated the pressroom. To some, it was a reminder of unused potential; to others, it was an intractable obstacle to progress.

Over the next year, we concentrated on typesetting. The income we earned by typesetting helped the Press survive and built some confidence. If we worked hard enough, we surely could gain the skills to keep the organization afloat. But it was Rinpoche's energy and vision that provided the inspiration to continue. He spent many hours encouraging us to appreciate the value of the work we were doing. As each new piece of equipment brought demands for new skills, he urged us to regard Dharma Press as a training ground. Here were opportunities to develop personal strengths and skills, while also helping to preserve Dharma works in Tibetan and make translations available.

Press worker: "Rinpoche's support was crucial—people could feel completely defeated trying to learn new technical skills by teaching themselves. Each failure was a real blow to self-confidence. It was so easy to excuse ourselves and say it was simply impossible to succeed. But Rinpoche had a very different attitude toward mistakes. If you did not hide them, they showed you exactly where you needed to concentrate your efforts and what you needed to improve."

In 1974 a smaller, more modern Harris press was bought so that printing of Dharma books could continue. Full-color thankas were soon printed on the new press, followed by the third volume of *Crystal Mirror*.

This equipment would also allow us to take on some outside printing jobs once again.

Each stage in production required a specialized skill we had not yet mastered, which then made it next to impossible to link the stages together smoothly. No one could keep track of the mistakes, let alone the time, money, and materials lost in the efforts to remedy them. In the daily chaos, work might be stripped incorrectly, but the error not noticed until after printing, requiring reprinting of the whole job. While a project could be properly printed on one side, the sheets might be mixed up by someone unfamiliar with paper-turning; then the second side would be printed upside down. If the project made it all the way to the cutter, a mistake in cutting could ruin it. Missing art might have to be tipped in by hand after a book was bound. Even on a straightforward job, we could spend hours picking through the completed work to find even five good samples to show.

Under pressure to learn so quickly, and unaccustomed to working together as a team, we found ourselves easily caught up in emotional situations and personality conflicts, which could drain energy away from our efforts. Aware of this volatility, some of us nicknamed the organization "Drama Press." Motivations were constantly fluctuating because we had begun work without clearly understanding the challenges we would face, or the demands that would be made upon us as the Press developed. When our association with Nyingma involved more work than we expected, some of us broke our commitments. Even when we had started to gain confidence, someone might suddenly lose heart and decide to leave; others simply could not afford to work more than a few months, for the Press could only partially reimburse living expenses. As a result, the productivity of the most experienced workers was limited by the need to constantly train new people.

Press worker: "There was a lot of transience among the early workers. I think we as Americans have little sense of loyalty and commitment to work. There was not always real appreciation for the learning opportunities because the work could be so frustrating. On the other hand, there was a very creative feeling and a freedom to participate in a number of different ways. Work has a way of putting people in touch with the gut, especially when the material reward is small. You begin to lose all the airy-fairy notions of 'the spiritual lifestyle' and develop a more practical viewpoint."

TNMC student: "The shifting of interest and the changing membership in the early years could be seen in all our organizations. In the beginning, many people were dreamy idealists; they became discouraged pretty quickly and left. Others stayed long enough to learn skills, but they became excited by prospects outside the organization and left. Those of us who have persisted long enough have begun to see what an unusual learning opportunity we have been given."

Dharma Mudranalaya meeting with Rinpoche, in spring, 1986: "At the start, it might be hard to envision the far-reaching purposes of Dharma Mudranalaya. In easy times we can accept these purposes in an idealistic way, but when work becomes very challenging, motivation disappears if we do not know and value what we are working for. So we also need to look at what we are gaining from work right at the beginning. As our body and mind move into action, our being is engaged in the world; we can see concentration, energy, and awareness manifest directly. As we learn how to develop these aspects of our being, genuine pleasure and satisfaction grow. We gain better results for our efforts, and this brings even more satisfaction. Once we understand how work develops positive qualities and strengths, we can support ourselves more consistently when faced with difficult situations.

"Gradually, as knowledge expands, a fuller vision begins to motivate us, and we view our efforts as ways of creating long-range benefits for others. The idea of benefiting others becomes more than a far-off dream; it becomes an actual possibility that offers more reliable inspiration than our original self-centered goals."

To improve skills and knowledge, we visited successful printers and typesetters to study their operations. By 1975 we had joined professional printing organizations, the staff had grown to twenty-five people, and our output was increasing in quality and quantity. We produced seven new Dharma Publishing books, as well as *Gesar* issues, twenty-five full-color thanka reproductions, and *Sacred Art*, a portfolio of twenty thanka prints. Catalogues and brochures were printed regularly for TNMC, Nyingma Institute, and TAP.

It was exciting to see our technical skills improve, but we still had much to learn. Almost every Dharma book required some new technique we had not yet mastered, and we could not always make accurate time estimates. Sometimes the Publishing staff could not predict when various manuscripts would be coming into typesetting. We often felt caught in a whirlwind of scheduling problems. Jobs for outside customers seemed to be more straightforward and made us feel a part of the business world. When we began having difficulty scheduling Dharma Publishing books, Rinpoche halted outside work so we could reorient our efforts.

Press worker: "We were beginning to see ourselves as a 'real business.' As people began to feel a little bit skilled, the confidence was channeled in the wrong direction. Our emotional investment in building a business at times overshadowed commitment to the founding purposes of the Press."

Soon thereafter, the legal status of Dharma Press was changed to express its purposes more fully. Dharma Publishing and Dharma Press were incorporated together under the name of Dharma Mudranalaya. The 1975 Articles of Incorporation of Dharma Mudranalaya described the Press's purposes: 1) to promote, foster, encourage, publish, teach, and disseminate the Tibetan Nyingma tradition of Buddhism; 2) to present the living spirit of Buddhism to the Western world; 3) to preserve, protect, publish, and disseminate the texts and thoughts of ancient Buddhist scholars; 4) to encourage, assist, and cooperate with related religious organizations on the same or similar paths; 5) to provide assistance for contemplative study by worthy persons in the course of preparation for the position of Master of Dharma of the Nyingma school; 6) to provide assistance for the continual spiritual development of worthy persons in the Nyingma traditions of Buddhism.

Reconsidering the founding purposes of the Press inspired us as we produced the ten Dharma Publishing books completed by the end of 1977. Several of these books contained color and black and white photos, unusual layouts, and color plates inserted by hand. Equipment acquired through the years had now made the Press a full book production facility, and the purchase of additional bindery equipment further extended its capacities. That spring Dharma Publishing and Press attended the American Book Association convention in San Francisco. We were becoming known for the quality of our work and had won several awards for superior book production.

Our production skills were definitely improving, but business skills had not yet matured—we still had difficulty with long-range financial decisions, balancing the budget, and meeting schedules. As we foundered again, Rinpoche called a halt to outside work and began a series of evaluation meetings. Throughout January and February of 1978, we prepared charts and graphs of cash flow, job schedules, and everything else we could think of. But this approach did not reveal the underlying difficulties. As the meetings wore on week after week, the more subtle problems of motivation and uncertainty were expressed for the first time.

We knew now that we had the potential to reproduce Tibetan texts and art and to print quality Dharma books. But we had to acknowledge our uncertainty about how to bring spiritual vision into the working world. Our reluctance to take responsibility and dedicate our full energy to the founding purposes of the Press was undermining our success. Encouraged by Rinpoche, we resolved to develop a stronger sense of purpose that would allow us to meet the challenges we faced.

Press worker: "The Press runs quite independently compared to some of the other centers where Rinpoche guides each project closely. This independence has been both a blessing and a challenge. We have the opportunity to make decisions and develop leadership, and this seems very healthy and satisfying for Americans. We like to take charge and try new things, and I think Rinpoche has encouraged this while constantly reminding us of our deeper purposes. But we get so involved in our own way of thinking that his message just doesn't get through. Sometimes Rinpoche has to do something very dramatic, such as stopping outside work, so that people wake up. Taking the initiative without a very broad perspective and deep devotion to the purposes of the Press does not lead in the right direction. Fortunately, when we start to 'tilt' in the wrong direction, Rinpoche catches us before we fall."

Management Changes

In 1978 we made changes in our management style. For years we had worked under the leadership of a few people, relying on them to make decisions. Now all of the older workers were encouraged to take more responsibility for managing the Press. Several committees were formed, but all members would have input in decision-making, while being personally responsible for specific areas of expertise. Women workers now came to the fore, and began taking on more responsibility for management and business decisions.

Women participating in all of the Nyingma Centers have learned skills of many kinds, ranging from the intellectual work of editing and research to the heavy physical labor of sculpture, sand blasting, and plating. Though Odiyan crews are all men and the Institute dean has traditionally been a man, the staffs of TNMC and Publishing, and the management staff of the Press have in recent years been predominantly women.

Press worker: "I have read that the Nyingma tradition holds women in esteem, but I did not know how that would apply to me in my work. Even when I was working on projects where several of the men had more experience, Rinpoche repeatedly encouraged me not to rely on them for advice, but to find out for myself and make independent decisions."

Throughout the summer of 1978, Rinpoche encouraged everyone at the Press to learn different skills. One who knew stripping now practiced pasteup; one who did pasteup now learned typesetting. The steps involved in each type of work were clarified through detailed job descriptions, which were written down and circulated to everyone. While this approach to learning seemed to scatter our energy at first, in the longer run we gained a broader perspective on all aspects of book production. When we began to better understand how to connect one job smoothly with another, each of us could do our own jobs more efficiently and coordinate the stages of production more effectively. This broad perspective also supported the democratic participatory style of management that was gradually evolving.

In learning new skills, we gained greater insight into ourselves. As we switched jobs, we found the same kinds of problems coming up in new situations. In time, it became more apparent that attitudes and psychological patterns play a substantial role in everyday work, and especially in learning new technical skills. Someone who became easily confused doing pasteup now saw the same kind of confusion arise doing typesetting. One who hesitated and doubted himself did so learning stripping just as he had while operating the camera. If we studied our attitudes and how they manifested in our work, we could see that technical difficulties were not insurmountable problems. If we could bring awareness, concentration, and energy into balance, we had the ability to work through these obstacles and obtain substantial results. Now that we had more experience, the advantages of Rinpoche's approach were more obvious.

While we were beginning to see the effects of our patterns individually, we did not see our reluctance to take responsibility as a group. Participation in weekly staff meetings supported our efforts at management and lifted morale, but we had not yet learned how to make "horizontal management" work.

Press worker: "People were really uncertain about leadership and did not trust each other to work for the benefit of the whole organization. No one wanted any one individual to be too powerful, but we did not know how to make decisions as a group. So we just struggled along for quite a while, trying to keep the work going as best we could and trying to grasp the essentials of real business management."

Our technical skills improved with the experience of producing three books by Rinpoche—*Kum Nye, Openness Mind, Skillful Means*—and *Crystal Mirror V.* The two-volume set of *The Life and Liberation of Padmasambhava* contained fifty-eight full-color thankas and parchment overlays. By 1979 the quality of our work was clearly improving. We produced *Buddha's Lions,* which contains eighty-six two-color line drawings and reproductions of three hundred Tibetan folios, and *Tibet in Pictures,* a two-volume work with more than two hundred black and white photographs. Both books were produced in case-bound, high-quality editions.

Rinpoche continued to give extra time and energy to the Press. Encouraging us to appreciate our improving skills, he urged us to develop the inner strength and awareness to persist through difficulties and make good decisions. Finally we began to realize as a group that if we took more initiative to investigate problems, they would not arise so often or be overwhelming. Our committee meetings focused more effectively on thinking through each step of a decision and actively inquiring into mistakes to find constructive solutions.

Press worker: "Becoming aware of the limiting patterns and gathering the energy to change is not easy. What is easy is convincing yourself that a situation is hopeless or that everything is just fine, without actually looking at the truth. When we began to look directly at the quality of our energy and motivation, we began to understand our problems. The best medicine for our difficulties was for each of us wholeheartedly to take on the obstacles in our jobs — the very activities or tasks we had been tempted to avoid."

In a smooth, easy situation, we might not notice negative attitudes so clearly. But long hours spent on complex projects with tight deadlines brought negative attitudes to the surface: confusion, resistance, lack of confidence, and laziness. Now that we were more willing to look closely, we found that the difficulty of the work was not just an obstacle to realizing our goals. It also created a special opportunity for knowledge.

Since all steps in book production are closely interrelated, the influence of one action upon another can be traced in detail. Examining the production process is an excellent way to study karma, the laws of cause and effect. While we were all familiar with the term karma, here was an opportunity to directly experience how karma operates. As we looked more carefully, we could see that positive attitudes and energy created one kind of result, while negative attitudes led in a very different direction—not only creating much pain and unhappiness, but also poor results in our work.

In 1980 we began to examine new systems that might encourage individuals to take more personal responsibility for their attitudes and the quality of their work. Efforts were made to develop ways of giving individuals feedback so that they could see consequences of actions and attitudes more clearly. Rinpoche sent proposals to the Press, urging us to look at *how* we were working.

One way to evaluate attitudes was to make a checklist of qualities we wished to strengthen, and let people give each other feedback on progress in each area. Attitude could be measured in terms of qualities such as confidence, honesty, responsibility, respectfulness toward others, concentration, openness, supportiveness, and patience. To measure general working ability, another checklist noted ability to handle stress, consistency of effort, productive use of time, and willingness to implement recommendations. Checklists were also created to help us recognize problem areas such as carelessness, sloppiness, reluctance to make efforts, manipulative behaviors, and a number of other difficulties.

Memo from Rinpoche in November of 1980: "This situation at Nyingma is unique, for you have freedom to express yourselves; you are encouraged to learn and develop both skills and internal awareness; and you are given responsibilities that are as challenging as any you could encounter in a work situation. At first there may be errors, waste, or duplication, as well as the tendency to hold back or excuse failures. In the process of internal development, however, the clarity and confidence that we develop within ourselves will manifest in efficient and productive efforts that yield results. Good results are the expression of a healthy mind.

"This evaluation system is not intended to discourage or find fault with individuals, but rather to discover effective ways to help one another. It is hard to see the consequences of actions unless we have repeated them many times and gained direct experience. Now it may be possible to see this more clearly. If you have comments, suggestions, criticisms, or ideas you would like to see included, please communicate them. Your thoughts and help in developing this process will be appreciated.

"Although we have not yet reached our ultimate goals, the process of learning can be stimulating and productive. It can result in lasting contributions to the Dharma, to the growth of the community, and to our own internal health."

While the evaluation system attempted to measure attitudinal growth, another system was implemented at the end of 1980 to measure working skills and productivity. The new system included daily time sheets, time estimates for each type of task, and monthly reports. From time to time, outside evaluations have also helped us sharpen awareness of inefficiencies and generated interesting new ideas. Consultants who have reviewed our operations have also encouraged us by acknowledging the value of the results we have achieved by following non-standard business procedures.

Press worker: "Over the past years we have implemented different systems to evaluate productivity, but it remains difficult to compare our way of working with regular businesses. Our priorities are different, and our money management is different. Rinpoche strongly recommends against borrowing, for example, while most American businesses borrow as a matter of course. The Nyingma approach is: If you need money for new equipment or more supplies, then learn to work better, become self-sufficient. Pay everything on time, or you will not be paid on time. These 'working ethics' may not fit with modern business practices, but they are solid, almost old-fashioned—and hard to implement in full."

As we developed greater awareness of how attitudes, work satisfaction, and the quality of results were interconnected, Rinpoche continued to expand and deepen our efforts by laying out an overview of his approach. Focusing on a larger perspective was particularly inspiring to us now, for it strengthened the realization that we could change old attitudes and habits.

Memo from Rinpoche, December, 1980: "Most of you have become aware of problems and how they arise. Many people in the world do not even recognize the nature of their difficulties, but you can see this now. You have entered the next stage of not totally confronting problems and not dealing with them directly. If you look more deeply, not just at the outward results of your actions, but at your internal attitudes and feelings, you can begin to overcome your resistances and learn to apply skillful means to whatever you do. When internal obstacles arise, try to face them directly. Communicate with yourself, instead of defending yourself or pretending. In this way you are working on yourself while you are working at your job.

"The confusion of the world is reiterated in our personal confusion and our inability to communicate. The inability to communicate reveals a lack of self-understanding. Support each other to overcome this muddiness, and work together without claiming territory or holding on to self-centeredness. Instead of competing with one another, help each other to understand the nature of our human problems.

"Learn to value doing your work well, and take it on as a stimulating challenge. Work can become a very effective way to a deeply integrated, concentrated mind. In turn, the quality of awareness we bring to our work is reflected throughout every aspect of our lives.

"I have said this in many ways, in books, lectures, and articles, and I know you know these things. I sincerely wish that one day those who have had some experience of the spiritual path will comprehend that the inner nature of work is an integral part of the path to enlightenment."

In our daily committee and work meetings, we made a point to encourage each other to uphold a basic openness and honesty, and not to become entangled in personality conflicts. Each of us made specific commitments to be more positive and to be open to constructive criticism when any negativity arose. Rinpoche recommended that we study *Skillful Means* together in weekly classes, which helped to bring the members of the Press closer together as a team and a community. We also clarified the chain of responsibility at the Press by reviewing the various committees and redefining their functions. Over the years, group meetings and classes, linked with evaluations and efforts at better communication, have become a part of our way of working.

Press worker: "Doing group evaluations was time-consuming. After a while, we stopped meeting formally for this purpose. But the meetings had taught us how tricky giving each other feedback could be. 'Feedback' can turn into criticism and meanness if you do not know yourself well or do not recognize your own weaknesses and strengths; if you do not have strong self-confidence and real feeling for other people, the competitive side comes out. You may even enjoy putting others down so you feel important, or so you are not the one blamed. Beneath ordinary communication lie all these hidden currents. The bottom line is: Everybody is out for himself. The truth of this shows when times get rough. We went through many hours of struggle and confusion, learning the importance of real honesty and good communication skills the hard way. We still have a lot of room for improvement, but at least now we know what skills and openness are involved."

Press worker: "Classes and meetings brought up a lot of issues, some of which we had no idea how to handle for a long time. Some of these areas still cause us difficulty. People at the Press are all strong individualists, and we each want our own ideas to succeed. At the same time, people are afraid of full responsibility. We say we want to achieve a certain goal, but we are not willing to do what needs to be done to succeed. Issues of responsibility and authority also get confused with power struggles. Very gradually we have seen the harmful effects of these self-centered attitudes. Lately, the group as a whole has developed more caring and more ability to take a larger view."

Press worker: "Looking back now in 1986, it seems striking how the members of the Press have matured in their management abilities over the last five years. We have evolved a way of organizing that actually functions well on the basis of consensus, but it depends on people really contributing. Meetings did not use to produce results; now, we can reach definite, shared conclusions in a reasonable length of time. We have been trying to develop away from procedure and toward communication, not always successfully, but that is our direction. People do not always embrace cooperation, but often they do. At least we know *how* to cooperate now."

Innovation and Teamwork

By 1979, seven years of book production had prepared the way for the production of the *Nyingma Edition of the Tibetan Buddhist Canon*, the companion volumes of the *Research Catalogue/Bibliography*, and the *Guide*. Even so, the volume and difficulty of the work ahead seemed overwhelming. We did not know how we were going to balance this work, which would bring the Press no income at all, with our other commitments. We needed more sophisticated skills, better planning, and much more self-confidence.

The plates for the nearly 52,000 text pages of the *Nyingma Edition* were prepared in a pyrofax process at rented facilities. Pyrofax film can be transferred directly to plates, eliminating costly negatives. In 1979 the Press received the first shipment of plates and began printing the Tibetan texts, running the press continually day and night to keep up with plate production. Organizing the plates for the 120 volumes required continual attention.

Inventory control and organization for this project were far more exacting than usual. The high-grade, acid-free paper had been milled to order, and it was not certain we could get more if we ran out. We had allowed for a certain percentage of reprints, but with quality such a high priority, we were reprinting for relatively minor errors. To add to these difficulties, we found that the building we were renting was being sold. Halfway through printing the *Nyingma Edition* texts, we had to stop operations, pack all equipment, plates, and printed sheets, and move to a new location. This made it necessary to reorganize and check everything.

We were asked to finish printing the texts and the *Guide* by July 1980, in time for the dedication of the Odiyan Stupa. The schedule was tight, but feasible if no unforeseen problems arose. In June, several Dharma Publishing workers came down to the Press to speed up work on the *Guide*, which had to be typeset, proofread, pasted up, printed, and bound in three weeks.

Press worker: "Most of our other work was set aside, as work on the *Guide* preempted equipment and staff. We had no time to think about the impossibility of getting all this work finished on time—we were too busy doing it. All stages of the work blended together with a smoothness we had not experienced before. Proofreading finished only a few hours before the last signature had to go on the press. The first books were bound early in the morning and delivered to Odiyan on time."

Processing galleys for the introductory pages of the new edition challenged not only our technical skills, but also placed great demands on our equipment. The Harris TxT typesetting machine could not handle the numerous Sanskrit diacriticals we needed, as well as the thousands of charts. Stretched beyond its capacity, it began to malfunction more often, and much time had to be devoted just to keeping it running. Machine malfunctioning caused extra work for proofreaders and pasteup workers as well; the level of frustration was rising, slowing production and eroding morale. Facing the same problems day after day, we felt that the harder we worked, the harder the work became. The project seemed to stretch out endlessly before us, and it became difficult to believe we would ever finish.

During this time, the Big Press became an invaluable asset. Its two-color capacity enabled us to print the 232 thanka reproductions for the *Nyingma Edition* without undue difficulty, though controlling resolution and color intensities required continual adjustments. Each thanka required eight passes through the press; many preliminary runs were needed to obtain good registration. For our pressmen, printing the thankas was an exercise in concentration and mindfulness that continued for many months.

The extensive art work in the *Nyingma Edition* also challenged the abilities of our camera, stripping, and bindery staff. Each volume contains twelve color pages which called for 1,600 masking operations and four hundred additional plates. Thanka printing alone required five plates for each thanka, a total of more than a thousand plates in all. Thanka prints and protective parchments had to be inserted by hand, which added to difficulties in collation and in sewing the volumes.

Press worker: "Since we were using the very highest quality materials, many specially designed to our specifications, costs were running higher than we expected. We were asked to make a strong effort to estimate our needs accurately and avoid duplication and wastage. We became particularly concerned about our diminishing supply of paper. It did in fact run out at a crucial moment in printing and was replaced at great cost and effort. Expenses mounted as we began binding; we had to budget funds for cover material, gilding and gold-stamping supplies, satin-embossed slipcases, custom-designed stamps, shrink-wrapping materials, and even specially made crates for shipping. Losses ran fairly high, in part because of our inexperience with such large projects, which contributed to materials wastage and duplicated efforts. At industry rates, such duplication would have been prohibitively costly, but for Dharma work, we had to do the very best we could, even if it meant repeated efforts and more expense."

By spring, when we were deeply involved with work on the *Nyingma Edition*, we had more business from local customers than we could handle. Rinpoche urged us to try to meet these commitments as well by focusing on skillful planning.

Memo from Rinpoche, spring, 1981: "Since we are 'living in caves,' that is, not making so much contact with many people socially or in business conferences, we need to actively gather more information on how to save time and money, what supplies are best for different purposes, etc."

By the end of the summer we were certain we could not meet our schedules with the existing staff and outdated equipment. We tried to define the cost-benefits of various types of new equipment and submitted a variety of suggestions on staff changes and expansion for Rinpoche's consideration.

Memo from Rinpoche, fall, 1981: "You say you need more people—but I think you need to understand relationships and how to use people's time fully. Rather than more time, you need better quality energy inside the time. I know that everyone is working hard and putting in long hours. This is not the critical element. You do not need to work longer; you need to look at where energy is wasted. This will open up creativity.

"To take full responsibility as a group, each and every member must have a duty in regard to management. The energy currently is too fragmented and polarized. Every single person must develop a problem-solving view that sees the long-range benefit of the group as a whole and envisions the success of our projects."

Press worker: "I didn't see there was an organizing skill that I needed and that I did not already have—the ability to recognize all the separate tasks that needed to be done, assign time to them, and make sure they got done. To the extent that I was aware of all the things to do, I put my energy into avoiding them. At our organization, when there is a tremendous amount to do, but there is not yet a clear path of action, the momentum of the work does not slow down for you to catch up. Everybody does the best they can while you figure things out. Someone once said that life is like learning to play the violin by giving performances in front of large audiences. That's a good description of how we learn."

To meet all of our obligations, we needed to improve managerial skills as well as production skills. But most of all, we needed a very positive approach to these challenges. Each Press member signed an agreement to do everything he or she could to ensure the success of the Press and to let go of personal blockages; to participate wholeheartedly and pass knowledge on to others; support the management committee and to acquire management skills of their own; to be responsible for specific goals and to help in refining and reviewing all general goals and procedures.

In preparation for collating and binding the volumes of the *Nyingma Edition*, we researched and acquired the new or used equipment that would be needed — special sewing machines that could handle oversized books, a gilder, special stamping equipment, book presses, and a shrink-wrap processor. Since gilding is seldom done in modern book production, obtaining a gilder and advice on using it took extensive research.

After considering various methods of book binding, Rinpoche selected the reinforced French-groove method, a seventeenth century technique that produces an unusually durable volume. This procedure adds extra linen tapes that extend from the spine in between two layers of cover board, securely joining the spine to the cover. One of us volunteered to study the technique and take responsibility for the binding process.

Press worker: "I enrolled in evening classes where I learned the French style of binding. It is said to last over three hundred years, and the books bound in that period have held together quite well into modern times. The course instructors recommended this method as the very best way to bind the *Nyingma Edition*. But they scoffed at the idea of trying such a labor-intensive, difficult technique on the scale we proposed—13,000 volumes. Despite such discouragement, we adapted this method for large-scale production. We started teaching our bindery people this technique and purchased the necessary equipment and materials. The workers learned fast, and soon were inventing better and quicker ways to produce the number of books needed."

Press worker: "Rinpoche thought it would be a beautiful gesture if we could gild all the volumes of the *Nyingma Edition*, so I went to New York to learn how to do it and to train on the equipment we were buying there. I heard the old familiar story: The instructors explained that it might be possible to gild such oversize books, but certainly not in the volume we proposed. But I completed the training anyway and brought back prototypes. After experimenting, we found a way to gild 13,000 volumes efficiently."

When the printing was drawing near completion, Rinpoche received reports that sewing and binding would take nearly two years with our three-person crew. Suddenly many assistants were available—members of all the Nyingma Centers came to the Press for a few months of very intense work.

Memo from Rinpoche, spring, 1981: "As we complete the *Nyingma Edition*, organization and efficiency will be extremely important. Specifically, make sure your procedures are clear; mesh each operation with the next, and be certain all stages are understood by each crew. With new people participating in this work, it is especially important that those in charge know all the aspects of each part of the production. I will provide an additional fifteen part-time people from TNMC to help and a list of more recommendations."

We immediately mapped out the production stages, organized materials, and set up more work stations. As Dharma Publishing workers helped with collation and checking, TNMC workers gravitated toward the bindery. People accustomed to sewing fabrics now found themselves sewing books. A group of workers from Odiyan arrived just in time to help move large quantities of materials, and contributed their energy to the momentum that was rapidly building in all phases of the work. When they returned to Odiyan several weeks later, new volunteers arrived from the Institute. Before long, the *Nyingma Edition* project occupied nearly all of the pressroom, and most of the Press workers were spending at least part of their time collating, checking, or binding the volumes.

Memo from Rinpoche, June of 1981: "I know that you all are very busy and are working hard to complete the Kanjur and Tanjur. But today I have a special urgent request to make. I am asking for everyone to give the utmost energy to complete the binding and shrinkwrapping of ten to fifteen sets of the Kanjur and Tanjur by July 16. I know this request may be shocking and very sudden, but I have a specific purpose for these sets, and I hope you can contribute the intensive energy necessary to reach this goal.

"It is also very important to complete the entire project as soon as possible, and so I would like to ask that another thirty sets be finished in approximately four weeks. Now is the right time to finish! You may feel that our work is always done on tight schedules, but this project has already far exceeded our original schedules, and I am very concerned that we may not finish if work continues to go slowly."

Interview with Rinpoche, 1982: "To complete the Kanjur and Tanjur project, the staff of Dharma Publishing and Dharma Press had to face an endless series of challenges and make many personal sacrifices to overcome them. The task of overseeing so many different activities was a constant strain. Sometimes it seemed that just one more new problem would be more than anyone could bear. Now that the work is nearly finished, we know that all the effort has been worthwhile. As a result of our work, we can be sure that the texts of the Dharma will be available for study for many years to come. I regard this as one small service I have been able to perform for humanity. Perhaps in future years, there will be growing appreciation in the West for the valuable resources contained in the Kanjur and Tanjur."

Throughout the finishing process, each volume was checked by a team of four to ten people—twice for paging errors before it was sewn, and once for accurate assembly and quality after it was bound. When most of the binding was finished, the checking and finishing teams continued their work for nearly six months.

In terms of volume and complexity, this project, finally completed in the spring of 1982, was more than a hundred times greater than any job Dharma Publishing or Press had ever undertaken: One hundred and eight copies of each of 120 volumes—12,960 volumes—were printed; 13,292 text plates and 2,632 front matter plates were required to print over five million text pages and more than one million front matter pages; over

400,000 special insertions were made to add full-color art pages. All the individual volumes were collated, checked, sewn, gilded, casebound, cleaned, numbered, jacketed, slipcased, and shrinkwrapped.

Press worker: "We had shifts working around the clock, seven days a week. Rinpoche had suggested we perform this activity as though it were a special ceremony. We needed to be especially mindful of the nature of the materials we were working with, and act with great awareness and respect on the level of body, speech, and mind. The energy was very high and occasionally would get scattered, but through the right intention, obstacles dissolved and the goal was attained."

Working in the World

The experience and skills developed in producing the *Nyingma Edition* supported us in producing the *Research Catalogue/Bibliography*, which entered production soon afterwards. For a time, organization was even more difficult, as we worked to resume normal operations and incorporate production of the *Catalogue* into the flow of backlogged jobs. Although this complex work went through many proofreading cycles, sets of eight volumes of the *Catalogue*, printed and bound in the same high-quality format as the *Nyingma Edition*, were completely finished in the spring of 1984.

The energy generated in producing the *Catalogue* began to expand as we reinvested it immediately in a series of new Dharma books. In 1983, we typeset and printed three beautiful books in the Translation Series: *The Voice of the Buddha*, *Mother of Knowledge*, and *The Marvelous Companion*. All three were intricately designed, with full-color reproductions, line drawings, gold-stamped covers, and gilded edges. *Crystal Mirror VI* and *VII*, illustrated with maps, color reproductions, ornamental type, and other unusual design elements, followed soon afterwards.

Producing Dharma books no longer seemed so difficult. We were beginning to feel real satisfaction with our products, and so was Rinpoche. He pointed out how much we had progressed in gaining both confidence and skills. If we could appreciate the nature of our own success, accomplishment would continue to build upon itself indefinitely. The encouragement he gave us helped us see how we could encourage ourselves and support the accomplishments of others.

Memo from Rinpoche, spring, 1983: "I am pleased and impressed with the Dharma Publishing catalogue and with the cooperation, skills, and fine attention on the part of the Press that made it possible. Look at the quality of the work we can now accomplish! We have come a long way in fifteen years. It is difficult to accomplish much working alone, but together our efforts are magnified and truly worthwhile.

"There have been many frustrating complications during these years, but you have persevered and taken an active role to produce works of enduring value. Your help has made tremendous achievements possible, and I am forever grateful for your support. I hope you understand how valuable your time has been. Of all the ways to use your time and energy and skills, work that endures is the most worthwhile. Dharma work benefits you and creates opportunities for others.

"As we produce more translations, we will be increasingly able to express the beauty and meaning of the

Dharma, building upon what has been done to further understanding of the Dharma in the West. You are all now a part of this good work. May you appreciate the value of your participation, the beauty of the books you have produced, and the significance of your successful completion of these projects."

As we grew more confident in our competence and interacted more effectively with customers and suppliers, the aspiration to perfect our skills and become more professional grew stronger. Compared to the 70s, there is now a more widespread respect for professional skills; people seem to have a new sense of commitment to work, which makes it easier to accept work as a path of learning and achievement.

When we tried to evaluate ourselves, we saw several very strong points. The small size of our staff had given us unusual opportunities; many of the older people knew a wide variety of skills, which gave the group as a whole an unusually comprehensive understanding of all phases of book production. Our sales people knew the business well because each of them had been involved in other departments for many years.

Press worker: "The ingredients for success seem to be good production skills, especially color printing; good sales; good equipment; and good attitudes, such as confidence, cooperation, and vision. All four of these must be maximized at the same time. People have to start thinking bigger, taking risks, making careful decisions, and taking greater responsibility. There is a 'critical mass' of serious, older Dharma students that must develop before all four factors combine synergistically.

I think starting about 1984, all the elements needed in this creative combination existed at the Press."

Press worker: "Though most of us were quite highly skilled by 1984 or so, I did not feel strong confidence until recently. By 1987 I could recognize that we *are* highly skilled. For example, our typesetting department stresses high-level skills. We do 'set-up'—writing computer formats—rather than typing manuscripts into the computer. With their computer skills, our typesetters can create special designs for charts, headings, and lists that we would not have imagined possible several years ago. Our pressmen know the different presses inside out. An experienced pressman can coax high-quality work out of an older press or even run the antique Big Press so effectively that it outproduces the new Heidelberg. Camera, stripping, and bindery workers are able to support very elaborate designs; their skill opens up many new avenues of design for Dharma Publishing books. How much we all have learned over the years! How much more will we learn during the next five years? The possibilities seem to expand before us."

Dharma Mudranalaya meeting with Rinpoche, in spring of 1986: "Though many of you began working here when you were young and had no training, you have done fine work. We have not followed a traditional business approach; we learn by doing rather than by formal training. Nevertheless, you should feel very proud of your accomplishments. When you do good, solid work, satisfying your customers, creating a fine product—whether it is a beautiful book or a loaf of bread—you do not need to feel embarrassed in front of anyone, even highly trained professionals. The distinction between amateur and professional is not so important as the quality and care, a genuine love of the work. Something created with an attitude of true craftsmanship has an intrinsic value, a beauty of its own, and a genuine impact on others, sometimes even long-range effects we would never imagine."

We now knew firsthand the difference in satisfaction between producing work that will be discarded in a few weeks or years, and investing time and energy in work that endures. Especially when we completed a new Dharma book, we appreciated Dharma work as inherently valuable. When we could step back and consider the long-range value of what we were doing, we could recognize a larger purpose to what we were learning and the great value of the support from Rinpoche and our co-workers. The powerful energy generated when a group works well together and the inner strength developed through challenging work were beginning to sustain us more consistently.

But working in the world was still our biggest challenge. Our very wish to increase our skills and efficiency encouraged us to look at ourselves through the eyes of the business world. How did we "measure up" professionally? How good were we compared to the typesetting and printing companies that offered similar services? How good were our personal skills compared with recognized professionals in our field?

Professionalism is associated with position, income, and personal power, none of which were stressed in our organizations. Our democratic approach offered us no organizational ladder we could climb; we had no high incomes that would prove to families and others that we were successful. Although we had come to the Centers to develop a spiritual way of life, some of us now found ourselves attracted to values we had once scorned.

As we compared Dharma Press with ordinary businesses, we found that individuals reacted in different ways. Some who had worked at the Press many years seemed to mistake the skills and confidence they had developed for personal power; then they might be tempted to look for a job that would let them enjoy more authority. Some were more fascinated with how much money they could make with their technical skills. Others seemed not to have fully resolved their feelings about the value of challenging work, and might be troubled by yearnings for an easier, more regular life and a simpler, less demanding job.

TNMC student: "I think everyone at Nyingma experiences periods of inner conflicts. It is confusing and very painful to be caught between our original purpose and the pull toward material values. Desires lead us back to the familiar realm of personal gratification; the spiritual direction leads us into the unknown. Desires are strong and familiar and have support from all sides, while the spiritual path turns out to be much harder than we expected. When we are aware that time is passing, we must face the question—what direction do we want for our lives?"

Because such conflicts are not easy to resolve, we may sometimes try to live and work in the community without clear purpose and commitment, ignoring our unanswered questions or hiding doubts and fears. But unresolved questions resurface in difficult times when work is especially frustrating.

TNMC student: "Once they take hold, doubt and dissatisfaction feed on themselves, draining our energy and limiting our vision and our ability to get results. Our actions lack the concentration that invites creativity into our lives and the drive that inspires us to purposeful action. When we lose a sense of purpose, and our results are not satisfying, then we may feel compelled to prove ourselves in standard business or professional careers. It becomes a vicious circle."

While work with Nyingma is based on an approach that is new to us, we have grown up with the attitudes and priorities of modern society. Leaving a community to follow a more familiar lifestyle or to go "our own way" can feel healthy, independent, and mature. But the groups we graduate into may not offer us the freedom we expect. Those who have left our organizations have often seen that their ability to accomplish is limited by the need to gain recognition from others, jealousies, and competitive attitudes. In coping with the pressures involved in working and living today, we may find ourselves more dependent on others than we had expected, and less free of emotional conflicts than before.

Press worker: "The business world is very competitive, and the Press has a competitive kind of atmosphere. People can become very involved with comparing themselves to others, measuring one group or department against another, and comparing the Press as a whole to other companies. This comparing reflects an underlying insecurity about ourselves, which we may try to resolve by putting ourselves in a favorable light. This competitiveness seems to be part of human nature. Ten years of work at the Press has allowed me to see it clearly in myself and others. We spend so much time worrying about ourselves, and so little caring for others. This self-centered insecurity doesn't change one bit if you go out into the regular working world. At least here we have a chance to practice a different way of being."

We began to realize even more clearly the value of mutual support as our organization expanded, and we wanted to attract more workers. In 1983 we had tried taking on a number of volunteer workers who wanted to learn specific skills. Since many of them were not interested in the community and its special training, or in furthering the goals of Dharma Mudranalaya, the foundation for developing motivation and purpose was lacking. Most of these volunteers soon left. In 1984 it seemed important either to recruit people who were interested in our approach to learning, or else to become more skillful at communicating our purpose to potential workers. It was clear that in either case, new workers should have more active support for their own process of learning new skills and new attitudes.

If we could emphasize a positive vision of growth that each new worker could aspire to and offer wholehearted support for the efforts of everyone working at the Press, we would create a healthier, more inviting environment for new workers. Our management style depended on all our workers making an effort to foster certain positive qualities in themselves. In the last several years, we had developed a committee particularly responsible for management. Older, long-time students were elected to this committee, which was gradually gaining the confidence of the workers. Everyone was encouraged to take as much responsibility as they could for communicating with the committee, as well as for handling their own departments.

From Dharma Press Minutes: "Managerial qualities: responsiveness to the broader perspective of benefiting others; high energy; ability to cut through obstacles; ability to do creative problem-solving; ability to do long-range planning; persistence and follow-through; good communication skills; ability to work skillfully with emotions, one's own and others'; willingness to be accountable; holding a wide view based on the welfare of the whole group; qualities that make the person an example of someone committed to spiritual growth."

The need to train new workers brought up some interesting psychological patterns. Often more experienced workers will hold back from teaching new ones, partly out of lack of communication skills and partly out of unwillingness to take more responsibility. This leads to duplicated efforts, difficulties in adjusting to staff changes, and a general air of distrust.

Press worker: "When I first started to work here, I was uncertain of what I was supposed to do. It seemed no one could explain to me in detail what my job really was. When I made mistakes and got into difficulties, then they said they thought I already knew what to do. I should have asked more clearly for help and information, but I was afraid of looking stupid. I can see now how attitudes of fear and guilt keep transmitting themselves from person to person."

Sometimes we might feel that we are just minding our own business and should let people make mistakes as part of the learning process. But we need to look closely at our own motivation.

Dharma Mudranalaya meeting with Rinpoche, in spring, 1987: "The learning process can require such a long period of time that individuals sometimes regard their hard-won knowledge as personal treasure. It may indeed be treasure, but keeping it for oneself spoils its deeper value. Knowledge naturally leads to greater responsibility, but hoarding cuts off this process. Older, more experienced students really do have the ability to transmit something to others; they know how to keep their balance better than new students; they know how to work hard; they have a broader perspective, and they understand their minds better. If they opened their hearts, they could support the efforts and strengthen the motivation of new people."

Press worker: "Having spent a lot of time training new people, I see two very important issues. One is that people generally do not appreciate the time and effort that goes into teaching them. They are more concerned with whether the supervisor is controlling them or criticizing them. And secondly, effective teaching involves much more than showing someone new skills. I can see now how I taught people work attitudes, and not all of them were healthy ones. For example, I myself did not know how to work well with mistakes, and my own unskillful approach of blaming myself or my co-workers conveyed itself to new people. When I look from this perspective, I see we older people are probably responsible for a lot more than we realize—both the positive and the negative attitudes here at the Press."

Advice on cooperation from Rinpoche: "Instead of supporting one another's weaknesses or sympathizing with negativities, we can encourage clarity and strength. If we have become skilled at supporting ourselves and in communicating, we can support others as well. Sometimes even a simple word or two or a light-hearted gesture can make a difference when a co-worker is feeling isolated or confused. When our hearts are open and our minds are clear, we can help each other through difficult times in genuinely supportive ways."

Memo from Rinpoche, in February of 1983: "Most members of the Dharma Press staff consider themselves students of the Dharma. Committed to spiritual growth and to the spread of the Buddhist teachings, they use their work as part of their practice, in keeping with the teaching that insight and appreciation are available within every activity.

"New volunteers at the Press can use their work as an opportunity to explore the value of Buddhist teachings in their own lives. Accepting work as a form of practice and combining it with study of the Dharma books we have produced, individuals can quickly increase self-awareness. Participating in an environment conducive to practice, new volunteers can pursue self-understanding in their own way."

Press worker: "Each of us starts out feeling that the spiritual and the worldly are two separate realms; we distinguish between Dharma practice and work. Slowly, people are beginning to understand that the two can be integrated, or better, that they are not actually separate in the first place.

"If you want to learn about the human spirit, you look into your experience, whatever it may be. We can learn from both positive and negative experiences. Once we realize that we have more options than we thought, we can learn to react in new ways; difficulties can become rather interesting."

Press worker: "The value of the community experience at Nyingma is that it teaches us the commonality of human nature and shows us the tremendous power we have to transform our situation, not just as individuals, with everyone for himself, but through working for a common goal."

Press worker: "I think many people have moments when they recognize that their small personal problems are the same as society's. But to feel this continuously evokes a desire to turn away from the truth. I would not have the strength to maintain steady conviction, to apply knowledge and vision, and to repair each imbalance in my life without the support of others."

The concept of a Sangha, a supportive community that offers all its members the opportunity for realizing their full potential, is relatively new in our society. Yet, having tasted some of its strengths, we can perceive the value of group support when this support is guided by knowledge and vision. If we wish to realize the freedom and creativity possible for human beings, a supportive group offers a way to pool our energy and resources to accomplish far more than an individual working alone. Working together toward a common purpose, we have begun to experience the benefits of bringing spiritual values into the working world.

Developing Efficient Strategies

By the end of 1983, we were hoping to take advantage of modern technology that promised to give us the capacity to produce books more efficiently, to accomplish more complex designs and even create special typefaces. Dharma books often required much work done by hand, and computerized typesetting might eliminate some of the steps. If the new equipment could handle all of our typesetting work more effectively, it would allow us to make larger contributions to support Odiyan where costs for art projects and finishing work were rising all the time.

The more skilled we become, the more appealing is the thought of new equipment. Newer equipment will often seem to be the key to producing more high-quality work, generating more funds, or solving certain types of problems. Always working within a tight budget, we have had to weigh these factors carefully to determine if the cost of expensive machinery is justified. Over the last several years, we have found that such decisions are not always easy to make. They require both long-range vision and the ability to penetrate emotional confusion to identify the real causes of various kinds of difficulties.

To modernize our typesetting department, the first step was to develop a computer linkage with the TxT that would minimize the limitations of the older outmoded typesetter. This would also allow Dharma Publishing editors to use word processing programs on personal computers to generate original manuscripts on disks. These disks could then be sent to the Press where computer operators could add codes to the text.

Press worker: "Installing the typesetting programs that linked the word processors to the TxT required many months of work with programming specialists. Since we had not been able to afford the most advanced software, we were working with new, untested material. It was frustrating but exciting to be one of the first two or three users of new software, and we worked closely with the designers of the programs. Since we were using the software to perform types of work it was not originally designed to do, we uncovered many 'bugs' as we put it through its paces.

"The process of refinement continued for many months. Each time the designer revised the software to remove a 'bug,' it would take our staff the rest of the week to integrate the change into our operating procedures. By week's end, the 'bug' was out, but the new procedure had created its own 'bug.' It took a full year before we were satisfied with the operation of the new system. Once we had begun, we had no choice but to continue until we could make it work for us efficiently.

During this time, we had to struggle to keep up with our work schedule."

The typesetting department was the first area of the Press to be computerized. The effects spread in ever-widening circles. The new technology greatly simplified the first stages of book production. Alternate strategies for typesetting could be developed to eliminate much of the work of pasteup. By writing computer formats, typesetters could now be relied upon to create typeset pages with folios, runningheads, and even charts and captions already in place. This allowed most pasteup functions to be turned over to typesetting, freeing pasteup artists to learn new skills in other departments. Simplified coding allowed editors to prepare design samples and do basic typesetting. Our sales strategies also began to change as we became capable of doing different types of work more effectively.

Learning new skills and acquiring new equipment opened up new opportunities, allowing changes in work flow and personnel. But to take advantage of these possibilities, we had to work with our resistance to learning new skills.

Press worker: "Most of us were reluctant to make the change because we saw ourselves as keyboarders, not computer programmers. The skills required are completely different; I imagine the same thing was true for editors who found themselves sitting in front of computer screens and pasteup people beginning work in new departments. Sometimes changing jobs can be very refreshing, for each type of work has its own flavor. In this case, resistance to learning was high."

Press worker: "Computers alternately excite and intimidate people. There seems to be so much we could accomplish, but the actual operation requires great concentration and great faithfulness to procedure. What we get back is precisely what we ask for, with each incorrect command clearly carried out! Until we knew how to run the system well, it was very easy to blame human errors on the complexity of the machinery."

Publishing staff: "When we started working with computers, the possibilities seemed very exciting. We wanted to do editing and typesetting; we hoped to develop a system for storing and retrieving research data. We talked to programmers and got all kinds of wonderful ideas. But to implement the ideas and play creatively with new options, we have had to go through a long learning process that is often tedious."

Press worker: "I would judge that our computer systems have not always given us good return for the time, money, and effort we had to invest in them. It was a long time before we became very skilled and could accomplish good results. Now no one would dream of returning to the old-fashioned way.

"But for a number of years, we were obtaining very mixed results. There were underlying emotional confusions and fears that distorted our ability to see what needed to be done. We were trying to solve problems with machinery instead of with knowledge — above all, self-knowledge. Because we lacked clear vision and commitment, the high-tech machinery only accentuated our confusion. There is a great computer hack saying that seems to apply across a very broad scale: Garbage in, garbage out!"

Press worker: "For several years, we could not get an accurate perspective on what would work best for our purposes. By the time we could make a tentative decision, the field and the market might have changed! We were making predictions and promises, and people were counting on us, but what could we guarantee? We did not have the confidence to make a decision and then do whatever was necessary to *make* it work or the flexibility to turn mistakes to advantage."

TNMC student: "Knowing when to persist and when to change tactics seems to be one main key to success. If you watch Rinpoche at work, you can see him sometimes stay on top of something for a long time, coaxing, prodding, even forcing it to be successful. Then other times, he will change strategies and try a different approach. Because he is intent on results, he never ends up empty-handed. Whatever happens he will never give up once he has begun."

Once again we faced decisions about the pros and cons of new equipment when the time came to purchase a new press. By 1984, we were considering how to improve our printing capacity. The 29-inch Harris press, on which all the *Nyingma Edition* texts had been printed, was worn out, and our greater volume of work required a replacement. Our first thought was to immediately obtain a used press while developing a long-range plan to purchase a new one. For years we had wished for a Heidelberg press. Although extremely expensive, it is considered the industry's best two-color press. In light of the artwork we wanted to reproduce, the Heidelberg's accurate resolution and speed made it an ideal choice. When Rinpoche encouraged us to proceed with plans for a new press, we were surprised.

Press worker: "Rinpoche's philosophy is to maintain old equipment in good running condition and keep using it as long as possible. You can see this clearly with the Big Press. Who but Rinpoche would insist that press would be worth repairing? We all thought it was a crazy idea! Now the Big Press is a great producer. But most companies do not operate this way. They purchase new equipment, run it for seven to ten years and then dump it. If someone bought used equipment from us, it would be in good shape, but we cannot count on others holding our viewpoint. Sometimes we have not been able to tell what condition a piece of equipment is in until we start asking it to do very challenging work."

Though a new press was very expensive, it proved to be a good investment. At first it offered much more capacity than we really needed, but it did not take us long to make good use of it.

The new press was delivered in 1985, in time for production of *Copper Mountain Mandala*, our most beautiful book to date. This five-hundred-page volume was printed on heavy coated paper to bring out the beauty of the full-color photographs and ornamental art that appeared on most of its pages. Every page was tinted a special copper color; the books were elegantly hand-bound, gold-stamped, and gilded.

That year we produced the *Dhammapada* and began a new series of thanka reproductions. The *Dhammapada* was our first attempt to present verses in Tibetan script facing the translation. Our first printing used color to emphasize various topics within each section.

Although most of us felt that the color was not coming out well, we did not think to call attention to it. When the finished book was submitted for review, it became obvious that the result was not satisfactory. Although many copies had already been printed, the design had to be changed and the pages reprinted. Once again we saw how much more is involved in efficient production than new equipment and the most up-to-date techniques. We have been trying to take more initiative to question work passed to us, if we can foresee any possibility of later difficulties. The more we are willing to take individual responsibiity and develop a larger viewpoint, the more consistently successful our projects will be.

By 1986, we could all see clearly that the original projections about the benefits of computer systems and equipment had not been completely accurate. Although some stages of book production were smoother, productivity had not increased as expected. In coping with new technology, we were tying up staff that could have been producing other benefits. Throughout that fall, it was easy to feel discouraged.

Memo from Rinpoche, October, 1986: "You must think seriously about the blockages and problems you are now experiencing. Look back at all our memos, see the patterns. Go over each topic and think carefully; answer each question raised in the memos.

"I know you are working hard, but if your motivation is negative, the result is not likely to be good. Doubt and self-criticism only undermine enthusiasm. If guilt, resentment, or hatred are what fuel your action, then your work becomes a form of self-punishment. If you do not care for yourself, you cannot develop the caring and intelligence that will bring success.

"The Buddha taught that each one of us can take control of our lives. Look to where you are doing well and build on that. Look ahead, expand consistently. If you have learned something about the Dharma over the past years, use that wisdom. Wisdom is sharp and clear; it leads beyond ordinary knowledge. In the end, we have to be grateful for the obstacles we encounter, even our personal negativities and emotional problems. Without difficulties, wisdom cannot be born."

Year after year, Rinpoche has pointed out that the way to meaningful and successful work in the world is to develop clearer perceptions and understanding. So often we had seen the truth of this, but it can be hard to acknowledge how much we have learned and begin to act upon it with conviction.

Press worker: "Besides inexperience or lack of technical knowledge, there are many currents beneath the surface that decrease our abilities to plan and perform well: competitive attitudes, closed communication, unwillingness to give beyond a certain point — people here have very strong opinions. Working at the Press with complicated machinery also seems to accentuate any inner difficulties. This makes it very easy to blame the equipment and adds to confusion about the source of our problems."

From a talk by Rinpoche, spring, 1987: "Often our problems seem to exist in the external world. But the difficulties may not lie in the work we are doing, the tools we are using, or even with our procedures. Outer difficulties usually reflect inner attitudes. It may be here that we need to search for the solution to our problems.

"As long as we regard our activity through the lens of emotion, emotions will color our view. Judgments and decisions cannot be made properly; our energy cannot flow freely, and vision grows very narrow. Can you imagine being completely free right now of all negative emotions? How would your work appear to you? Where would your difficulties be?

"The mind is like a fine, thoroughbred horse. If it is not well-trained, it causes no end of trouble, but once it is tamed and disciplined, its excellent qualities are revealed and can be developed. Now it becomes our best companion and reliable partner."

Press worker: "After much experience, I finally could see that we block our own commitment to succeed by telling ourselves that we are trying, that everything is all right, or that nothing can be done. If the project takes longer than expected, then we say it is really all right to miss the deadline. Or we excuse ourselves because we tried. Or we say it was crazy to try to meet such a deadline, that no one could possibly do this job. After more experience, we find out that so-called impossible projects are possible. If we have the heart, we can do it."

With more experience in meeting challenges, we have discovered that the possibilities for accomplishment are greater than we had imagined. From this new point of view, our original reasons for not being able to accomplish something are ways we excuse ourselves. But in the beginning these reasons feel very real; we believe in our own limitations, which are supported by what people around us believe as well: An untrained person can not *possibly* do this job; no one can work *that fast*, etc.

In 1985 Rinpoche urged long-time students at all the Centers to consider how they worked with time pressure. We wrote short essays, which were collected and passed around. Having gained new insight from sharing experiences, some of us felt our attitudes toward time change. For example, working to meet a deadline, we feel caught between the force of time and the force of habit patterns. A tremendous pressure can build up until we let go of the reasons that tell us *why* we cannot succeed, and why we should not even try.

Once we give ourselves wholeheartedly to the work, we find ourselves in a new situation. Accepting the possibility that we *could* meet our deadline, we have the opportunity to interact directly with time. Knowing our time is limited awakens us, transforming pressure into energy we can use. As vision clears, we can focus on priorities and determine what is most worthwhile. We do not bog down in indecision and fear. Letting time's momentum inspire us, we can respond to the challenge before us in a creative way.

Advice from Rinpoche in *Skillful Means*: "Confusion, tension, and depression all contain energy that can be used for us as well as against us. When we can calmly face our difficulties without trying to escape, without trying to manipulate or suppress our feelings, it is possible to see something that we have never seen before. We may realize that we simply do not want this pain any longer. We can then discover within ourselves the motivation to change the habits that lead us into difficulties.

"We can use the energy of our emotions to skillfully cope with our problems, to rediscover the clear interplay of mind and senses that allows our energy to flow in more positive directions. Our emotions are really only energy; they become painful when we grow attached to them and identify them as being negative. We can transform this energy into positive feelings, for ultimately it is we ourselves who determine these reactions. The choice is up to us: We can dwell on negative emotions, or we can take their energy and use it to encourage a healthier response to our problems."

Publishing staff: "For a long time, I felt very pressured trying to work fast and accurately at the same time. The job was difficult, the time was short, and Rinpoche was urging me to finish the project. I felt trapped, and I blamed one thing after another, but I could not see what was really trapping me. Now I see that what traps me is my own lack of knowledge and confidence, my own work habits, and my psychology. I very easily become afraid of making a mistake; I feel guilty when I know I am not working well, and my mind then gets distracted in making excuses. These emotions and thoughts create intense pressure. But because I am so used to believing in them, I have had trouble letting go of them and dealing with the work directly."

From a talk by Rinpoche, spring, 1987: "It is easy for the mind to become 'stuck' inside certain kinds of emotions once they arise. As soon as we feel some emotional energy surface, we give it a label—confusion, anxiety, guilt, blame, anger. Then there is a moment when we are not completely sure, so we act out the emotion. We step onto the stage and play the part. Soon we completely forget we are on a stage, and we become really involved. Like a good audience, we suspend disbelief. Now we *are* confused.

"It may take much practice to penetrate this mind-play because it is established very quickly and seems thoroughly believable while it lasts. But when we begin to notice this role-playing that the mind performs, we can take more responsibility — we can be the director. We can treat the mind more lightly and playfully, freeing ourselves from conflicts and confusions. This inner understanding of mind will support great accomplishment and enjoyment."

Skillful Means at Work

In February of 1985 we formed a new organization, Skillful Means Press, a non-profit mutual benefit corporation. The skills, equipment, and experience gained through our efforts to produce the *Nyingma Edition* and other innovative projects had allowed us gradually but steadily to expand our operation. While Dharma Press continued to produce high-quality Dharma books, the new organization rented equipment and space from Dharma Press on a time-sharing basis. Skillful Means Press contracted with Bay Area businesses to do fine-quality typesetting and printing.

Although they were not producing Dharma books, workers at Skillful Means Press considered their work Dharma activity. They continued to use their jobs to foster self-understanding, to bring the principles of the Dharma into the ordinary business realm, and to support Nyingma Centers.

Formally stated, the purposes of Skillful Means Press include: 1) providing an opportunity for members to participate in working together as spiritual practice; 2) promoting and encouraging the attitude that work is inherently valuable as spiritual practice; 3) promoting and encouraging the attitude that accepts the welfare of all beings as the goal of every activity; 4) supporting the activities of institutions and organizations dedicated to the transmission of Buddhist principles in the West; 5) supporting activities, institutions, and organizations that foster the firm foundation of Buddhism as a living force in the West; 6) supporting activities, institutions, and organizations that promote the study and transmission of the Dharma in the West.

In February of 1986 Rinpoche sent a long essay on "Working Ethics" to all the members of the Nyingma community. Workers at Skillful Means Press found it especially inspiring.

Press worker: "Many of the people at the Press hardly ever see Rinpoche. At Publishing and TNMC he is involved directly everyday. Sometimes I feel like the Press is very far away from the activities at Padma Ling. But when I look back at the memos, I see Rinpoche's constant concern and care. People who do not often get to see him read his memos with great attention."

We were asked to read and discuss the ideas, and to make an effort to bear these principles in mind as we worked. Discussion groups were formed at each center, and comments were invited. People returned to this essay for guidance and inspiration many times.

Excerpts from Rinpoche's essay: "In this country the spiritual path is sometimes viewed with suspicion as a form of escape from responsibility and the realities of daily life. But the distinction between the worldly and the spiritual is one imposed from the side of worldliness, not from within the spiritual tradition. In Buddhism the foundation of practice is the intention to benefit others, and this naturally means playing an active role in the world. If we truly want to be of benefit, to be able to offer beings protection from fear, there is no better way than to manifest our commitment through work. Each individual has a unique path, but each of us can help guide others simply through expressing our own convictions through our actions."

Skillful Means Press has added an interesting dimension to our interactions with the modern business community. In founding SMP, we had to take into consideration a completely new set of legal requirements such as payroll taxes, workmen's compensation, social security, medical and dental plans. Because the formal structure of the new business was different, new types of records had to be kept and different forms filed. Our inexperience caused some confusion at first, but we quickly learned the basic steps. SMP also had to improve sales techniques and be prepared to handle an increasing volume of jobs, while carefully scheduling the use of equipment and space with Dharma Press.

Sales representative at SMP: "When I first started doing sales, I could not even see this job as me. I was just doing the job because it had to be done. But along with this lack of participation was an underlying need to be successful. Eventually, I found a way to create a momentum and use my will. I was very successful and could attain goals I set myself. But my success was not satisfying because it was mostly for show. When I began concentrating not on the number of sales, but on an honest interaction with other human beings, my sense of satisfaction greatly increased."

Sales representative at SMP: "Sales can be trickery and flattery, bribery and show biz. Or it can be an open heart. Rinpoche has told our salespeople that the only way to be successful is to have an open heart! When I sell with an open heart, customers feel a bond that transcends any outward appearance, and they will be loyal beyond all reason. Who would believe that sales could be an excellent spiritual practice?"

Though some spiritual principles *seem* removed from ordinary business practices, most translate directly into what Rinpoche has called "working ethics:" making good decisions, assuming full responsibility, expanding self-centered concerns and short sightedness. Dharma Press and Skillful Means Press are both training grounds for developing long-range vision, determination, patience, and motivated, creative ways of working.

TNMC student: "Learning to make good decisions at Nyingma seems very difficult. We do not have a one-dimensional plan of how everything is supposed to operate or where exactly everything is heading. There is no mechanical way to come up with the right answers. People at each different organization have found good decisions require tremendous sensitivity. It is important to look at a situation from different angles, trying to see the possibilities and predict the consequences of various lines of actions."

Since our goals are manifold, decisions must lead to well-balanced results in more than one area: benefit for the Dharma, benefit for others, increasing knowledge or skills, strengthening our organizations, and supporting the community. Which difficulties can become interesting challenges? Which are too much for us to take on at this time? What is the purpose of each project and how do they fit together? Which projects take priority at different times? Which decisions can be made quickly, and which require long consideration?

With each passing year, Rinpoche has urged older workers to take as broad an overview as possible, to be responsible for finding ways to bring resources and people together in the most fruitful fashion for the benefit of all. Though we rarely feel able to expand our point of view very far, we know now that such vision and devotion to a higher purpose are the basis for developing successful leadership.

A well-balanced, long-range approach is not the province of the head or the heart alone. Rinpoche describes it as a combination of the two, in which intelligence moves beyond strict logic or simple emotional response. The heart will guide us toward cooperation with others, toward more honest self-understanding, and toward deep appreciation of a larger vision. The head will compare and analyze causes and effects from the past, tracing them into the present and future. Each situation calls for varying proportions of different kinds of intelligence.

Press worker: "I believe Skillful Means Press has been very successful in some ways and less successful in others. Our skills are good, our sales are good, but our attitudes as a working team are still not fully developed. We need to practice wanting all the departments to succeed, supporting each other, and improving communication. If these more heartfelt qualities develop, then I am sure sales and skills will also improve."

TNMC student: "There are *always* hidden blind spots, connected with emotional confusions or fears— places where we just don't want to take responsibility, or possibilities we would never consider, or things we simply do not know. Rinpoche can always detect these blind spots, but more and more we are learning to recognize our shortsightedness and correct it."

A careful plan does not necessarily have to be complex. Modern business people are often not satisfied until they do elaborate breakdowns of all possibilities, presenting options and alternatives in detail. Rinpoche does not seem to work this way, though he encourages investigating and analyzing.

From a talk by Rinpoche, spring of 1987: "When intelligence is deep and sharp enough, it is possible to penetrate to the heart of a situation, to find the crucial points that need to be addressed or the root causes of the difficulties. A simple direct path can then open before us, cutting across complexity, which is no longer necessary to have a complete picture. As we connect with a vision of great meaning, and know clearly what we wish to achieve, then we can see what response each situation requires. This is skillful means in action."

Over the years Rinpoche has encouraged us to develop clarity of purpose and longer-range vision. As SMP was established, he again urged us to consider our goals and to keep priorities straight.

Press meeting with Rinpoche, January, 1986: "It is important for the staffs of Dharma Press and Skillful Means Press to clearly examine their goals. In America there is great emphasis on short-term satisfaction and not so much on long-term values. But eventually, people look to the longer run and appreciate what holds up. So books based on real knowledge and human values will eventually be appreciated. Making such books available for the future is extremely important work. The books we have published may seem to have little effect now, but these books are not like novels that will disappear. They will endure a certain length of time, and speak to a certain audience for a particular period of time. They will be a means for Americans to contact knowledge in their own language.

"By American standards, Press workers are making a big sacrifice because you work so hard for so little money. But you have the opportunity to make a real contribution, to direct your energy toward worthwhile goals. So you must ask yourselves what your real goals are, each of you personally examining your deepest desires. The point and purpose is not to make money or to learn business practices for their own sake.

"Our purpose may be difficult for people in this culture to understand right now. In the past, the Indian scholars and masters who went to Tibet to translate Dharma texts for the Tibetans were considered national heroes. It is true that our contributions are very small compared to those of the past. Still, the introduction of new knowledge is extremely important, even if people today don't see anything special about what we do. Later, when a deeper appreciation for new alternatives develops, there may be more understanding. If you have a long-range vision, in the end, more energy and knowledge will come to your support."

An appreciation of the benefits that grow out of our actions provides reliable motivation, while developing determination and confidence in our abilities builds the basis for creativity. Over the years, there has been a slow but steady growth in awareness and in responsibility, which is reflected in successful projects.

Press worker: "Even when we ourselves become discouraged, we cannot deny what has been accomplished. I must admit that many days I spend most of my time in a pretty low state of consciousness, just doing my job, focused on my own problems. But somehow, our work has been uplifted by something larger than each of us individually. The concrete results prove it—the books, the stupa, the temple, the successful organizations. And I do have to acknowledge that I have learned something, not just skills, but things about myself that I will never completely forget. I have seen my selfishness in its many different guises; but I have also experienced other moments when I recognize the deeper potential of human nature in myself and others."

Press worker: "I continue to face many challenges at the Press, in the work itself and in working with other people. These challenges are the stepping stones that have allowed me to grow and benefit the community. The benefits I have received include the satisfaction of my desire for inner freedom, for going beyond my limitations, and for spontaneity and joy in working with others. These continue to grow naturally as I offer my efforts toward a larger purpose.

"When I face new difficulties, the practice that I find most effective is to examine my goals, to take a hard look at what effect my action is having on others, and to attempt to listen openly to the feedback others give me, though it is not always easy to hear. Can I go beyond praise and blame, like and dislike to trust a deeper inner knowing? Can I learn to take appropriate action?"

In the future we hope that it will not be necessary to take on outside contracts, and that all of us can dedicate our skills to preserving and offering the teachings of the Dharma. We do not know what the future will bring. But relying on our experience and encouraged by Rinpoche's vision, we are confident that we will find a way to continue our activities.

Inner confidence has gradually become the basis for a new sense of security and freedom. Most of the experienced members of our organizations now know that they can engage unfamiliar situations, confident that they can find a way to work with difficulties. Knowing our work is truly worthwhile has given us the inspiration to persist through problems and disappointments. These experiences help develop a kind of psychological strength that does not fear the future. Even financial difficulties do not need to worry us unduly. Each of us has numerous skills we could use to support ourselves and our projects if circumstances change.

Press worker: "I think it is quite common for people, even rich people, to worry about money, for there is a great sense of instability in society. The news about homeless people on the street, for example, makes you feel a little anxious—anything could happen. Misfortune might strike; you could lose everything, and be left completely discouraged. At Nyingma we live comfortably, though modestly; we have student savings and so forth. But the real basis for security is knowing you can take care of yourself—financially, emotionally, physically. This brings real freedom that not many people feel today. Our work and our education have taught us how to be independent."

Advice from *Skillful Means:* "Traditionally, education has been the process of learning both the knowledge and skills to take a truly responsible place in the world. But today, education usually provides only information, and fails to teach us to use it well in our lives. We do not learn about the true nature and extent of our responsibility as human beings.

"Work gives us the opportunity to educate ourselves, to incorporate higher values into our daily experience. By caring for our work, responding fully to it, we can begin to understand the nature of our responsibility as human beings. As we respond to our work, we develop our capacity to respond fully to all of life. The qualities of caring and responsiveness are the greatest gifts we have to offer."

Each of us has realized in varying degrees that spiritual practice can be brought into everyday life. Accomplishing something of value in our ordinary world requires intelligence, devotion, and a wide range of excellent qualities that spiritual traditions recommend as the basis for human development. With each passing year, it is clearer to us that these attributes support the best in everyday life; they uplift and guide our working ethic, our attitudes toward other people, toward our environment, and toward work. Guided by a spiritual vision, we do not need to retire from the world, but can act creatively within modern society. We have been fortunate to participate in a vision that inspires us to move beyond self-gratification, to channel our time and our energy into enduring and meaningful gestures for society and for the future. Our work has been both a rare education for us and a valuable opportunity to bring benefits to others.

NYINGMA

INSTITUTE

NYINGMA INSTITUTE

Opening New Horizons

The Nyingma Institute, formally incorporated in the spring of 1973, extended to the general public the opportunity to investigate the Buddhist teachings and explore their value for Western disciplines and ways of life. To lay a solid foundation for study and practice, Rinpoche focused on basic teachings common to all schools of Buddhism, while offering introductory experiential programs to encourage Westerners' interest in the Dharma. These nontraditional courses in relaxation and psychology promote balance, peacefulness, clarity, and encourage deeper inquiry.

The Institute's first program was Rinpoche's Human Development Training Program, offered primarily to educators and mental health professionals, people most likely to be interested in the Nyingma insights into the nature of mind. If a dialogue with Westerners in the helping professions proved fruitful, these established professionals might be able to convey to many people the practical benefits of Buddhist psychological insights. When the announcement for the first Human Development Training Program was mailed in the spring, the search for a suitable building was intensified. A well-designed but dilapidated older building was located soon afterwards, but we were unable to take possession until June 1, about three weeks before the program was to begin. Renovations were still in progress when participants began to arrive. It was soon obvious to the new students that programs at the Institute would be different from what they had expected.

First HDTP participant: "On June 24th the arriving 'students' found clean, if spartan quarters, and were a little surprised to be handed brooms and mops. This was not the smoothly staffed American institution they were used to; instead they were expected to help keep the place clean, clear the garden of broken glass, and help prepare and clean up after meals. Our very arrival was an immediate lesson in the Buddhist secret of survival, a philosophy which urges the acceptance of life as it is, rather than an effort to meet expectations. The Institute was the opposite of all that is institutional: Nobody could be a passive recipient of food, lodging, and instruction without becoming part of a community. Similarly, the instruction was often socratic, involving direct experience and very little book work."

During the Human Development Training Program, Rinpoche inquired more deeply into Western understanding of human consciousness, offering in turn the perspectives of his tradition. Drawing upon Tibetan medical practices, Rinpoche explained the close interconnection of body and mind, and introduced physical relaxation exercises, called Kum Nye practices, which effectively relieve tension and stress. Participants practiced basic meditation techniques for observing the nature of thoughts and emotions; they also learned some simple visualization exercises to promote concentration and clarity, and techniques to heighten awareness.

These introductory practices laid the groundwork for basic Buddhist practices such as shamatha and vipassana (tranquility and insight meditation). Though perfectly safe and not at all esoteric, these practices had a powerful effect upon many participants, for they promote the integration of heart, mind, and body that we often lack today. Later programs based on these HDTP courses became very successful.

Most HDTP participants became interested in sharing what they had learned with others; some applied what they knew in their practices or formed the nucleus of meditation groups in their own communities. Others joined the Institute faculty, where they began to train in teaching relaxation and introductory courses on Buddhist psychology. Some became members of TNMC, establishing a long-term relationship with Nyingma Centers.

HDTP participant, a counselor: "In an age where there has been so much fad and fancy concerning Eastern religion, meditation, and related topics, it is a breath of fresh air to know of a program and a man who are genuine representatives of a tradition of great richness and value. I have personally benefited from this experience and share these feelings with several other clinical psychologists, psychiatrists, and psychoanalysts, who were my colleagues at the Center. I find that these techniques and the experiences they evoke have been of great value in extending my professional work as a psychotherapist, and are consonant with the best psychological principles of my profession."

Social worker, HDTP participant and later Institute staff: "I find Kum Nye of particular value in teaching patients how to achieve deep relaxation without dependence upon tranquilizers. In a more general application, the Buddhist philosophy of personal responsibility for one's own destiny has a unique perspective, which can deepen Western cultural values in that direction. This has certainly been true for me; it has deepened my understanding and compassion for myself and those with whom I work. I am much more effective in my work as a result of my Nyingma experience and because of the continuing practice which Tarthang Tulku has inspired me to sustain. I would like to continue my association with Nyingma."

That summer, Rinpoche made establishing the foundation of the Institute a high priority. Classes in basic Buddhist concepts and history begun at Padma Ling were developed into courses in Abhidharma, the basis of Buddhist psychology, and courses that introduced the principles of the major schools of Buddhist philosophy and logic. These introductory classes were led by students trained and supervised by Rinpoche, while visiting scholars, attracted to the unusual programs being developed at the Institute, offered courses in their specialties. Rinpoche continued to lead seminars and programs in meditation, philosophy, and psychology.

Through 1977, the Human Development Program was offered each summer, supplemented by intensive summer sessions in philosophy, Tibetan language, and approaches to health that involved healing and balancing the energies of body and mind. The number of participants in HDTP continued to grow, as graduates of the program recommended it to friends.

Rinpoche devoted much time and energy to developing programs that would offer Westerners of all backgrounds and interests access to the wisdom preserved in his tradition. Weekly classes in psychology, philosophy, art, and language were balanced by meditation and relaxation courses; Kum Nye relaxation programs were now adapted to the special needs of children and the elderly. Weekend programs focused on specific philosophical issues or meditation techniques. As programs were organized on Eastern and Western approaches to physical and mental health, Western specialists in psychology, medicine and education joined the Institute staff for various periods of time.

Jesuit priest: "From all of this [academic courses and retreats at the Institute] I have grown to appreciate the immense wisdom of Tibetan Buddhism, and the importance of making the riches of this tradition more available to Americans and to the West in general. Perhaps in the future your institute will serve as a place where representatives of living traditions, East and West, can come together to share the treasures of wisdom."

Psychiatrist: "Above all else, I am impressed by the general atmosphere, which remains open to many divergent views, and the willingness of the people there to engage in open discussion and research."

By the end of its second year, the Nyingma Institute had attracted over 2,500 people from all walks of life and had become a lively but serious forum for exploration and study. Some participants had become deeply impressed with the scope and depth of a Buddhist education, which is quite different from our traditional approach to learning.

Excerpts from a letter from a philosophy professor, 1975: "You have asked why I am spending much of my sabbatical year studying so remote-sounding a subject as Tibetan Buddhism at the Nyingma Institute. In a nutshell: Of the new psychologies, philosophies, human potential and spiritual movements that have journeyed to or sprung up in the United States in the last decade, none seems to me more valuable and more relevant to our problems than the tradition of Buddhist Tibet. Since the first seminar, I've continued to take seminars and courses at Nyingma Institute, whenever I could get to California. I've heard from everyone—clinical psychologists, teachers, physicists, doctors, artists, psychotherapists, parents, students—only expressions of satisfaction, and usually of surprise as well. What is it then that takes place?

"The Nyingma Institute opens new horizons. The Lama is introducing hundreds of Americans to aspects 'overlooked' in our society . . . Throughout the variety of sessions, certain themes appear and re-appear: self-centeredness as our basic problem, with its anger, possessiveness, hatred; the fictitious character of the ego, a function of clutching behavior that tries to hold forever what is in reality a process to be lived and appreciated; enhanced seeing, hearing, tasting, feeling, and being present as remedies for the deprivation of information caused by automatic labeling; the integrative force of heightened awareness; the equation of compassion and enlightenment. This isn't spiritual exhortation as found in most of our religions, nor the short-term adjustment without regard for the human spirit, as in much psychotherapy, but — I think — an almost unique combination of the practical and the intellectual, the empirical and the rational, the pyschological and the spiritual."

This "opening new horizons" combined introductory meditation and relaxation techniques for exploring consciousness with a down-to-earth approach focusing on personal responsibility and independent thinking. Though initial exposure to these new ideas is exciting, putting them into practice is harder than we expect, for we are learning to study ourselves. Institute students who attended classes over a period of time found that the "study of consciousness" was the study of one's own mind — its potential and its limitations.

Institute student: "From the start my experience at Nyingma was bittersweet. I was nourished beyond all expectation by the practices, by the people, and the environment; at the same time I could feel my anxieties, insecurities, and resistances greatly intensified, exaggerated, and revealed for all to see. I was confronted by my own limitations.

"The people at the Institute proved to be natural and human, being themselves with good-humored acceptance. I could feel a genuine caring quality. And yet there was also something sober and sensible about Nyingma. Throughout my first interview with Rinpoche, I was secretly hoping he would tell me what to do with my life.

But rather than tell me to join his community, he advised that I relax and quit trying so hard. In my generation it became all too common to drop out of society and seek easy answers to the difficult issues of life, often surrendering one's freedom and intelligence to a guru or higher authority. Again several years later when I asked the staff if I could move in, they encouraged me to wait."

Branches of the Institute were also attracting new students. A branch institute established in Phoenix, Arizona during 1972 was offering classes. In November 1975 the Rocky Mountain Nyingma Meditation Center was incorporated as a non-profit organization. In 1976 the Phoenix Nyingma Institute staff founded another institute in Tucson where weekly classes would be offered; Phoenix and Tuscon were soon sponsoring projects to raise funds for Odiyan and TAP. That same year in Colorado, a Boulder fraternity house was renovated and became the new home of the Nyingma Institute. All faculty were graduates of Rinpoche's HDTP in Berkeley, and had many years experience in higher education and experiential learning techniques.

Newsweek, September, 1976: "Many serious intellectuals have embraced Tibetan Buddhism both as a philosophy of consciousness and as a flexible system of applied psychology . . . Tarthang Tulku offers Western psychotherapists training in Buddhist methods of treating neurosis and psychosis by 'taking refuge in your own self to find out who you are.' "

Study and Practice

In 1975 a Buddhist studies program was established to give serious students background in the history and teachings of Buddhism. The focus would be on basic teachings as presented in the Sutras (the Buddha's direct teachings) and in the shastras (commentaries by outstanding masters of the tradition). Tibetan language, art, and cultural studies were integral to this program, as were meditation courses; students took at least one course in meditation each quarter and participated in week-long retreats at least once a year.

In an early Institute catalogue, Rinpoche expressed the broad view of human education that characterizes the Tibetan traditions: "The Tibetan Buddhist tradition has always held that intellectual effort, in whatever form, is valuable only insofar as it aids growth and realization as a human being. These objectives can only be accomplished through a thorough understanding of the nature and functioning of the human mind and by the exposure of self-imposed limitations that prevent openness, balance, and compassion.

"The study of Tibetan Buddhism is far more than the undertaking of an academic discipline in the Western sense. It is a comprehensive learning process that relates to every possible situation and to every moment in our lives. Over a period of time, the effects and significance of such study deepen and take root. Finally we are able to arrive at a knowledge and an understanding that no circumstance can undermine."

In Tibet the Dharma had been introduced in a carefully planned fashion to lay a foundation for deeper understanding and transmission. In America, Buddhist teachings have been introduced much less systematically; over the last century different texts and teachings have been chosen for translation largely out of the translator's personal interest.

Crystal Mirror VII: "The early contacts between Buddhism and the West were accidental and made little lasting impression. In the nineteenth century, scholars began to study Buddhist history and languages, but only toward the end of the century did Westerners begin to follow the Dharma as a path to realization. Despite the widespread activities of Buddhist groups from every school, each busy giving teachings and initiations, basic knowledge of Buddhism in the West remains limited."

The approach to Buddhist studies outlined by the founder of the Nyingma Institute is to present the most basic teachings common to all schools of Buddhism, teachings about the Buddha, the Dharma, and the Sangha that provide a genuine framework for further study and practice. With such a background, students can benefit from studying Dharma history, the growth of different schools and philosophical traditions, and eventually approach more advanced teachings. Students coming to the Institute would not become Buddhists and enter a full-fledged training. Rather they would begin to explore a tradition new to their culture.

From an Institute meeting with Rinpoche: "It is remarkably difficult to teach the basics. So many people are fascinated with what they believe to be the exotic or the esoteric. If fundamentals are presented—the four noble truths, the eight-fold path, the law of karma—people grow impatient, convinced that they already understand. When intellectual familiarity is mistaken for realization, the profound depths of the foundation teachings are missed. It would be easy to offer initiations and mysterious ideas that would attract a lot of people. But to create lasting benefits, it is important to present the basic teachings first and to bring them alive so that people begin to look at their own lives in a new way."

In preparation for the Buddhist studies program, we investigated and initiated procedures for registering and licensing the Institute with the state. It was important for the Institute to be able to offer scholarships, grants-in-aid, and certificates of eligibility to foreign students. While these administrative tasks required several years of effort, they were essential to the goal of establishing a sound educational facility.

Credit for course work at the Institute was given by local universities and colleges at the undergraduate and graduate levels. We began doing research on accreditation and on adapting cataloguing systems used by university libraries. We compiled a bibliography of translations and books on Buddhism for new students; books in the new Tibetan Translation Series and the volumes of *Crystal Mirror* soon became valuable resources for introductory courses of several kinds.

From the outset, the Institute offered an unusually dynamic environment for study and practice. Buddhist studies students could study with Rinpoche and visiting scholars, and interact with professionals investigating the value of the Dharma in their fields. After a time, serious students could share what they had learned by teaching introductory classes and giving Dharma talks for the general public. Balancing receiving with giving created an open atmosphere for exploration.

Institute student/instructor: "Teaching at the Institute was different from teaching in our usual college environment. I felt fairly confident in presenting historical information I had studied, and directing students to useful books. But the students enrolled in these classes were persistent in asking why it was important to study history and learn unfamiliar terms. How did this relate to meditation? How would knowing these things make any difference in their practice or in their lives?

"Finally, I had to acknowledge my personal uncertainty. I expected some of them to quit on the spot, but my admission cleared the air—we were on common ground. A few volunteered their opinions, and soon we were involved in discussing the nature of ignorance, and how expectations and fixed ideas limit our capacity to learn—which I had just demonstrated. The experience we were sharing began to connect with Buddhist concepts more meaningfully: We were all learning together from direct experience."

By 1977 over four hundred students were enrolled in quarterly courses, more than one thousand people were attending special weekends and seminars, and ten students were participating in the Buddhist studies program. The small number of these students made possible an intimate student-teacher relationship in which progress was closely monitored and programs shaped according to individual needs. A degree program and a certificate program were designed as formal courses of study requiring several years of intensive work to complete.

A recent survey of Buddhist traditions (*World of Buddhism*, London, 1984) described the programs at the Institute: "The form of Buddhism taught in the Nyingma Centers is firmly based on the traditions of the rNying-ma-pa school, and it is presented and practiced in a way that allows Americans to combine its study and practice with daily professional life. The learning of Tibetan and Sanskrit is encouraged, to open the way for a proper understanding of the sources, and the Nyingma Institute has succeeded in gaining high recognition for its achievement in the field of Buddhist studies."

The Institute curriculum continued to be refined. Language studies included several introductory courses that prepared students to read texts in Tibetan as soon as possible. Philosophy courses were frequently combined with language courses as more students studied Tibetan language.

The philosophy and psychology courses covered five specific areas. Basic surveys of Buddhist literature and reviews of Hinayana and Mahayana philosophy developed a basic understanding of Buddhism. Three areas of in-depth studies followed: specific philosophical traditions such as Abhidharma, Yogacara, Madhyamika, and Logic; presentations of Mahayana path structure; and a special focus on Tibetan Buddhism. Tibetan texts were studied with visiting scholars in conjunction with a number of these more advanced courses. Though in no way comprehensive, the courses gave students an introduction to serious textual study and helped foster an appreciation for the vastness of the Dharma teachings.

Institute student: "It did not take long to read the introductory materials on Buddhism available in English — there were not many available, especially ten years ago. But once I had learned enough Tibetan to begin reading texts, there was so much to read, I could not believe it. Though my understanding was limited, to read the actual works of a master such as Vasubandhu or Asanga was a very rewarding experience."

Buddhist studies students were encouraged to participate in meditation courses and retreats to develop their individual practice. Meditation courses were based on tranquility and insight practices, and often included elementary Abhidharma teachings on mind and mental development. Special discussion groups were offered to help students apply the teachings and integrate practice and theory in their own lives.

The combination of practice and theory made the Institute a unique place to study. Western universities offer only academic subjects, leaving personal applications and experiential study up to individuals. The Institute's approach raised interesting questions about the learning process for participants.

Institute student: "As students new to the Dharma, we often are confused about the relationship between study and practice. Some of us are interested in study, not practice; we want to read texts and gather ideas as a sort of imagined shortcut around the hard work of practice. Some of us believe we can gain meditative success without study; we are interested in the Dharma, but reluctant to engage in serious studies, thinking that intellectual work would actually detract from meditation."

From a talk by Rinpoche in spring of 1987: "Traditional sayings that urge us to reject the intellect have many levels of meaning and cannot be literally applied to every situation. The properly functioning intellect has been highly valued by many eminent Buddhist masters, who spent untold time and energy offering teachings that sharpened and refined all aspects of the mind.

"Traditionally, study and practice are said to be the necessary support for each other. My teachers urged this point of view upon me, and I strongly recommend that the two be balanced. It may be that Dharma study is not necessary for everyone, but it is difficult to guarantee enlightenment without any knowledge of the Dharma.

"Individual students have their own motivation and interests that inspire them, and this must be taken into consideration. But if a student is willing to put effort into both study and practice, as best he or she can, eventually it will be clear that Dharma studies have a flavor that is very different from ordinary intellectual studies."

Institute staff meeting, spring, 1976: "The differences between the Nyingma Institute and other Western educational institutes in organization and administration may make it difficult for us to be accepted in traditional Western terms. Oriented toward Buddhist ideas and ideals, we may appear 'unobjective' or 'one-sided' in the eyes of some academics. But the Institute's purposes are served by developing the students' capacities to understand, practice, and share what they learn."

The Institute's approach to human education did not readily fit into the categories of Western educational associations that gave accreditation. We made efforts to devise joint programs with neighboring institutions that gave courses in Western philosophy, religion, and psychology so that our curriculum more closely resembled the expected format. It was difficult, however, to reconcile different approaches and standards. So the Institute continued to offer its own distinctive programs, knowing that our students could independently study the non-Buddhist subjects they found helpful or interesting.

In 1979 the Buddhist studies program was redesigned to follow the traditional Nyingma approach more closely. Foundation courses were laid out on the plan of an encyclopedic work by Lama Mipham, a nineteenth century Nyingma master. Readings were taken from major shastras, and included Abhidharma theory, the three yanas, the four truths, karma, the conditioned and the unconditioned, and the history of Buddhist philosophy. More advanced courses varied each quarter, focusing on classical texts such as the Abhidharmakosha, the Prajnaparamita Sutras, and works by great masters such as Nagarjuna, Asanga, Vasubandhu, Dignaga, Dharmakirti, and Shantideva.

We continued to assemble more materials for the library, Manjushri Vihara. Systematic efforts to acquire Buddhist texts and all available translations, as well as essential research materials, had been begun in 1975. The library now contained over 5,000 volumes. We also had the complete English translation of the Pali Canon and a copy of the Cone Tanjur on microfiche.

In 1980 the students in the Buddhist studies program were given the opportunity to put their studies to good use on Dharma Publishing research projects. One such project was the research needed in conjunction with preparing the *Nyingma Edition*. Several students began to work full time at Publishing, applying what they had learned while beginning a new kind of education.

Institute student: "I started to work for Dharma Publishing during the *Nyingma Edition* project, and I rapidly gained a completely different appreciation of the Buddhist tradition. The sheer volume of knowledge and the remarkable efforts made by those before us became real facts to me. Over several thousand years, centers had been established all over Asia, and one culture after another had been profoundly influenced by Buddhism. I had studied the accomplishments of great masters at the Institute, and I knew a little about the most important texts, but I was completely unprepared for the vastness of the tradition through time and the scope of the subjects included in the Canon.

"At the time, I was especially impressed with how much I was learning from assisting on research for the project. Later, I realized that this was a special opportunity for me to give something back to Nyingma, to offer something in return for the education I had received at the Institute. Putting what we have learned to work and making even a small contribution begins to change our approach to education. Rather than considering only what will benefit us, we begin to consider what we need to study to become of use to others. This opens up new areas we would never have thought interesting, and our education grows more balanced and integrated."

Other Buddhist studies students and instructors now took on commitments to staff the institutes in other cities. One instructor traveled to the Institute branch in Tucson, where more classes were offered in Kum Nye, introductory Buddhist philosophy and psychology, and beginning meditation. A new dean for the Institute in Boulder was sent from the Berkeley Institute. Reinvigorated with fresh leadership, the Boulder Institute offered full-time classes for the first time since 1978. Now responsible for supporting the education of others, or working on preserving the texts of the tradition, we found a new aspect of our education opening before us.

Opening Up Limitations

In 1978 Rinpoche took a leave of absence from public teaching to prepare several books and to supervise the expanding activities of all the centers. New vice presidents of the Institute, selected in 1978, began to take more responsibility. Instructors began to compile teaching manuals. Rinpoche continued to advise and train Institute staff; his books and materials from Dharma Publishing provided the core for many courses. The basic structure had been created, and Institute staff had been given the necessary tools. However, a great challenge remained. Could students effectively share what they had learned? Could the staff implement the creative vision behind the Institute?

After the first six months of working with this new challenge, the staff composed a planning report, which covered the following topics: faculty development, community development, and new course development; guidance counseling, assessing educational needs, developing more outreach programs, and enrolling new people; improving communication and decision-making and clarifying for ourselves the Institute's founding vision; making plans for the library and for research programs; improving funding, market research, advertising, and the recruitment of volunteers; and improving physical facilities. Plans for fall and winter quarters were presented in detail. Financial data for the six months up to June 1978 were tabulated, as well as projected expenses and income. But despite all these plans, the staff had not yet touched some basic issues.

Memo from Rinpoche, June of 1978: "There are many places in your report where you create a positive impression, but the basic approach is not strong enough. Finances need more attention, and enrollment is not high enough; faculty needs to be more interested and involved, and the administration more energetic.

"When I was growing up in Tibet, the people of my village would spend the winter months talking about racing their horses. Everyone grew excited by the competition and tried to prove in discussion which was the best horse. And so we have the saying: 'The horse proves his own worth in the running.' Results and accomplishments are more important than all these words. Here are some areas that need attention and improvement.

"You need to know your own mind and support each other in healthy ways that do not promote each others' weaknesses and emotionality.

"Rather than relying upon any status you may have in your position at the Institute, you need to develop more genuine self-respect.

"The right atmosphere must be maintained, so that the environment is not loose and uncontrolled. If you watch yourselves, even your physical manifestations, how you dress, walk, and move, you will see what needs more discipline. The Institute is not a gathering place or an information center.

"Try to be more aware of how the students act and think. Is a deep exchange of ideas taking place? Encourage the faculty, and find out what they need and what their problems are. You should know exactly what is being taught and whether it is effective.

"Cultivate enjoyment in your work, and try to make real contributions to the programs. Consider what you are learning in doing this work.

"Try to develop a better sense of time, not rushing at the last minute or making quick decisions. You need planning and careful consideration based on accurate information and follow-up.

"You may believe that your roles limit you, but everyone's potential is limited only by the discipline and energy they are willing to invest in their endeavors. Since there are serious people studying, our programs have great potential. So magnify your effort, and open up more dynamic energy. Do not hold back or define your limits. If you can penetrate the cloudy mind, you can make a substantial contribution.

"Being a part of the spiritual community, you could be even more capable than average business people, for the qualities you learn here can only benefit your development. Meditation, concentration, awareness, devotion, love, truth, caring, and compassion can be applied to any situation with very effective results. So take good advantage of your opportunity!

"If you can open your heart to the challenge that lies ahead, I am sure that solutions will come. Our work is not necessarily easy, but it is deeply important to preserve and transmit the Buddhist traditions. I hope one day you will understand this."

Institute staff: "In retrospect, I am aware of our great reluctance to engage the situation and the challenge directly. This fundamental resistance caused difficulties for myself and others. At the time my particular resistance was connected with holding on to a narrow vision. Now I can see the opportunities the situation offered; but then, I went from one thing to another without considering how my work connected with Rinpoche's vision or how my tasks furthered the Institute's purpose. Every responsibility, large or small, that I was given gave me great scope to use my knowledge and to learn. But I was mainly interested in things I could identify with a spiritual life, like meditation practice. I did not understand that participation in the day-to-day operation of the Institute was an important part of my practice, even though Rinpoche told us this clearly many times."

Institute staff: "I believe a lot of our difficulty was lack of discipline. At the Institute it was easy to feel that talking and planning were productive. Sometimes we would have a great burst of energy, and then ride along on a wave of enthusiasm. The results didn't show for a whole quarter. Then we would make another heroic effort to plan and publicize the courses. Rinpoche kept urging us to work at our peak all the time, but it would be a number of years before any of us were able to make disciplined, consistent efforts."

Institute staff: "When I began to see how extensive Rinpoche's plans for the Institute were, I was not certain I could take on so much responsibility. I would make my limited effort to help, but I did not want to be held accountable for something I felt was beyond my capabilities. If I had wholeheartedly participated, I could have used this opportunity for more accomplishment, expanding my limits instead of believing in them."

From *Knowledge of Freedom:* "Unable to penetrate the protective layer of reasons and excuses we create around ourselves, we undermine our ability to accomplish even our most cherished goals. We let things go, subverting our own efforts to take the actions that could make the crucial difference between success and failure.

"Slowly, a sense of messiness, of things undone, builds up. Our time goes by, filled with confusing inner debates. We begin to move and think more slowly; it becomes difficult to organize our thoughts and actions, and we begin to care less about whatever we are doing. We do not plan as well as we could; we leave things out and keep making mistakes we could have avoided, then create more rationalizations to explain to ourselves and others why this is happening.

"Although we may feel the force of this pattern as a palpable presence undermining our deepest feelings and aspirations, we are so used to holding the familiar sense of limitation close to our heart that we cannot let it go. Even if we want to change, we feel we cannot do anything on our own; everyone else is doing the same thing in their own way, so who will support us if we try?

If we do manage to make a start, others threatened by our attempts to increase our confidence and strength may try to undermine us. Lacking the compassion and energy to wake ourselves up to a larger view of what we can be and do, we eventually allow ourselves to believe that we cannot do what we set out to accomplish."

In our organizations, people sometimes have difficulty supporting their potential by acknowledging their own abilities. If they compare themselves to Rinpoche, they place him in a different "category," and lose the benefit of his example, while shortchanging their own intelligence and aspirations.

TNMC student: "When Rinpoche urges us to try something new and difficult, we often think that while it might be easy for him, that does not mean it is easy for us. He seems to have a special sense of timing, as well as knowledge and incredible persistence so that his efforts come out well. Yet I have heard him say that the main difference between him and students at Nyingma is the practice of self-discipline."

From a talk by Rinpoche, spring of 1987: "If you want to open up your full potential, a disciplined attitude is crucial. It allows you to begin exercising your intelligence and integrating body and mind. From such training flow forth all excellent qualities: dedication, integrity, consistency, caring, and deeper awareness. With these, you will be able to overcome obstacles and open the doors to all kinds of knowledge. The steps you need to take will become clear, and you will be able to implement your vision. This is not magic—it is hard work and discipline. Even greater knowledge arises from a more disciplined mind."

Desire to study the Buddhist tradition deeply and seriously takes time to develop. Often we on the staff studied what was most interesting to us or what was related to the particular courses we were teaching. Rinpoche had strongly recommended that we study as much and as widely as we could, and that we inspire students with the desire to discover the wealth of the Dharma. Once he encouraged us with the advice of the Nyingma master Paltrul: "When you are older, there will be time for practice, so now while you are young, it is best to study as much as you can."

Institute staff: "We needed to find ways to bring the basic teachings to life for others, to present them so that their real value would shine through for the modern world—teachings about cause and effect; the relation between the inner mental and emotional realms and the world of objects and events; the forms of mind conditioning that entrap people; the futility of self-centered pursuits; the possibilities of inner harmony and self-knowledge that clear up confusion and conflict, bringing meaning into human life."

Only as we personally see how the teachings apply to our own attitudes, emotions, views, and actions, can we begin to put them into practice. As understanding grows, our ideas of learning and communication begin to change. Rinpoche often reminds us of the value of a living understanding, which directly communicates to others the benefit of increased self-understanding. Institute staff had the opportunity to learn more about their own attitudes by seeing themselves at work, interacting with students, other instructors, and with Rinpoche.

Institute staff: "Once I had obtained a little bit of knowledge, I 'forgot' where it came from and how I had learned. It belonged to me to use as I chose, to support my own ideas, my own importance. This is not something we do deliberately and consciously; it happens inadvertently and almost automatically, based on how we have learned to think and feel over a long period of time. We naturally seek our own advantage and use all our resources to that end. Fortunately, Rinpoche will point out how self-importance shows through in my voice, even when I cannot see it in my actions. Accepting this has been very difficult, but I have learned to listen more closely to what I say and *how* I say it. Interestingly enough, it has become much easier for me to understand Rinpoche now and much easier to communicate more effectively with others."

Working with Rinpoche has opened our eyes to ways that we support or undermine others in communication. Because his style of speech is quite different from that of Americans, we have seen how much communication relies upon shared background, shared assumptions and views. Anyone who has taught, for example, knows how easily one slips into a role of "expert." If we use the accepted jargon and speak with a certain inflection, we are respected almost automatically. If someone's speech patterns differ from ours, we may assume the person is uneducated, and we quickly grow impatient.

Institute staff: "When I am not able to understand Rinpoche, I have assumed that he is the one who is not understanding. I am sure this assumption is operating for many of the professional and business people he interacts with, at least at first. They seem to patronize him, while seeking their own advantage—though I would wager they learn more from him than they would be willing to admit! While I found this amusing, for a long time I did not apply what I noticed to myself. When I did not understand Rinpoche, I tended to switch into the same patronizing mode. My command over the language gave me a subtle sense of superiority. Then I tended not to listen carefully to what he was saying or ask for clarification.

"Certain that I could help him, I just took charge and did it my own way. Having manifested confidence, I had to play out the role. But my results, as well as my way of going about getting them, were often quite different from what was wanted or needed. Eventually, my reactions showed me that my primary motivation was a need for recognition and approval. If I had really wanted to help, then I would have been more attentive and made certain communication was perfectly clear."

From a talk by Rinpoche, spring of 1987: "The self has practiced ways of presenting itself with gestures and language so that it will communicate confidence, accomplishment, and knowledge. But inside, these may not really exist. The confidence may not hold, the accomplishment may not be very substantial, and the knowledge may not go very deep. If we catch a glimpse of this unreality, in desperation we hurry to cover it up. We fabricate something to hide behind—a smokescreen of excuses, rationalizations, and eventually, as a last resort, emotional dramas.

"But we ourselves are caught in our creation. We believe our stories and so do not take any action, either in the world or in ourselves. Many years of energy can be wasted in this way, while all we gain is an uncomfortable, unproductive life. We may suspect that we have somehow been tricked, but the smokescreen becomes harder and harder to penetrate because it grows thicker over time. So whenever we sense this screen developing, we must penetrate it right away. Then our communication with ourselves and with others will be more genuine. Such understanding is the basis for real confidence, accomplishment, and knowledge. Now we have something of great value to share with others—real knowledge of ourselves."

Focus on Long-Term Programs

As the 1980s began, the Institute focused on developing sustained training programs to introduce a variety of different approaches to human education. During the 1970s much interest had centered on East/West comparative studies and on scholarly studies of Buddhist philosophy. Now the Institute began to offer the basic Dharma courses in new programs suited to a wider audience. Experiential programs in Kum Nye and Skillful Means were attracting new students; many more individuals were now prepared to undertake longer retreats of several weeks. Rinpoche gave the staff guidelines for developing and supporting long-term programs. Over the next decade, this emphasis would help many Westerners appreciate the Dharma as a guide to understanding that can benefit anyone who is seriously interested in self-knowledge.

Kum Nye is a special system of relaxation and self-healing based on exercises Rinpoche selected from the

Tibetan traditions of healing, meditation, and medicine. These practices offered the immediate benefits of relaxation, while also preparing interested students for meditation. Kum Nye had been part of the curriculum of the HDTP for seven years and had formed the basis of several special seminars. In 1978 Rinpoche presented the theory and practice of Kum Nye in a two-volume book and developed a teaching manual for the Institute staff.

Weekly classes in introductory, intermediate, and advanced Kum Nye, as well as week-long Kum Nye retreats and weekends, had been offered for several years. The first long-term program began in the fall of 1978, a nine-month course in Kum Nye and meditation practices, designed as a Kum Nye teachers' training. This program, which has been offered each year since its inception, combined relaxation, calming, and alertness practices with the study of philosophy and psychology.

The Kum Nye intensive programs have provided opportunities for participants in Institute classes to deepen their inquiry. They also attracted many people who would not initially have been interested in Buddhist studies or meditation.

Beginning Kum Nye practitioners are often looking for helpful techniques to resolve personal difficulties such as work-related stress or emotional conflicts. Practitioners commonly obtain greater benefits than they expect, for Kum Nye develops a deep sensitivity to the body and mind, and supports a fuller self-understanding based on direct experience of emotions, thoughts, sensations, and feelings.

Deeper self-understanding offers us the support and protection our bodies and minds need to prosper in the midst of the pressures of the modern world. Three or four hundred years ago, ways of life must have been quieter and much more "spacious." Certainly there were problems and sorrows, but the space of the world was not "taken up" by so many objects and so much information. Now our inner and outer landscapes are full of the things we have created over the centuries, things we must think about, care for, fix, or replace. We spend our time sorting them out, rejecting one, pursuing another; with so much material to deal with day after day, our minds naturally feel pressured, and our bodies are subjected to constant tension. When our space and time and energy are all "preoccupied" in this way, we are left with little inner freedom and little time for reflection.

The endless excitement and rush of events in modern society also takes its toll. Thoughts, feelings, and sensations are relentlessly stimulated and agitated. In the confusion, we easily forget how to take care of ourselves. We do not recognize our own feelings and have difficulty sorting out our own thoughts.

From a talk by Rinpoche, winter of 1986: "Over time, pressure and tension demoralize and damage the human spirit. Loss of confidence, reluctance to take responsibility, and the feeling of being pressured, even controlled, are warning signals that our human spirit is being subjected to a dictatorship of some kind. But no matter where we look, it is difficult to find the root cause of pressured, anxious feelings. While we can point to certain events that seem to 'cause' our tension, we forget to ask a more important question: Why do we allow such things to control us? If we had the knowledge to direct our lives more skillfully, we could develop more inner freedom and confidence."

Long-term programs seemed to generate deeper interest in the Nyingma teachings. Some Kum Nye graduates began more serious study in Institute classes; others took jobs at one of the Nyingma organizations to deepen their understanding through work. Some continued to study Kum Nye and and trained to become instructors. As the number of instructors increased, we could offer Kum Nye courses in Europe and South America. Interest in Kum Nye abroad has continued to grow since the first programs in 1979–1980.

In 1980 a three-month residential Kum Nye training program, an integrated course of study with all-day sessions, offered an opportunity for a small number of students to live and study intensively at the Institute. The third nine-month training program was designed for those who could attend evening sessions. Week-long Kum Nye intensive retreats were offered all year long.

These long intensives were the first results of the staff's attempts to create full-fledged, multidimensional programs. The inner steps of each kind of program had to be worked out in detail, combining practices, readings, and discussions, while each session had to be flexible enough to address the specific concerns of different participants. As the programs grew longer, instructors needed to establish long-term relationships with students. It was essential that we find ways to guide this learning process so that the participants became fully engaged in developing their own inquiry. As we gained more experience with these practices and with the learning process itself, we became more effective at helping students enrich their own understanding.

Skillful Means programs were introduced at the Institute in 1979, one year after the publication of *Skillful Means*, Tarthang Tulku's book outlining the relationship between work and spiritual values. These teachings, which take a very direct and practical approach, have demonstrated the effectiveness of self-knowledge in the everyday working world.

The essence of the Skillful Means teaching is knowledge in action, applied meditation and theory, using work as a ground for observing and learning from each experience. Once this approach is learned, any kind of work can support the learning process. Skillful Means is the basic practice of everyone working at Nyingma.

The book outlines three stages in developing a new attitude toward work: recognizing the attitudes and habits that rob work of significance and turn our daily experience into dull routine; implementing new attitudes that will support much more satisfying experience; and sharing our results with others. Together with readings from the book, discussions and communication exercises provided the core of the Skillful Means program at the Institute.

For a number of years, a bakery was run by the Institute as a Skillful Means project and an experiment in creative work. All income from the bakery was donated to Odiyan to support the building of the country center. A bakery established in Colorado also operated for a number of years.

The Skillful Means approach inspired a variety of new courses. Two courses in communication were designed for business executives in the fall of 1980 and the winter of 1981. Another course was created in problem-solving for professional working women, while a special seminar focused on changing attitudes toward work. A summer program in 1983 combined relaxation and stress management techniques, lectures, simulated work situations, evening seminars, contemplative exercises, and individualized counseling. By the autumn of 1984, enough interest had been generated for an intensive Skillful Means program.

As always at the Institute, the main challenge was to present new courses in ways that would effectively deepen understanding of human nature. Even though Rinpoche's books were rich in teachings, it often took years to work out successful programs that addressed the needs of different kinds of people. The major difficulty was that we first had to understand and apply these teachings in our own lives. Though we were all practicing Skillful Means, many of us were uncertain about its underlying principles.

Skillful Means instructor: "Despite the gentleness of the presentation, Skillful Means reflected my resistance to work with such penetrating accuracy that at first I could not bring myself to read it; eventually it became my primary source of inspiration. In a soft, friendly voice, Skillful Means told me what I had never heard before: I am responsible for the quality of my experience. All experience offers learning opportunities.

"A theme keeps coming up in my Nyingma experience: constantly going beyond self-imposed limitations and accomplishing what had once seemed impossible. This going beyond is very different from the habitual way of being in the world; it requires a concerted effort in real-life situations, supported by awareness, relaxation, and conceptual study.

"All this focus on work may not appeal to some people; indeed it did not appeal to me when I first came to the Institute. But what I am finding is that it does not matter what limitations I bring to the work. Simply being present with a willingness to participate is rewarding and exciting. There is a spirit of doing that is not based on external criteria. There is no success or failure since we learn from our mistakes.

"The work is a cauldron in which our old habits are heated up and come to the surface. For all the talk about changing patterns, there is no attempt to repress how we are. We need to see the patterns, not hide them. So we don't waste much energy repressing our old ways of acting or feeling; we just work. Work in this community seems to help people change more effectively than any psychotherapy I have ever seen."

From *Skillful Means:* "We have a responsibility to work, to exercise our talents and abilities, to contribute our energy to life. Our nature is creative, and by expressing it, we can constantly generate more enthusiasm and creativity, stimulating an ongoing process of enjoyment in the world around us. Working willingly, with full energy, is our way of contributing to life. Working in this way is working with skillful means."

The year 1979 also marked the beginning of a long-term program based on *Time, Space, and Knowledge*, which had been published late in 1977. The new vision offered a basis for joint inquiries between science and religion, while opening an independent inquiry free of all dogma. But such a path, which relies on individual intelligence, openness, and honesty, is rigorous. Rewards are directly proportional to efforts.

1977 Institute staff: "In Rinpoche's summer intensive on TSK I saw how important it was to practice on our own initiative. Although performing the exercises properly was not easy, the more effort class members put into it, the richer were the discussions and the more everyone benefited. It became clear that this was a very serious inquiry, and that motivation for study and practice had to come from the individual."

Advice from *Time, Space, and Knowledge*: "An integrated natural intelligence, unfragmented into reason, emotions, sensations, and intuition, is our greatest treasure, and our key to progress. Exploring our realm of experience with such intelligence can be an inspiring undertaking. By integrating a theoretical approach with one that is more experiential, we can actually begin to change our lives."

During 1978 Rinpoche continued to train several TSK instructors, who began to offer courses. By 1979 two nine-month programs were held at Berkeley, one in Petaluma, two at the Institute in Arizona, and one at Odiyan. Numerous workshops were planned for New Mexico, Los Angeles, Chicago, Houston, Boston, Boulder, San Diego, Seattle, and New York. In 1980 another series of nine-month programs was held at the Institute.

Participants in these programs contributed to *Dimensions of Thought*, a collection of articles on TSK by philosophers, psychologists, and scientists interested in studying the vision.

TSK News in *Gesar*, 1980: "TSK has been in print for two years and now leads Dharma Publishing's sales. Such an upsurge of reader interest at this point is unusual, and Dharma Publishing is finding the reasons difficult to analyze . . . Translation rights have been requested from countries in Europe and Asia."

After participating in the nine-month program in 1979 and the classes that followed, advanced students were ready for the intensive program offered in 1981–1982. Dawn of Knowledge enrolled fifty full-time students in a ten-month program that brought in guest speakers and explored TSK's relationship with Western disciplines. A four-day conference, co-hosted by the Dawn of Knowledge Program and the physics department at the University of California, was attended by over five hundred people.

The translation of TSK into Dutch and German stimulated interest abroad, and several study groups formed in Germany and Holland. The first issue of the *Journal of Time, Space, and Knowledge* came off the press in March, 1982. This issue included an interview with Tarthang Tulku and articles by well-known physicists, philosophers, and educators.

After the TSK conference and the Dawn of Knowledge Program, classes continued to be offered each quarter, though new long-term programs took several years to develop. Since the TSK vision is very subtle, some instructors found it quite difficult to teach. When word spread in 1986 that Rinpoche was at work on a tenth anniversary sequel to TSK, planned for publication in 1987, TSK teachers were very pleased.

TSK instructor: "I have heard that this new book, *Love of Knowledge,* will introduce many helpful background ideas to deepen understanding of TSK. Some people find TSK extremely tough reading, even with a class and guided practices as support. So I am looking forward to this new book, for myself personally, and for teaching purposes. There is apparently another volume coming out as well, one especially related to the more subtle levels of TSK, and that one I am most interested in. It seems to be time for a 'flood of knowledge!' I am sure we will soon be offering additional TSK courses of several different kinds."

Making Transitions

In the fall of 1981, a new dean was appointed at the Institute, and the former dean began a three-year retreat at Odiyan. Many of the previous staff and faculty were now working on the *Nyingma Edition*. As a new staff was assembled, new directions opened up. More emphasis was placed on outreach programs, which had begun in 1979 when Institute teachers led programs in Europe and Australia. Now Institute staff traveled to Europe and South America. Response was good; participants in these programs soon set up new study groups and began attending summer courses in Berkeley. A year-long course was offered one night per week to help train graduates of the Kum Nye and TSK programs as new instructors; reading programs and meditation practices were designed to give them more background in Buddhist studies.

Institute staff: "The administration of the Institute is regularly changed every three or so years. At first there is a great surge of pioneering energy. You can see all the new things you want to do, and all the mistakes made before your time. After a while energy wears down, and you may not accomplish all the things you imagined in the beginning. There follows a period of indecision, discouragement, and anxiety when initial plans do not work out. As the three years draw to a close, you begin to look at what you can pass along. It becomes very important to leave something stable and positive behind so that someone else will have something to build upon.

"Then you begin to see how everything you thought you did yourself was actually built upon what had been done before. Feeling that we cannot accomplish anything because we have no experience is a limited, personal way of looking. In fact, we have tremendous backing, and we can tap these resources."

Members of each new administration usually go through a period of uncertainty as they find ways to implement the vision behind the Institute.

Institute staff: "As our new administration began, people compared the situation to earlier times, as far back as the time when Rinpoche was teaching here. Then the task ahead seemed impossible. How could we match what he accomplished? New faculty members were needed, for our teachers trained in Buddhist philosophy were now working on the Kanjur and Tanjur. We had no experience in administration or publicity. For the moment, our financial situation was uncertain."

Despite financial difficulties, it was essential that the resources of the Institute be used properly. Any income from classes had to go back into education and could not be used for household purposes — the house had to remain self-sufficient. To ease the financial strain, the staff turned back their living expense reimbursements for almost a year and focused on developing better publicity strategies. Outreach trips brought in some funds, but it was difficult for the Institute to advance the traveling expenses for an instructor's trip.

Institute staff: "Publicity for the Institute has never been our strong point. We do not promise 'quick fixes' or great excitement, and this makes ordinary public relations more difficult. It also seems true that we are just not good at advertising ourselves. This may not be all that bad in itself, but it means that people do not find out what we have to offer, and that we have periods when we struggle financially."

Memo from Rinpoche to Nyingma Centers, 1982: "The Institute and its difficulties are an example of the problems Nyingma Centers should be examining. As members of the Board of Nyingma Centers, we need vision; we need to understand the whole picture. Sometimes one place is weak and another strong. How can the stronger parts support the weaker ones?

"Consider all the jobs we are doing: We run many projects at once; we do fundraising, teach philosophy, perform scholarly research, counsel students, and practice art. Throughout all these efforts, we are trying to operate not just on the business level, but also on the psychological and the spiritual levels. How does all this keep going with such a small group of people? If we take this for granted, then we ask no questions, we do not challenge, and we do not take responsibility. Suppose each one of you had to start our organization from scratch alone. How would you conduct activities? What would you do?"

Institute staff: "Looking back, I would say that at first we did not really understand the meaning of full responsibility. We kept repeating to ourselves that we would do the best we could; but in the back of our minds, we did not feel we could really be held responsible. This undermined our efforts.

"We needed vision and energy to overcome our disadvantages, which at first really immobilized us. But if we held back for fear of making a mistake, our situation only grew worse. The feeling of crisis heightened our sense of responsibility—finally, we could act because we had to. Although we were successful only to a minor degree, our actions set the stage for new developments that have continued. More outreach programs evolved, the house has gradually become more self-sufficient as longer retreats were offered, and many new people have had the opportunity to learn something about the Nyingma teachings."

This same kind of challenge has faced new deans at the institutes in Tuscon and in Boulder.

Branch dean: "I had only a couple of days with my predecessor, whose work I admired greatly, to learn how to run the center. Doubts started to creep in as I faced the void ahead. What did I want to do here? How would I fill this gap? The previous dean had been at the peak of his teaching—I was just beginning. Though I couldn't see it then, I was gripped by fear: fear of being judged, fear of failure, of having gotten in over my head, of not knowing what to do. Comparing myself, and in some cases being judged by others, tightened me up so that I lost touch with my own positive qualities.

"Gradually it became clear that such comparisons were keeping me from doing what needed to be done. The financial problems actually helped turn the situation around. I had to feel the heat of impending failure before I could thaw out and respond. The positive effects of such pressure are that it compels me to think creatively about how to use my time and resources to best advantage; I have to be greatly concentrated and relaxed in order to work quickly. Negative feelings are stirred up and stripped away. I am much more alive to the beauty and possibility in each moment. We generally wait for a crisis before we find a way to be disciplined and creative. Why not live with that depth of engagement all the time?"

In the midst of such challenges, we may recognize the preciousness of time and see how our lack of motivation holds us back from effective action. We may acknowledge occasions when our lack of attention, lack of intelligence, or lack of caring have caused trouble. But as the feeling of crisis passes, our new understanding fades. Rinpoche keeps reminding us that if we do not awaken clear vision now, we may not have time to accomplish much of value. Although it is difficult for us to hear this from someone else, experience proves this is true.

From *Skillful Means:* "Whenever we start something new, we may find ourselves anticipating the obstacles that could arise, and the limitations we must face in ourselves and in others. Although we feel enthusiastic about our work, we may also feel constrained by an underlying sense of fear that we might not succeed.

Because we are afraid to put all of our energy into our work, we undermine the force of our involvement. When we begin to look for the easy way out, we put more energy into finding excuses than into work itself. Because we give only partial attention to our work, we make frequent mistakes, misinterpret instructions, and begin to fail."

Over time, members of our organizations have begun to see how fear of failure inclines us to ignore our situation. When we are less oriented toward seeing the job done than we are toward being the one who succeeds, then both failure and success reflect on us, not as neutral and helpful feedback, but as pronouncements about our worth. Lacking confidence in our ability to learn and grow, we do not wish to discover mistakes or problems. But if we can accept mistakes as guides to show us where we have room for improvement, then even if we have made a false start, we can correct it so that the problems do not multiply.

From a talk by Rinpoche, spring, 1987: "Our situation is much more flexible than we ordinarily think, so that even if we have made mistakes, we can still change. Though our old mistakes may still cause us some future difficulty, there is no reason to keep repeating them devotedly! As soon as effort is wholesome and honest, it is easier to follow through in our actions; discipline builds on itself, each moment of care and effort making the next effort easier. Then even if there are difficulties, we do not feel guilty, for we have begun to do our very best and we know it. Each difficulty becomes a way of gaining in knowledge and strength, and each challenge we face becomes our teacher and friend."

New Approaches to Learning

In 1984 the Institute administration was changed, following our policy of rotating certain positions every three years. The dean of the Institute began a new job at Dharma Publishing, and the dean of the Boulder Institute returned to head the Institute in Berkeley. An experienced instructor from the Berkeley Institute now became the dean at Boulder. The new Berkeley administration focused especially on the long retreats and intensive programs introduced in the beginning of the 1980s. For many years the Institute's programs had centered on evening classes and weekend seminars. The new direction created a fresh and interesting atmosphere that attracted new students.

Institute staff: "The atmosphere at the Institute has always been attractive, but when the number of retreats was increased, it was even more inviting. There was a new feeling that the Institute was more open to the outside, encouraging more involvement. At Rinpoche's suggestion, the Institute offered long-time students new opportunities to participate in Nyingma Centers activities by establishing an Associate Membership. Older students could now meet together and find ways of contributing their energy and ideas."

With Rinpoche's guidance, a new nine-month program in Nyingma practices was now developed, drawing on all types of Institute teachings. The focus of this program changes each year so that students can benefit from repeating it. One especially successful program was based on topics from *Gesture of Balance*; other themes have included the nine different vehicles of the Nyingma tradition and the life of the Buddha.

Institute courses continued to be developed and refined. The five programs at the Institute — Introduction to Buddhist Psychology and Philosophy, Meditation Courses, Tibetan Language, Kum Nye, and Skillful Means — were now structured into a balanced course of study requiring two to three years to complete. A concluding course was added to integrate the five programs. An intensive residential retreat focusing on human development was offered: the four-month Nyingma training program, in conjunction with a two-month Nyingma training program.

Institute staff: "The four-month program in combination with the two-month program is a very special sequence. Rinpoche designed the program of the first four months in detail, giving us a set of specific meditation practices with specific guidelines for instruction. These practices heighten awareness, revealing the potential for much greater clarity. People develop a strong sense of direction that goes beyond the psychological and encourages them to see more, without telling them what to see or how to be. The following two-month program develops themes from *Knowledge of Freedom,* bringing a deep questioning attitude to the clarity and calm arising from the earlier practices. I have seen new possibilities unfold rapidly for participants in these programs, and teaching them is very rewarding."

Knowledge of Freedom, published in 1985, inspired a new course that focused on questioning experience as a path to more comprehensive knowledge. Discussions and guided meditations helped students discover a wealth of hidden meaning in each chapter of the book. This popular course placed new demands on the Institute instructors, who found it challenging to teach.

Institute instructor: "Teaching people to question is harder than it may seem. Asking yourself important questions deeply and persistently is a very private and delicate undertaking. People learn to go through the motions of questioning and surely make interesting discoveries on the psychological level. But to move beyond the psychological, to question the whole set-up we call the psychological, is much more difficult. The mind tends to balk and stop short. Or else the inquiry goes intellectual, shifting into words and theories. To question ourselves without getting caught in our own language, we have to really want to know, almost desperately want to know without getting negative.

"The classes I taught were very hard for me. It was exciting and satisfying work, but not at all like teaching an academic course or even a meditation class. I could feel my own fear of teaching emerge very clearly. How could I take any responsibility for someone else's development? What did I really know that I could trust completely? There I was, with *my* question that threw me back to ground level. Now could I actually teach from within that open space?"

To help students question themselves directly, instructors encouraged them to clarify their thoughts in writing and analyze their questions and answers. Questioning their responses in class opened a productive dialogue that helped students explore their experience. Rather than coming to conclusions, students were urged to ask another question. The spirit of such open inquiry seems to be very Western and yet deeply connected to the most basic principles of the Dharma.

Institute instructor: "The Knowledge of Freedom class is the 'cleanest' course I have ever taught. It does not promote any particular view at all, but penetrates to the heart of our deepest issues of being human."

Another new program called Gestures of Balance was initiated by Rinpoche to accomplish special art projects. These projects offered students an opportunity to work together in the spirit of skillful means while developing a deeper appreciation for the beauty and significance of Tibetan Buddhist art.

Institute staff: "Students had always appreciated working in the kitchen or helping out around the house. People in the Skillful Means programs might work at the Press, but until the Gesture program, there was no project that focused energy here at the Institute. This program gave more people from study groups around the world the opportunity to work on Nyingma projects. Being here, working directly with us, is the best way for them to understand the value of the Nyingma approach. When they return to Europe or South America, they can share their experience with students there."

Since 1985, participants in Gestures of Balance have produced traditional forms for Odiyan, including hundreds of prayer flags, 100,000 tsa tsas and 1,080 small stupas. Nearly 150 fifteen-inch statues of Buddhas with elaborately carved haloes were cast in plaster and then finished in gold leaf.

Gestures of Balance projects unite meditation and theory with sustained creative activity that requires new skills and deepens sensitivities. Institute students have begun to see more clearly the value of an education that integrates work, practice, and study. The challenge of difficult and unfamiliar work has gradually opened up a deeper understanding for many participants.

Institute student: "Here it was again—the part I couldn't relate to. What is a tsa tsa? Why make little statues? Once we got started and I realized how much money this was going to cost, the old patterns of doubt sprang up again. Yet when I was involved in working on the project, I could feel these thoughts relax. I could appreciate how nice it was to work with the clay and create the forms.

"The project seemed to take over all the Institute. There were tsa tsas everywhere you turned. One benefit was very clear. The people who worked on the project learned to work together, overcame obstacles, and used their combined energy to accomplish things that just days before they had said they could not do. I began to realize some of my resistance was that I felt left out. I was kept out only by my own judgment and negativity because I didn't understand the forms.

"One day when Rinpoche came to visit, he spoke about the project. It wasn't often, he said, that we would have a chance to use money without creating any bad side-effects. He described the tsa tsas as tape recordings of a beautiful prayer for the benefit of all beings. Each time a tsa tsa was recreated by the mold, another prayer was made. Thinking of how world events were worsening, how countries were competing with one another to make bombs, I decided that making tsa tsas was not such a bad way to spend money. I also began to appreciate the idea that those very areas where I lack understanding and feel resistance are the areas where I might learn something new."

Throughout 1985 and 1986, a deeper appreciation of Tibetan Buddhist art was fostered by a series of exhibits at the Institute. "Fifteen Years of Dharma Publishing Thankas" was shown in 1985, while in 1986 the exhibit "Sacred Images" was held at the Institute as a benefit for the Stupa Fund. In the fall of that year three hundred people attended "Path of Beauty," a showing of more than one hundred thanka reproductions.

Setting up these exhibits is always an intensive group effort. Waiting until the last moment so as not to disturb ongoing classes and seminars, the staff and volunteers erect wall-size panels to display art, put up decorations, and clean the Institute before guests arrive. For the duration of the exhibit, the schedule at the Institute becomes very flexible. We create a small catalogue for each exhibit, a wonderful learning experience for us and for others. Every time we prepare an exhibit, we understand more about sacred art and have come to appreciate these opportunities to share its beauty with others.

Institute News Digest, winter, 1986: "Filled to capacity and beyond, and bursting with creative energy, the Institute is now enjoying a productive and eventful winter. 108,108 tsa tsas will soon be finished, and a slide show of this project has received enthusiastic acclaim. 250 of 1,080 stupas have been completed, and in April we begin the production of 1,080 statues of the Great Teacher Padmasambhava."

During this period outreach programs developed rapidly. As early as 1979, Institute instructors had begun to travel abroad to offer seminars and short retreats. Regular visits were made to Germany and Holland twice a year between 1980 and 1986 to offer classes in Kum Nye, meditation, and TSK. Austria and Norway also hosted instructors several times. In 1984 a ten-day retreat was held in Brazil for forty-five participants. Beginning in 1986 instructors traveled to Brazil twice a year to offer large workshops in Skillful Means, Kum Nye, and Knowledge of Freedom. By this time, ten Dharma Publishing books had been translated into major European languages: German, Italian, Dutch, and Portuguese. Study centers had been established in Germany, Holland, and Brazil. People from Japan have also been coming to study more regularly at the Institute in the last several years.

As the Institute reached out to more and more countries, increasing demands were made on the staff. We had to learn to present helpful teachings in short retreats or seminars, find ways to organize the study groups, and then help the groups maintain contact with the Institute. Since travel and arrangements are expensive, careful planning and organization were essential. The seminars and courses had to produce enough income to justify the original outlay.

Outreach instructor: "On the positive side, Institute outreach programs bring Rinpoche's teachings to many different people who might not become interested in Nyingma simply by reading books. Some individuals need a group setting, a chance for discussion and questions. Once they become more involved, they often read other Dharma Publishing books and develop a real interest. But sustaining this new development requires a lot of attention from the Institute. We have found the best approach is to invite serious students to come here to Berkeley. All the long-term outreach students eventually do this. This also helps the Institute and brings new people into our programs."

The process of setting up and guiding the new study centers opened a wider perspective for the Institute staff and the Nyingma Centers Board overseeing their progress. The Centers Board is responsible for general guidelines, organization, and management, while the Institute advises on course content. As we attempted to guide new groups so far from the Institute, we realized the importance of conveying the larger vision that inspires Nyingma organizations in America. We developed a much deeper appreciation for the vision and energy that have gone into establishing the Institute and the other Nyingma Centers.

Although our own knowledge of the Dharma is limited, we have had the opportunity to appreciate the contributions the Buddhist tradition could make to our culture. Guided by Rinpoche, Institute staff have learned how to engage the Western heart and mind in a genuine inquiry about the meaning and purpose of human life. Throughout fourteen years of offering courses and programs, the Nyingma Institute has found many different ways to encourage self-understanding and to explore the teachings of the Dharma.

At times the focus has been on formal Buddhist studies; at times more psychological and experiential introductions have been emphasized. Over the years, such explorations foster the deeper self-understanding fundamental to approaching the Buddhist teachings. Participating in making new knowledge available to others has made work at the Institute a rewarding path of learning. As appreciation for the deep wisdom of the Dharma grows, these precious teachings may flourish here in the West.

ODIYAN MANDALA

Laying the Foundation

From the beginning, Tarthang Tulku envisioned a country center that would accommodate a wide range of activities such as traditional Buddhist studies and translations, meditation and retreats, sacred art, and cultural projects. For the past twelve years, the desire to give this vision shape and form has inspired all the Nyingma Centers.

Preliminary proposals for a country center were drafted in 1972, and volunteers searched throughout northern California for land. Dozens of separate trips were made over several years, but nothing completely suitable was found until 1974. That fall, we located a large tract of land that had once been inhabited by the Pomo Indians. Exactly 108 miles northwest of Padma Ling, this property reminded Rinpoche of Oddiyana, the birthplace of Padmasambhava, the most powerful of the masters who transmitted the Dharma to Tibet. Set among rolling hills and surrounded by forested ridges three miles inland from the Pacific Ocean, this beautiful landscape was a peaceful and yet inspiring environment for future Dharma work.

By the spring of 1975 preliminary architectural planning and design were underway, together with the preparation of a detailed environmental impact report for county officials. On July 10, county officials approved the Odiyan plan and granted a use permit. On August 8 the land purchase papers were signed. The following day, August 9, the land was consecrated and named Odiyan, in honor of Oddiyana. In dedicating the land for the Dharma, Rinpoche performed special religious ceremonies and buried sacred relics at the center of the site chosen for the temple.

Rinpoche envisioned the Odiyan country center as a mandala with the temple situated at its center. In the Buddhist tradition a mandala is a dynamic, ordered arrangement of elements, a basic pattern that gives rise to creative action. Its fundamental structure is an inner circular space surrounded by four walls, with gates in each of the four directions opening to a landscape enclosed by an outer circle. Associated with each direction are specific colors, shapes, and a wide array of different elements related to the human body and mind, as well as to the larger cosmos. A mandala can be drawn as a diagram or painted as a thanka; its form can be reflected in the structure of monuments and buildings. In Tibetan art, mandalas were usually represented in two-dimensional drawings and paintings. To construct such a mandala architecturally would be a tremendous challenge, but very meaningful historically, psychologically, and spiritually.

Though excitement and energy were running high, some of our friends and acquaintances thought such a huge project was just a dream and unlikely to succeed. A few of Rinpoche's friends strongly recommended he start with something much smaller and more manageable. From one point of view, this seemed to be reasonable advice. Rinpoche had no background in construction or architecture; his students were mostly young and untrained in any field that could support such a project. There were few funds available, and many other important projects were awaiting attention.

TNMC student: "We certainly had no idea what we were getting into! There was a lot of excitement and enthusiasm, but very little understanding of how much work—psychologically and physically—would really be involved. But we were inspired by Rinpoche's ideas and wanted to help. Rinpoche knew, I am sure, that it was going to be very difficult, but once he feels something is really important, he finds ways to do it. I have heard him say that somehow the Dharma Protectors have always helped. This seems true to me—how do you explain the success of such a large-scale project without the staff or money or skills?"

Reflecting on the plans made some fifteen years ago, we see that Odiyan has come into being in a process that seems almost miraculous. Odiyan "could not" have succeeded but did. The land was found, buildings took shape, and a stupa and a temple were created, complete with art and ornamentation.

TNMC student: "Each one of us who has been fortunate enough to participate in the creation of Odiyan has had to stop and wonder. We can describe how the buildings were built, how the materials were purchased, and even how Rinpoche spent so much time overseeing these efforts. But considering that just one individual was doing all the designing and directing, and that an untrained crew of ten or twenty was holding the hammers, the creation of Odiyan remains a kind of mystery."

From another perspective, we can look back and see how vision, hard work, and discipline were the keys, together with persistence and willingness to take responsibility. With Rinpoche's constant encouragement, his example, and his supervision, it was possible to develop the strengths, skills, and knowledge to bring the vision of Odiyan into being.

TNMC student: "I remember when we first set up the country center office to coordinate the new work at Odiyan. Suddenly I was thrust into a fast-moving world of construction and fund-raising. I had to talk to architects and engineers about subjects completely foreign to me (I had been a dancer). My head was spinning trying to understand and remember what was said and then correctly explain this to others who needed the information. Somehow Rinpoche was always one step ahead, keeping track of the details. He cared so deeply for this new center that he just poured energy into it. When I tried to explain to him that I knew nothing of construction, he exclaimed: 'You can ask questions! At least the answers will be in your native language!' "

Now that the construction of Odiyan nears completion, we realize that none of us could have envisioned what Odiyan has become today, nor could we have imagined the remarkable process in which we were about to participate.

We began work in the fall of 1975 by renovating the few buildings on the property, an old farmhouse, a garage, and a barn. The farmhouse and the barn provided housing for most of the construction crew, and some later arrivals lived in their campers or trucks. The core of the construction crew consisted of TNMC students, none of whom had experience with heavy construction, architectural planning, or surveying.

We erected a shop and began work on the square rim structure that would enclose Odiyan's central courtyard, the future site of the temple. When the county approved foundation plans, volunteer architects and engineers instructed our novice crew in surveying, in laying a foundation, and in reading blueprints. After the foundation was laid, 2,500 feet of trenches were filled with concrete footings and laced with rebar. With the foundation in place, the basic structure of the mandala began to emerge. So did a pattern of poor planning that generated the need for a last minute rush. Sometimes we were successful in spite of lapses in planning and follow-through, but we could not always rely on having such "good fortune." Still, there were occasions when we felt this project had special protection.

Odiyan worker: "That fall and early winter we were working against time. The rains were due, and we had to finish the foundation before the dirt roads became impassable for our concrete trucks. Then in December, the weather turned sunny. Since this was unusual and not likely to last, the crew worked around the clock for eighteen days to prepare for concrete pouring. When the concrete trucks arrived, all the foundation walls were poured in one day. Just as the last truck drove out, the rains began once again."

By the winter, the building permit was received, and work began on the subfloor. For wall-framing, over 350,000 board feet of lumber were cut in the shop — the portable saw mill was one of our first pieces of equipment. The crew was convinced wood had to be purchased, though Rinpoche had hoped to use lumber from the land. In retrospect, he was probably right, but we were insistent. Soon timber became a major expense.

Because only one crew member was experienced at reading architectural plans, the wall sections were prefabricated; the crew could then assemble them on-site. Three sides of the rim structure went up in just ten days. Encouraged, our crew was working hard and well. During this period of rapid progress, Odiyan workers felt that the structure emerged almost magically.

In the springtime of 1976 the Nyingma master Ven. Dilgo Khentse visited Odiyan and conducted a religious ceremony to dedicate the site chosen for the future temple. He inspired the workers, reminding us of the tremendous value of these efforts for ourselves and for future generations.

That August H. H. Dudjom Rinpoche, head of the Nyingma School, visited for three days to give traditional blessings to Odiyan and all those involved in its creation. He held a ceremony and buried Dharma treasures at the sites of the central temple and the entryway pagoda shrines. He also gave advice on where to drill a new well. His Holiness greatly encouraged the workers when he remarked that the work being done at Odiyan was very meaningful for the future.

The rim structure, which contains fifty-two residential rooms, a large kitchen, and meeting rooms, was ready for roofing in the summer of 1976. The shape of the roofs was retained in the interiors of the rooms, with their distinctively vaulted ceilings, sixteen feet at their highest point. Each side of the rim structure had an opening where entryway gates surmounted by temples would eventually be built. Now these openings were marked off with prayerflags. One hundred fifty grooved redwood columns formed an inner gallery and outer porches. Elaborate lotus bases for each of the columns were cast in concrete, a process that took one worker six months. Fireplaces for the meeting rooms were constructed from rock on the land.

During the fall and winter of 1976 electrical wiring and plumbing were installed, a 60,000 gallon water tank erected, and a successful new well dug, precisely where H. H. Dudjom Rinpoche had recommended. A thirty-year-old forklift, the first heavy equipment, was bought and a foundry for casting statues constructed. We also began reforestation and clearing work on the land, a long-range project to reverse many years of neglect.

Beginning in 1976 Odiyan kept a number of domestic animals: several horses, a few goats and cows, a pony, and some chickens. In July of 1977, a herd of thirty-five mustangs from Nevada were given refuge at Odiyan after Rinpoche had heard they were dying of drought. Though we have had little time to ride and train horses, we tamed several mustangs, and plan in the future to give more attention to them and our growing domestic herd.

At the end of the first year, construction was off to a good start, and the crew was beginning to learn how to work together—a process that was to continue over more than ten years. As the work progressed, the crew received Rinpoche's continual guidance and support to establish good procedures and communication.

From an interview with Rinpoche in 1984: "To direct and coordinate all our various efforts, I constantly had to be aware of a whole range of activities. We were acting as our own contractors, subcontractors, designers, planners, and architects. We had some consultants helping to draw up plans, but every day I had to make informed decisions on legal, financial, and construction issues, on design and architecture, on community relations and policies for volunteers. Although I frequently attempted to delegate responsibility, I usually found the results were better if I stayed closely involved with day-to-day activities."

Finances required constant attention, for such a large construction project required sustained financial support. While Tibetans who know about the Odiyan center might imagine that we have had rich American patrons, Westerners might speculate that we have used clever strategies to raise money or have been unusually lucky. In reality, funding our projects has been a continuing struggle; hard work, careful saving and planning, and a high tolerance for shortages have been essential ingredients for success. Odiyan's expenses have been met by our savings and by individual contributions, a small but always helpful source of funds. Valuable support for Odiyan has been generated within the Nyingma Centers—the Institute, the Press, and the

Bakery. Financial summaries are recorded in the Odiyan history, *Copper Mountain Mandala.*

Because Rinpoche carefully controlled materials expenses and the workers were volunteering their time and labor, we could hold down the costs dramatically. For example, the cost of the rim structure came to less than $15.00 per square foot as compared to a commercial cost of $40.00 per square foot. On the other hand, we have had to guard against wastage of different kinds. We sometimes miscalculated materials needs, tying up money in unnecessary supplies; worse, unused supplies might not be properly stored and could eventually spoil. Over the years, we have seen how each small error adds up, especially when the budget is very tight. If we try to make good use of everything, even small items, gradually we can make substantial savings.

TNMC student: "Watching Rinpoche squeeze every last drop out of our materials has been a real lesson in responsibility. Perhaps because we have all grown up in America, we do not realize the real value of these things. We would throw away paper by the pound, as well as nails, scraps of all kinds, even left-over food. I have seen Rinpoche pick scraps up off the ground and turn them into something useful or even beautiful. I have heard he collects pennies—I don't know if that's literally true, but that is certainly his attitude."

TNMC student: "Wasting supplies is not just a matter of being irresponsible; it shows a particular attitude about time and money that seems very prevalent in our culture. When we feel skilled, we feel our time is worth something, and we do not want to spend it picking up nails. But we should look closely to see what we are doing with those few minutes. When you deal with projects that are the scope of Odiyan or the Kanjur and Tanjur publication, then all the little material losses add up. Taking both time and money into account is just good business, but it also develops a much more acute sense of how we use time."

Odiyan worker: "Some of the workers feel that there are times when Rinpoche deliberately holds back money as a kind of challenge, but I don't think so. I think it's just that the budget is always stretched to the limit. Whenever we've come to Rinpoche with a thoughtful, clear proposal for equipment or better material, he has always supported it. If we don't have a clear vision or good planning—well, Rinpoche has a sixth sense for any fudging or cover-up. If we set up situations that don't work because of our poor planning, and then come to Rinpoche with our problems for him to fix, we wind up using all his money and his energy without accomplishing anything in return. The challenge is to come at problems with the right energy. Then we can usually get results."

Learning How to Learn

Individuals working at Odiyan have had a remarkable chance to develop skills while applying them to create something of value for others as well as for themselves. Without serving any kind of apprenticeship, Odiyan workers found themselves carpenters, electricians, plumbers, and heavy equipment operators. Engineering and design skills, casting, plating, roofing, sheet metal work, welding, gardening, reforestation, and landscaping expertise—all these skills were required and had to be developed. In the beginning construction skills were most in demand; the work gradually called for more handcrafts and various artistic skills. In addition, management, record-keeping, financial planning, and communication skills were always important.

Odiyan has provided abundant opportunities for all workers to learn. Each person is allowed as much responsibility for planning and organizing a particular segment of the work as possible. Instead of doing the routine tasks of an ordinary construction job, workers are given a project to carry from the end of the planning stage to completion. This approach restores the pleasure and satisfaction of the craftsman to daily work, but it demands that each person learn more than one skill.

Our beginner's approach has actually proven to be helpful in some ways. We have solved problems experts told us were insoluble; we have pioneered new techniques and discovered new applications. Because many of our projects are unusual, we find ourselves working with materials we have never used before to accomplish something we have never seen anyone else do. Sometimes we do not know enough to hesitate. Because we want a certain result, we try something without knowing it was supposed to be impossible.

As long as we keep an open mind, being a beginner is an advantage, allowing us to learn new skills very quickly. If we have no great emotional investment in protecting a professional reputation, we may be willing to try novel techniques and materials and learn from mistakes. The lack of apprenticeship training in all our organizations, however, has sometimes tricked workers into a false sense of confidence.

TNMC student: "Suddenly we forget that we just learned how to do this work. Now we are arguing with others about the best way to proceed or giving Rinpoche a confident report about what needs to be done. A month ago, we were unsure of ourselves; now we are experts! But if it doesn't work out, then we can say: 'After all, we aren't professionals.'"

Odiyan worker: "In the beginning we really had almost no knowledge at all. Sometimes we just looked in the phone book for someone we could talk to for advice. Lots of times the things we were trying to do were things that even the experts hadn't done, so when we did get advice, we had to take it with a grain of salt."

To find out the techniques or materials needed for unusual projects, we had to ask advice, read and study, compare notes, and ask more questions. Frequently we thought we had a good technique worked out or had found the right materials; later, our experience proved us wrong. This pattern has repeated in all our organizations because we do not always realize when we have stopped our inquiry too soon.

Not asking questions reveals a reluctance to take responsibility for our work, but for many years we did not see this. Rinpoche kept pointing out that we had not asked enough questions, that we had not investigated carefully. Until we gain more experience, it can be difficult to feel capable of taking responsibility. Protection against mistakes increases as we develop awareness by questioning, evaluating, and analyzing. We have found that awareness is closely connected to caring and a sense of purpose; when we care deeply for our work and feel responsible for results, a lack of knowledge actually sharpens awareness and intelligence.

The concrete nature of the work meant that any lack of awareness or responsibility would manifest in poor results that would be easily noticed. Each step of construction required research into techniques, materials, and strategies. The scale of the construction intensified the seriousness of every poor decision, while the high expense of building materials meant miscalculations and mistakes were unusually costly. In 1976, for example, mistakes were made in installing a Corten steel roof, and the work had to be redone.

Seeing this pattern repeat, workers began to realize that the work provided a special learning opportunity. However, learning to use work as a means for gaining insight and self-knowledge takes time. Most of us had hoped for more formal teachings from a Tibetan lama and were frustrated when the teachings did not manifest as we had expected. Gradually, our expectations were replaced by more practical attitudes. Those of us who persisted through the initial disappointment could begin to use the opportunities at hand.

Odiyan worker: "One of the difficulties I had when I came to Odiyan was that I really didn't understand why the buildings had to be so elaborate. I didn't see why we couldn't just finish the construction and get on with the real work. I didn't realize the construction *was* the real work."

From an interview with Rinpoche in 1984: "The realities of work give students countless opportunities to explore their habitual attitudes and actions, and see their consequences. In a community dedicated to personal growth, self-knowledge and mindfulness are real possibilities, not just abstract ideals. For those who are willing to face the challenge, Odiyan has been a continuing lesson in the value of intelligence, awareness, and creativity, and a case study in the slow growth of deeper understanding.

"Odiyan offers us an excellent opportunity to carry out such an investigation. If workers respond to each new situation with resistance, looking for ways to avoid responsibility or holding on to their personal positions, learning will be slow. But if they can to some extent break through resistance, learning can be very rapid. Each instance of openness makes it easier to respond with intelligence the next time."

Our lack of knowledge and experience could have been regarded as a dangerous deficiency, a recipe for certain failure, or an excuse for every new mistake. Rinpoche's approach, however, is to work directly with whatever shortages, weaknesses, and obstacles exist to develop clearer awareness, stronger concentration, and steadier, positive energy. Without always knowing exactly how to proceed, we have attempted to follow Rinpoche's advice and have learned to work in ways we did not always believe would be successful. Again and again, we have seen that willingness, cooperation, discipline, concentration, and openness to new perspectives are catalysts for learning.

Odiyan Report from 1977: "Rinpoche teaches that awareness, concentration, and energy are the sources of creation, and that even without past experience, we can succeed when these three are fully applied. These three qualities will carry us past our limitations. The growing beauty of Odiyan seems to prove this teaching is true."

From a talk by Rinpoche, spring of 1986: "It takes time to learn how to develop concentration, awareness, and energy, how to use one's own natural resources. In the beginning, we may not know what we are doing. But concentration, awareness, and energy can develop naturally—from an interplay between knowing and not knowing. Under the proper circumstances, ignorance is not so bad. If it becomes a kind of sharp and clear questioning, then it is the close assistant to wisdom. Not knowing does not obstruct knowing, but rather makes room for it and calls it forth. But for this process to happen, not knowing must be supported by a positive attitude. So hand in hand with the sharpening of intelligence must come the nourishing of a positive, open attitude. And this, too, takes time to stabilize."

In all our organizations, we have noticed that attitudes shift over time as people begin to learn from their work how the mind and emotions operate. Feelings of enthusiasm, commitment, and excitement run high in the beginning, partly because we do not yet know how difficult the work will be. Soon, good ideas, criticisms, and proposals are offered as we try to take responsibility. But we find ourselves in competition with others for roles we consider important. It can be difficult to distinguish a desire for authority and control from a willingness to take real responsibility. Even when our intentions are good, we may come into conflict with others who feel they are also taking responsibility.

As we gain experience, we begin to see the underlying patterns of confusion and emotions. If we feel incapable of changing or do not yet know how to work with our own emotions and thoughts, our confidence and enthusiasm, which may not have been grounded in real understanding, blow away with the wind. Now we do not want responsibility even when it is offered. Fear of making a mistake paralyzes our energy.

TNMC student: "Before I had started to work at Nyingma, I felt very confident in myself. I did work I knew how to do, and I considered myself competent and responsible. At Nyingma, I eagerly took on unfamiliar work and enjoyed the challenge of teaching myself new skills, but I did make costly mistakes. I soon began to lose confidence and grew confused. I could not understand how working and practicing the Dharma could be making me less confident, less calm, less successful. I thought I had made a mistake to work at Nyingma.

"In time, I realized that my earlier confidence and self-satisfaction were not really very deep. It was mostly an act that I carried off successfully; others believed it, and I did too, because I never put myself in a really challenging position. Here, as we are tested in the crucible of experience, we see for ourselves how knowledge, skills, and personal qualities hold up; once we discover the importance of developing discipline and self-understanding, then a new kind of confidence begins to grow from a solid foundation."

The crew faced the same kinds of questions that all members of our organization have asked as we tried to combine a spiritual way of life with work in the world.

From an interview with Rinpoche, 1984: "Young workers are likely to have special difficulty as their involvement with Odiyan grows. Because of their inexperience, they may feel they are missing something by not being active in the outside world, or they may become easily disheartened by setbacks. Their family and friends may not understand what they are doing and may not support their efforts.

"On the other hand, older workers face their own set of concerns. As their time at Odiyan lengthens, they begin to wonder what they are doing with their lives. By conventional social standards, they are accomplishing very little. They have no career and no prospects; they are not building up assets or making a name for themselves. Is this really how they want to spend their remaining years of physical vigor?

"Filled with such concerns, the individual will usually arrive at a time when he is tempted to leave. Ironically, this often happens at the exact point when he is beginning to make real gains in awareness and responsibility. Responsibility involves commitment, and many people have a strong fear of making a commitment."

Until we became more familiar with these psychological patterns, it was hard to work consistently with full dedication as individuals and as a group. The small size of our crew and the large scale of the work required effective teamwork. When a project calls for so much willingness to learn and demands the growth of new attitudes and skills, the group dynamics can become very complicated. Individuals are all in different stages of growth, each of us working through personal struggles with our own confusions and weaknesses.

In the beginning, our crews did not know how to work effectively together. Rinpoche gave many guidelines, but we had to work out the specifics such as how to resolve disagreements or how to deal with different work styles. We began seeing all kinds of interesting interpersonal reactions related to issues of individual and group responsibility. Beneath the surface, most of us have a two-sided relationship with our jobs. We want our job for ourselves and resent too much help or advice. But we do not necessarily want to be the only one responsible or have to do all the work. When it comes to someone else's work, we greatly enjoy advising and critiquing—after all, we are not responsible.

It is possible, however, to have clear lines of responsibility without staking out such limited personal territory that we do not concern ourselves with important group responsibilities. When we find ourselves saying, "That is not my job," or "That is someone else's job," we need to look again. Are we minding our own business in a healthy fashion, or are we contributing to a shared avoidance of responsibility? Such attitudes are very contagious. No one else cares, so why should we?

In time, we found that difficulties in teamwork can actually increase as we develop better skills, for we usually develop a sense of territory to go with them. We feel comfortable and secure, and wish to protect our job. We may even hold onto work, afraid to complete it and continue on to something new and unfamiliar. If we do not transmit our skills to those who assume our old tasks, cooperation is blocked and time wasted. Sometimes we really do not know how to share knowledge. We may have developed our own style of working, which someone else might not be able to duplicate; we may feel uncertain of our ability to teach someone because we are self-taught and not professionally trained; or we may secretly want to see others struggle the way we did to learn "the hard way."

When we become short-sighted in this way, we can easily forget our higher goals. Our whole point of view then naturally reverts to our habitual way of evaluating our efforts: Do we have a good position? How much power do we have? What do others think of us? Working in a group can help us discover and open up these negative patterns, for we see our attitudes reflected in our co-workers. Sometimes it is easier to recognize various ways of refusing responsibility in others first; then we can begin to acknowledge them in ourselves. Seeing how patterns of manipulation and territoriality undermine the whole group helps us let go of destructive approaches more easily. Once we experience the benefits of cooperation, we can work more wholeheartedly as a team toward a common purpose.

Cooperation combined with leadership and individual responsibility supports effective teamwork, which is what we are aiming for in all of our organizations. Although our crews may have foremen and projects have coordinators, each worker takes on as much responsibility as he or she can within specific areas, while a coordinator centralizes communication and information within the group or with other groups. This style of working requires that each person have a strong sense of the purpose of the work, a solid appreciation for the benefits of working together, good communication skills, and an ability to take individual responsibility for the success of the whole project. As each person grows in understanding, the group as a whole works better.

As we would soon discover at Odiyan, none of these abilities develops overnight, but requires experience and consistent efforts. The inner development of the people and the growth of Odiyan's structure were intricately linked — one could not develop without the other.

Meeting the Challenge

By the spring of 1977, after nineteen months of dedicated effort, the rim structure was nearing completion. To celebrate the end of this initial phase of Odiyan construction, an Open House was planned for June 6 to welcome and thank those who had helped make Odiyan possible through their support and encouragement. It was also hoped that the second TSK seminar could be held at Odiyan during that weekend. The large amount of finishing work that remained had to be successfully completed before June.

Odiyan Office coordinator: "As the completion deadline approached, it became dreadfully clear that we could not meet the schedule. The naive, passive hope that 'everything would turn out OK,' like it does in the fairy tales of childhood, was abruptly upset. Passive hoping had to be replaced by resolute doing *now*. Actions, not thoughts about actions, were needed. Even communication became an action to make sure something was accomplished, rather than a conversation about some possibility for the future."

During May, up to eighty people worked at Odiyan day and night. The entire construction area had to be cleaned and the guest rooms completed and furnished. Work continued during the TSK seminar held on Friday and Saturday. Tiles for the walkway were set just before the guests arrived Sunday for the Open House.

Four hundred people attended the Open House, touring the land, viewing the models for the planned temple and entryway pagodas, and attending a short program. Seeing the progress that had now been made, guests and supporters began to realize more fully the scope of the vision behind the Odiyan mandala.

The completed rim structure now became the home of Odiyan workers. During the fall and winter, prayer wheels made at Padma Ling were installed in a small temple-room in the rim structure. With better facilities and some solid experience, the crew felt refreshed and confident. Work began on the foundations and framing for three of the entryway pagodas. The east entryway was left open to give heavy machinery access to the temple mound.

All through the cold wet winter, we worked on the entryways. Some of this work was not so difficult now because we knew the basic framing and foundation procedures. Our newest challenge was learning to frame a dome. The eight steel beams that define the dome were assembled off-site for the first entryway in the north, but we learned how to do the steelwork ourselves for the rest. Framing the north dome in wood proved unusually difficult. On the last day of dome installation, sudden storms came up throughout the day, often making it too dangerous to work. Just as the dome was completed, the thunderclouds cleared, and a rainbow could be seen stretching across the sky.

Through the winter and spring of 1978, we began constructing the temple mound, which required moving 12,000 cubic yards of dirt. Constant delays and mistakes plagued the efforts of the crew, but the causes for these disruptions were unclear. Eventually much of this work had to be completely redone. Rinpoche sent memos, encouraging workers, trying to broaden and deepen our approach to the difficulties.

Memo to Odiyan from Rinpoche, spring of 1978: "Work quickly and energetically now, and do your very best. You can fully rely upon awareness, concentration, and energy, so develop and integrate these factors. Then we can find a way to function effectively within the ordinary world despite the fact that it is dominated by greed, hatred, and confusion.

"We need to be good businessmen with solid, practical minds. When a businessman has every penny tied up in a project, he works from the gut. That's how we need to be. At the same time, we need to see every detail from a broad perspective, like the cosmic vision of the Bodhisattvas in the Buddhist tradition."

Work proceeded through the summer and fall as the south and the west entryways were framed. Drilling and pouring of piers for the temple foundation were completed, and the cap slab was poured. But difficulties continued to arise. When the drilling on the last pier was almost completed, the drill cut through an underground electrical cable, causing an unforeseen delay. When this was repaired, the steel columns for the second and third temple stories were anchored to the slab, and the steel beams were set in place. These beams, which were once part of a highway overpass south of San Francisco, were hauled to Odiyan by a trucking company specializing in long loads. The first load of steel beams got stuck a mile from Odiyan and required three days of work with heavy machinery to extricate. The second truckload went off the road, totally destroying the truck, but fortunately no one was injured.

It seemed that a better balance would develop when the largest prayer wheel in the West, prepared during many months at Padma Ling, was installed a half mile from the rim structure in the winter of 1978.

Odiyan worker: "This special prayer wheel was built before the stupa, which would later be erected around it. We worked at Padma Ling on the mantras, taping them together and rolling them onto huge spools. The spools were then transported to Odiyan and re-spooled onto the prayer wheel there. Rinpoche had instructed us to chant the Ye Dharma Mantra whenever we assembled prayer wheels. Sometimes while we were chanting the mantra during the unwinding of the spools, the tape would break. When we checked those places, we always found some mistake in the order or some misalignment. So I began to feel that beneficent forces were watching over the Odiyan prayer wheel. Although we installed this twelve-ton wheel at the end of 1978, the bearing system was not properly worked out, and we could not get it running reliably. Looking back, this seemed to be a reflection of the difficulties that were developing in this period of time."

The construction of Odiyan was making tremendous demands on the resources of other Nyingma Centers. Lacking wealthy patrons, we had raised money from within our own organizations and from numerous small donations, a time-consuming process that TNMC students have overseen for many years. Rinpoche has consistently tried to find ways to control the budget, but our income was less than half of our expenses. By 1979 our funds had been depleted. Workers were having trouble maintaining a sense of purpose as construction continued to run into one obstacle after another, and cooperation, communication, and teamwork were all weakening. The painful decision was made to halt construction at Odiyan for six months. A small staff maintained the grounds, while some of the crew took outside jobs to help raise more money for the future, and others worked at Dharma Press.

Rinpoche urged everyone to investigate goals, attitudes, actions, and values to strengthen our understanding and commitment to unfolding the vision. We were beginning to realize how difficult this work could be—could we face such a challenge? Often over the years, Rinpoche has encouraged this kind of penetrating questioning in the midst of difficult situations.

Nyingma Centers meeting with Rinpoche, in spring of 1986: "Questioning is essential to learning. But as soon as we begin to investigate, we can feel resistance. We sense confusion or conflict brewing, and we would rather not cause ourselves trouble. Or sometimes we may not feel interested, and it just does not seem worthwhile to make the effort to inquire further. We convince ourselves that we have nothing to gain; we believe we already have all the answers we need. So we insist on our right not to investigate! Here we need to challenge this belief squarely. What happiness and success have our answers brought us in the past? What are they based on, and why should we trust them?

"The last tactic is to create fear. If we open our investigation and begin to discover that we do in fact need more knowledge, then suddenly we also notice how ignorant we have been for so long. It is difficult to admit that we have lived so long without wondering what we were doing, or without noticing how we fool ourselves. If this uncomfortable, embarrassed feeling does not stop our inquiry, then a stronger fear may ambush us. What if it is too late to change? What if our situation is hopeless and nothing can be done to correct our confusion? How can we bear to dwell upon this? This is a very effective way to close the investigation.

"If we can question freely, without condemning or praising ourselves, we can release our intelligence. The fear, ignorance, and laziness that restrict our vision can be completely transformed."

By fall of 1979, the financial situation had improved. Having considered their own views carefully, the crew felt freshly appreciative of the possibilities Odiyan offered and eager to learn to work more effectively. We could see clearly that for Odiyan to succeed, the cooperative energies of many people would be needed, together with the guidance of a clear and selfless vision. Rinpoche gave permission for work to resume on the prayer wheel, and with a flood of relief, the crew gladly took on this task.

Odiyan worker: "After a fierce and stormy night of effort, the wheel finally turned, the small bell at the top marking each revolution. Rinpoche then began a land clearing project of several months that refreshed and revitalized both the crew and the land itself. Work became a gift, not a task, and with that fresh insight, we began construction on the temple."

Conversations with Rinpoche in October 1979: "If you work past your own personality, you will find real intelligence. Be patient, and instead of drawing on your emotions for strength, rely on the power of the vision. Don't worry about conserving energy. The more energy you generate, the more there is.

"When you learn to sacrifice a rigid commitment to your own position, ideas, and attitude, you quickly find that the gain can be tremendous. Energy and intelligence both are maximized. If we can do this as a community, we will be able to make a real difference in the lives of others. If we succeed, the inner mandala will unfold, and our efforts will not be lost."

Odiyan worker: "Although I really want Odiyan to be successful, and I want to finish projects, to follow Rinpoche's guidance, and to work quickly and energetically, I still find it quite difficult at times to maintain my motivation. There are times I feel resentful, times I want a girlfriend, more money—a more normal life. I lose sight of the fact that Rinpoche is supporting us so that we have the rare opportunity to devote all our time to serving the Dharma.

"Motivation seems to be a key element in accomplishment. The temple, pagodas, and stupa symbolize the results produced by motivation and commitment.

I feel Odiyan is essentially the result of one man's total commitment and vision. What kind of accomplishment would be possible if more of us individually could develop that kind of commitment?

"As I've grown to understand how much value our work at Nyingma has to offer the world, I have a deeper sense of confidence in what can be accomplished. Despite our negativities and shortcomings, we can help manifest something beneficial for others. Without the guidance of Rinpoche, how could I have been part of such a contribution?"

Odiyan worker: "At Odiyan there is the ongoing complexity of urgent construction schedules and deadlines; the dynamics of a large group of men living and working together ten hours a day six and one-half days a week; shifts of image and personality associated with changing projects; changing crew leaders and changing goals; precarious and unpredictable finances coupled with costly construction needs; living in a remote and isolated job site. All this is taking place within the context of a young spiritual community. The stability has been provided by a constant push toward accomplishment. Even when workers at Odiyan have failed to meet schedules, have worked ineffectively, and made large and expensive mistakes, a larger and comprehensive vision has illuminated the overall project. It is participation in this vision which allows Odiyan to continue."

Building the Odiyan Stupa

In 1979 Rinpoche began planning a stupa for Odiyan. While some of us had seen photographs of ancient Indian stupas, we did not really grasp the significance of building one. That year we began to learn about these ancient monuments, one of the most important and enduring symbols in the Dharma.

We discovered that throughout the long history of Buddhism, stupas have manifested the positive power of awakened knowledge. Building a stupa is a deeply significant act, for this perfectly proportioned architecture is richly symbolic and has profound effects on human consciousness and on the environment. Though people in our culture are not familiar with stupas, we perceive a similar uplifting quality in a soaring Gothic cathedral or an exquisite domed sanctuary. A sacred building has a subtle but powerful effect on feelings and perceptions. Constructing a stupa was a remarkable opportunity for

Odiyan workers to begin to appreciate the knowledge embodied in Buddhist architecture.

In the fall of 1979 preliminary drawings were made for the stupa, which was planned around a 113-foot-high steel tower upon a base 60 feet square. Rinpoche worked out the design, and the crew researched construction techniques that could be used to create exactly the required proportions. To define the shape, precast concrete sections would be assembled around the existing large prayer wheel, located a half a mile from the rim structure. A flyer mailed out to friends of Nyingma described the stupa project, explaining the significance of the stupa and inviting participation by contributing funds or time to its construction.

From *The Great Stupa in the West* brochure, 1979: "Wherever Buddhism has prospered, it has left its mark in monuments called stupas. Deriving from prehistoric burial mounds, the Buddhist stupa developed into a structure of great architectural magnificence, symbolic of the Buddha's heart. It is said that so long as these symbols of Buddhist teachings remain on earth, the Dharma will be preserved."

Perfectly proportioned according to the instructions given in Buddhist texts, the stupa reflects balance and harmony. Its qualities foster the equilibrium of natural forces, deterring natural disasters and diseases, and dissolving obstacles to enlightenment in the human mind.

The planned Odiyan Stupa would soon require all of our manpower, but for a few months through the fall and winter of 1979, work continued on other projects. Stucco and interior work was progressing on the entryways. We installed copper roofing on the west pagoda dome and began erecting steel beams for the temple. The beautiful shining copper holds profound meaning in the Nyingma tradition.

From an interview with Rinpoche in 1984: "The copper roofs at Odiyan, found on all the five temples, are dedicated to Padmasambhava, the Precious Guru. As a youth I had the chance to see the Copper Colored Mountain, a special monument to Padmasambhava at Katog monastery. Its splendid beauty was before my eyes when I resolved to make Odiyan a shining jewel, ornamented with copper."

By the spring of 1980, work commenced on the stupa. After the steel was erected for the first two stories of the temple, and the walkway around the temple was finished, the foundation for the stupa was excavated and the concrete was poured. A large crew, assembled from the other Nyingma Centers, joined the Odiyan workers. The goal was to complete construction of the stupa by Padmasambhava's birthday, which was less than four months away.

Preparing the precast was the most difficult part of the process. Forms, molds, and test pieces were done in April, and full-scale production began in May. To stay on schedule, crews had to work around the clock. A piece was poured, the crew napped while it set, and then unmolded it before pouring another piece. As long as we were extremely careful, we could remove pieces from the mold every few hours, but every piece needed extensive touch-up. A crane would then lift the precast into place, and workers assembled the sections.

Rinpoche arrived at Odiyan around the end of June to supervise final steps in construction. By then over one hundred volunteers had arrived from the other centers, and even people participating in a TSK retreat at Odiyan had joined in the work. At the same time, forty people at Padma Ling were creating interior murals and prayer flags to encircle the stupa. By calling on a huge crew, even though it included many inexperienced workers, a great joint effort could be made.

We have used this approach successfully many times to complete large projects. With proper guidance, an expanded team can quickly produce excellent results. Everyone who participated in completing the stupa recalls those weeks with deep satisfaction. Because the purpose and value of our work was clear, energy was high and determination strong. For some people this experience of working with full dedication became a touchstone for later experience.

The last twenty-four hours we worked steadily; no one slept. Just before dawn on July 22, after a life-sized Buddha statue was placed in the cupola, Odiyan's founder sounded the conch signaling completion of the first large stupa in the West.

In specific locations inside the stupa, Rinpoche placed hundreds of precious relics, some dating back many centuries and transmitted to him by his teachers. Ritual objects, relics of Buddhas, Bodhisattvas, and Arhats, and rare manuscripts were enshrined. Statues, mandalas, and 100,000 small, gold-painted ceramic tsa tsas impressed with the images of three Buddhas were stored within the stupa. An additional 100,000 tsa tsas were later created to line the inner walls. In Tibet a stupa with 100,000 images, known as a "bumpa," was considered very precious; the Odiyan Stupa now contained

200,000 images. The blessings from the stupa were also greatly enhanced by the enclosed prayer wheel, which activated three hundred million prayers for peace and enlightenment with each revolution.

The Odiyan Stupa contains remarkable treasures found nowhere else in this country. Within the stupa is an obelisk over one hundred feet tall, so heavy that it cannot be lifted by a group of workers. Around it are wrapped prayers and texts, printed in a particular way with special ink, and rolled up at a specially chosen time. While we do not fully understand the significance of these treasures, we can see that Rinpoche has made tremendous efforts to collect and preserve sacred objects in the stupa and the temple at Odiyan.

At the same time the stupa was completed, Dharma Press had just completed the printing of the texts for the *Nyingma Edition* of the Kanjur and Tanjur, and had produced the first edition of the *Guide*. The simultaneous completion of the stupa and the successful printing of these canonical materials seemed a most auspicious omen for the future of the Dharma in the West. On July 22, Rinpoche dedicated the stupa in a short ceremony, which was followed by a conference on the future of Odiyan with the theme "One Point is All Points." Several hundred people attended, and over a dozen speakers led workshops.

With the physical completion of the stupa, the benefits that the Buddhist tradition might bring to Western culture seemed more real to us. This ancient symbol of knowledge now stood upon American soil. The experience of creating it had given us a more profound sense of potential — new possibilities seemed to beckon to us all.

Over the next few months, residents at Odiyan noticed tangible changes in the land itself, as though the energy of the stupa were promoting gentleness and peace. More animals were attracted to the property, especially deer and flocks of birds.

Odiyan worker: "When the stupa was built, people from all of the centers came together for a short period. This very intensive activity under Rinpoche's guidance brought into existence the most significant symbol of enlightenment in the West. Opportunities to participate in such activities are extremely rare. We do not usually appreciate them until sometime later when the seeds that were planted begin to grow. The objects themselves, such as the stupa or the Kanjur and Tanjur, develop more levels of significance for us the longer we are around them."

Creation of the Temple

Once the stupa had been built, intensive work began on the temple. Designed by Rinpoche with great care, the temple was to have a Dharma Hall on the first floor, a library and twelve residential rooms on the second floor, and four residential rooms on the third floor; a huge dome would rise above the top floor. Using the same process we had employed for the rim structure, we framed the temple walls with prefabricated sections.

That fall, our crew roughed in and waterproofed the temple roof and dome before the winter rains began. In December of 1980, Rinpoche added a cupola to the top of the dome, bringing the temple's height to eighty feet. Through the winter, we milled lumber for the interior and installed rough electrical wiring and plumbing.

The following spring, we covered the temple roof with 72,000 square feet of copper, and plastered the interior of the dome. It was also time to fabricate 2,000 precast ornamental elements for the temple exterior.

During the fall and winter of 1981, the radiant heating slab for the Dharma Hall was poured, and red granite from Italy was mounted on the exterior walls and the columns. Balconies around the second floor were constructed and windows roughed in.

Once the structural work on the temple was completed, the primary emphasis shifted to art projects and finishing work, which continued throughout 1982 and 1983. Many of us commented on the noticeable change from the rough driving energy of heavy construction to the more refined energy of craftsmanship. Odiyan had definitely entered a new phase, characterized by an emerging gentleness and beauty.

We used the finest materials that we could afford to create the finishing touches which Rinpoche envisioned. Rooms were wood paneled and floors of hardwood were laid; wooden cabinets for the library were finished by hand, and intricate doors carved. Even doorknobs were specially designed, cast in Odiyan's foundry, and polished by hand. Stained glass windows and etched windows created by TNMC were now installed in the temple and entryway pagodas. A thirteen-foot-high stained glass window of the Buddha was created and installed in the stupa. Installation of windows began in late 1981, and many were completed in 1982–1983.

Sixteen windows with images of Buddhas and Great Bodhisattvas were sandblasted in the winter and spring of 1982 for the temple dome. Precast panels and ornamental pieces for the gallery, columns, roof corners, and bas-reliefs were also installed. The lower level concrete walkway around the temple was poured, and a fine marble walkway was laid around the building. Years before, TNMC students had salvaged this marble from Bay Area schools that were being demolished.

Construction of the multicolored terrazzo floor for the Dharma Hall was then begun. Small chips of glass, marble, and semiprecious stone were crushed and embedded into the elaborate mandala that Rinpoche had designed. Brass dividing strips between colors were bent by hand to fit the pattern. After six months of effort, the floor was ready for grinding and polishing—a process that continued for many weeks.

In the summer of 1982, Rinpoche arrived to supervise painting of the temple's exterior. Again, we used a team approach—forty-five volunteers from the Centers came to help. The painting of the entire temple exterior was completed in less than one month. The final touch was mounting a goldleafed spire to the top of the temple. At this time, Corten and copper roofs were installed on the north and south entryways, and work was begun on the east pagoda.

During fall 1982 and winter 1983, 112 prayer wheels, created at Padma Ling, were installed around the gallery of the temple. Steel frames were specially constructed to hold the wheels, which were covered with etched copper housings. Each large wheel was then topped with a miniature wheel containing microfilmed mantras, so that one revolution of the entire set generates over a billion prayers. While the new prayer wheel project was underway, another crew of ten completed and installed seventy-two windows designed for the temple.

Another Open House was held in June 1983 to celebrate the progress of the Odiyan mandala. Many donors and friends of Nyingma could now finally see the results of their gifts. Representatives of the media were also invited, and their reports generated a number of news articles over the next few months. To make the press brochures, we collected a set of photos and documents that later would be greatly expanded for *Copper Mountain Mandala*, the history of Odiyan that was compiled in 1984–1985.

By summer 1983 the temple was a truly beautiful building. Combining the solidity and massiveness of the earth with the light and spacious quality of the sky, the temple radiated power and intensity. The design was neither Eastern nor Western, but a special blend of both envisioned by Rinpoche for America. A detailed explanation of the shapes and forms of the temple can be found in *Copper Mountain Mandala*, but the care that has gone into each element is apparent to anyone who views the temples and grounds.

Odiyan visitor: "I cannot believe it—everything has been thought out so clearly and in such great detail. Everywhere I look, there is more to notice. Each little corner has a beautiful shape or color or ornament of some kind, and it all completely fits together."

The completion of the temple seemed to transform Odiyan into a realm of the sacred, evoking new possibilities and a richer way of life. The older rim structure had seemed almost like a fort from the days of America's past, a cavalry outpost in the wilderness. Many of us had enjoyed the "cowboy" energy, riding horses, wearing boots and cowboy hats. Not so many years before, this crew of heavy-construction, beer-drinking cowboys had been hippies and "flower children." Now the "cowboy" energy was shifting as the temple rising from the rim structure's center exerted a profound effect on the atmosphere of Odiyan.

The completion of the temple prompted serious questions about Odiyan's purpose, and how we would fit into the vision we saw emerging. Finishing the temple would clearly be but one stage in a longer process. Its completion marked the beginning of the next unknown step in the creation of the mandala.

Odiyan worker: "Our practice is to continually face up to what we are doing. It's hard work. You build up a vision of who you are, what your job is, what the world is; and then it breaks, and you have to build up another one, which is very uncomfortable. You have to ask yourself what kind of challenges you want to take on, how deeply you want to go."

Over the years, we had seen in ourselves the possibility of changing old patterns and realizing new potential. We had learned a tremendous amount, given a great deal, and had obtained real results. The decisive change in the environment and the work seemed to signal a time for changes in the people as well. Some of us had spent ten years building Odiyan and felt a certain fear of finishing and entering the next phase.

Memo to Odiyan from Rinpoche in July of 1982: "Changing your situation depends on wisdom, which grows out of knowledge. Knowledge does not come from wishful thinking or from abstract study. Real knowledge comes from dealing with challenges. When you act, alternatives open up. Your concentration sharpens, and you can become more incisive.

"The most basic kind of change depends on attitude and on the patterns of the mind. Changing mental patterns may not always be easy, but basically mind energy is very fluid and very pliable, so deep changes are possible. If you reshape a piece of steel, you still have steel left at the end; if you melt it, you still have molten steel. But if you reshape a mental pattern, it is simply gone, with no residue. That kind of change can be the most dramatic and powerful.

"Realizing how much freedom and control you actually have can be frightening; so much so that you resist being aware. Usually, right at the moment when you are about to slip into a neurotic or destructive pattern or make a wrong choice, there is a moment of awareness. But if you have reasons for not wanting to be aware, the moment passes unacknowledged, and later you may not even be able to remember it.

"If you want to deepen your practice, work on keeping that awareness active. Use it to challenge counterproductive mental patterns until they just disappear. If you could do that, think what you would be able to accomplish. Imagine having no blockages, no negativities, no resistance. Think of the benefit to Odiyan and to the Dharma, and to yourselves."

Our old impatience with basic mindfulness practices, and our desire for advanced Buddhist teachings have decidedly changed over the years as we have begun to realize how much preparation is involved. Our work is one very useful way of preparing for more serious study, by building up the strength and clarity we need; but we may hesitate to let go of it to engage in full-time practice, preferring the familiar to the unknown.

This new venture into the unknown seemed closer at hand by 1984. Starting in 1980, a few of the older students had entered traditional three-year retreats. In the beginning, many of us were skeptical of the retreats, wondering whether even older students could endure the long period of solitude. But it was now clear that Americans could actually complete such a long-term practice. One student had finished and others had begun. To continue with such a challenging practice, they must have gained something of value. What changes would such a retreat engender? What could we accomplish?

Over the next few years an unusual collection of American Dharma students would undertake retreats: a government administrator, a psychologist, an educator, and a stockbroker. Some of us wondered if Rinpoche was experimenting with test cases of American consciousness! These Nyingma retreatants seem to represent certain strong traits of the American spirit, and their experience will be very valuable for all of us.

TNMC student: "When I think of the meditators and yogis of the Tibetan tradition, when I consider the great persistence and endurance needed to succeed at genuinely transforming consciousness, I really wonder how far any of us will be able to progress."

TNMC student: "Three years of retreat seems like a very long time from one point of view; but it is not much time out of a whole life. Can we expect miraculous changes from spending five percent of our life on retreat? Nobody that finished the retreat has walked on water yet. But the idea of retreat grows more appealing to me with each passing year. Who can say how much I, or anyone else, might be able to accomplish or what the long-range effects of such a retreat might be?"

Interview with Rinpoche, spring, 1986: "It is not yet clear what the future of the Dharma in the West will be, even though the Dharma has so much to offer. You might say there is tremendous room for improvement because modern life is so full of suffering. If the ideal of human perfection is introduced, then people in this society can compare and see if they feel a desire for more knowledge. Then it is up to them. How far are they willing to go once they know what is involved?"

Ornamenting the Mandala

Reflecting the natural refinement process inherent in creativity, Odiyan has gradually been ornamented with more precious materials. In the early days, the crew hauled lumber, hoisted steel beams, and poured concrete. Later we laid wood floors, installed copper roofing, and hung granite panels. By 1984 we were working with gold, silver, and copper, three precious substances that symbolize the Buddha, the Dharma, and the Sangha. Rinpoche has spent many hundreds of hours designing the ornamentation and supervising its creation. A huge portion of our budget was now going toward art projects.

During the summer and fall of 1983, almost two thousand copper fascia ornaments were mounted on temple and pagoda roofs. Chusrin, mythical crocodiles that serve as temple guardians, were cast in fiberglass, copperleafed, and attached to the corners of the temple roof. Hydronic and solar heating systems were also installed; hardwood floors were laid in the entryway pagodas, and carpeting was laid in the temple.

The following winter and spring, we painted interior ceilings of the entryway domes with lotus petal mandalas. Silkscreened wallpaper and curtains were added to the pagodas, together with stained glass lampshades for the temple. During this year we cast twenty-five small Padmasambhava statues in the Odiyan foundry using the lost wax technique. Since perfecting this delicate technique is very difficult, nine out of ten early efforts were failures. We began to investigate alternative techniques such as electroforming and have also cast many small statues in nonmetals.

In that same winter and spring of 1984, a plan to decorate the inside of the temple dome with etched metal plates was underway. The results promised to be very beautiful, but the cost would be a smaller crew at Odiyan and added financial concerns. Eventually, the original plan was expanded to include decorating the stupa, greatly increasing the cost. Rinpoche selected each traditional drawing to be used and designed the plating patterns in silver and gold on copper.

From an interview with Rinpoche, 1984: "In 1983 after seeing the golden stupas of Thailand, I decided to plate the Odiyan stupa in metal. Gold seemed the best symbol of the Buddha's compassion, love, and blessings, but financially this seemed impossible. Instead I decided on silver, a universally acceptable symbol of radiant light and purity."

The texts to be etched onto plates included the highly revered Bhadrakalpika Sutra, which names each of the thousand Buddhas of our fortunate era. Two sets of rare mandalas were also included, as well as texts from the Kanjur, prayers, and auspicious symbols.

Since having this work done professionally would be prohibitively expensive, we had to learn how to do it ourselves. Our crew had a little experience with plating, and Rinpoche encouraged us to do research. Our goal was to etch the texts onto copper and then plate them in various patterns of gold and silver. Although experts told us that the process would be impossible without expensive equipment and long training, we persisted. Some workers had had formal training in chemistry and engineering, while everyone by now had many experiences doing something "impossible." Convinced that we did not have to give up on the idea, the crew began experimenting in the spring and were eventually producing acceptable plates. The process of preparing the plates in three metals required two full days per mandala for a three person crew: eight months of work for the entire set.

That summer the stupa was covered in 2,800 silver-coated copper plates, which were installed in a special sequence. The manpower needed for this installation was more than three-fourths of the Odiyan crew: fifteen people from June until September.

Odiyan worker: "Other people spend twenty-five years doing one thing; here we spend two months, or at the most two years, and then go on to the next thing. It's like living many lifetimes in one lifetime. It may sound confusing or exhausting, and it is, but it is also wonderful . . . there is a sense that we're really doing something to live up to our full potential, to take advantage of the opportunity we have."

Once again, we found ourselves far behind our original schedule, unable to estimate how long the installation would take. Some plates had to be redone, adding to the delay. Finally, by September, the project was complete, and Rinpoche conducted a ceremony to celebrate the ornamenting of the stupa.

From an interview with Rinpoche, fall of 1984: "We greatly enhanced the power of the stupa by covering its surface with canonical texts and mandalas. I do not believe any stupa on this planet has ever before been adorned with the words of the Buddha and images of powerful mandalas. In the centuries to come, as breezes pass across the surface of the stupa and the sunlight reflects the words and images, the teachings of the Dharma will radiate throughout the world."

Over 1984 and 1985, 364 exterior prayer wheels and 120 interior prayer wheels were built and installed in the temple. In 1987 prayer wheels from various locations at the Centers were transferred to Odiyan to form a ring around the base of the stupa. Later in the year a second ring of prayer wheels was installed along the walkway encircling the stupa.

Elaborate crystal chandeliers were now designed by Rinpoche and constructed by Odiyan craftsmen. The chandelier for the Dharma Hall is over seventeen feet long and nine feet wide. Four smaller ones were built for the entryway temples. To create the elaborate designs for the chandeliers, 70,000 crystals were required.

Spending so much time and money on art may seem extravagant to people today. When we consider the poverty of some parts of the world, or the desperate need for funding for education or medical research, we find ourselves wanting practical and immediate results for our money. But the art connected with an ancient knowledge tradition transcends monetary values to foster the priceless wisdom of enlightenment. Such art is a good investment, for it affirms the value of human beings and makes knowledge available for the future. With greater knowledge we would have the potential for resolving many problems that defy solution today. At the same time beauty itself is a way of knowledge. If the beauty created at Odiyan inspires individuals to contribute to the store of human knowledge, then it is well worth the cost.

From an interview with Rinpoche, 1984: "If you think in traditional religious terms, spending money on Odiyan is like taking the energy that people have used in creating the money to begin with, and transforming it into the Three Jewels: the Buddha, the Dharma, and the Sangha. It is an act of alchemy—the transformation of money into beauty. Beauty naturally heightens awareness and leads to knowledge, liberating the power of the mind. We have all inherited a treasure of vast knowledge, but we need to find access to it. Beauty is one path to this treasure of knowledge."

Odiyan has become a repository of sacred art from many Buddhist lands. Its collection includes ancient statues, precious wall hangings, and ritual instruments such as conch shells, drums, cymbals, and trumpets. Sacred art objects have been gathered together in an array of precious materials: ivory, jade, turquoise, coral, and lapis lazuli; silver, gold, bronze, brass, copper, and crystal. Through the years, Rinpoche has made extensive efforts to collect treasures of Tibetan, Indian, Nepalese, and Chinese Buddhist art. Preserving such precious objects in a setting such as Odiyan is important; religious art viewed only in museums and private collections is removed from the environment that brings forth its deeper meaning and beauty.

Rare blockprint and manuscript copies of sacred texts are preserved in Odiyan's library, together with twenty-five sets of the *Nyingma Edition*, each of which includes more than two hundred full-color thanka reproductions. Library walls are lined with texts shelved behind decorated glass doors. The collection of traditional art and precious objects has been enriched by art produced by TNMC in a series of special projects, as well as by prints of traditional thankas reproduced by Dharma Publishing.

TNMC student: "There is so much art at Odiyan— almost one hundred life-sized statues, more than one hundred smaller Buddhas, thousands of little stupas and tsa tsas, as well as murals, thankas, and mandalas everywhere. I do not believe most monasteries in Tibet had such large collections. But I doubt that most Nyingma students realize that. None of us really comprehends what a treasure we have here in America."

Odiyan worker: "At Odiyan I've learned to appreciate how art appears out of nothing. First there's an idea, and then gradually it takes on form. At each stage it becomes more permanent, more real until finally we have a result that will last for hundreds of years. In a way, all of Odiyan is like that—creating this beautiful reality out of thin air. But it's not magic—every step along the way is a challenge."

Odiyan worker: "I became interested in the Tibetan tradition first through the art and the iconography. I was attracted to the beauty, and the use of color, and to something else I didn't understand that seemed to relate to the spiritual significance of the images. I would say that the art as I have experienced it here is very strong and very clear, and not based so much on pleasing the emotions. It runs to something deeper. The level of workmanship that is practiced at Odiyan communicates something not readily available in the West. It's like a courtship—as if the art were constantly finding new ways of opening our hearts."

Odiyan worker: "I do not understand the meaning of a lot of the shapes and forms we build, but more and more they're a part of me. I feel lucky that sometime in my life I've been able to see a building with the power of the temple, or that I've had the chance to walk around the stupa. I think anyone who comes here senses that."

In 1984 a more beautiful environment for the temple and rim structure was envisioned by Rinpoche. By creating a lake all around the outside of the rim structure, we could put the temple complex on an "island" in the center of the lake. The vision of the shining surface of the water and the flashing copper roofs seemed to belong to a heavenly realm.

In the summer of 1984 excavation began—a process of moving 60,000 cubic yards of dirt. The lake, which begins about sixty-six feet away from the rim structure, is square in shape and ninety feet from bank to bank. Bridges were designed to span the lake in each of the four directions. The lake was planned to be four to five feet deep, containing approximately six million gallons of water. The water level might fall each summer due to evaporation, but a new well we had dug nearby would allow us to replenish the loss. It seemed to us that the crucial loss of water would be through the soil, but the cost of installing liners was far beyond our reach. When Rinpoche insisted on additional research, we sought the advice of geologists. They determined that the claylike soil at Odiyan could, in fact, be compacted to form a natural barrier to water.

Seeing the value of this kind of persistent inquiry, we realize how often we unthinkingly rely upon what we are told by authorities instead of taking responsibility for a complete investigation. After we had begun several new excavations, we saw once again the need for higher levels of responsibility. Several large new buildings were being added near the rim structure to house the Press and to provide extra space for conventions and meetings. By fall of 1984, excavation on the lake and buildings was falling behind schedule; if the winter rains began before the work was completed, much damage could be done. Fully acknowledging and taking responsibility for the difficulty was the only way to begin solving the problem: Responsibility calls for action.

A third time we saw this same pattern when the protective coating we had applied to the silver-coated plates on the stupa began to deteriorate. We realized we could have conducted a more thorough investigation in the beginning, instead of relying on advice from a few experts and not pursuing more alternatives.

As our work shifted to more expensive materials and involved more refined and complicated techniques, it was all too easy to depend on advice from experts. Work at Odiyan has shown us very clearly the high cost of not taking *full* responsibility for results. The first step is investigating as carefully as we can; then we must be willing to recognize and acknowledge mistakes at any point in the process; and finally, we must have the energy and confidence to take action to remedy problems. Unfortunately, our feelings and ideas can block this process.

Odiyan worker: "I've often become proud and arrogant when given new jobs. Once my energy has gone into my ego, communication with others is difficult, and I fail to acknowledge my own mistakes. All this might just seem like interpersonal problems. But Rinpoche has repeatedly proven to us that the cost of our pride can be actually measured in the dollars wasted in needless mistakes. Since I've always had enough money, I've been reluctant to look at the cost of my time and the materials I'm working with. For a long time this practical approach didn't seem to fit in with my 'spiritual' values, and I could not understand why a spiritual teacher would spend so much time talking with us about money and funding."

From a talk by Rinpoche, spring of 1987: "To take real responsibility requires a tremendous amount of self-understanding and self-control. Developing these capacities is not as easy as we might think, first because we imagine we already possess them. This assumption leads to confusion when mistakes and problems arise—how could they have happened? Once we realize that we need more awareness, stronger motivation, and very stable, balanced energy, then we begin to find our balance and develop inner qualities we can rely upon.

Maintaining balance through all kinds of situations is very challenging in the short run, but in the long run it results in virtuous activity."

In January of 1985, a training program based on *Knowledge of Freedom* combined with Kum Nye relaxation practice was begun at Odiyan. Extending over several months, this program helped evoke a clearer awareness of emotional patterns, open up communications, and support the possibility of deeper knowledge.

Odiyan worker: "The Knowledge of Freedom class has undergone many changes—from open and enthusiastic dialogue to arguments, heartfelt challenges, and dull and sleepy states of mind. But behind all this, there has been change for almost every individual and the community as a whole. Communication is now more straightforward, more open, with more challenging and satisfying questioning taking place. Questioning plans and procedures is now viewed as healthy rather than as attempts to undermine. I feel the Odiyan community has progressed tremendously through this book and the training program. The possibility of affecting positive change has never been so close."

In the summer and fall, new prayer wheels were installed in the temple gallery, and work proceeded on the bridges and new buildings. Landscaping and grading, earth-moving, and other kinds of site work also continued. Four islands were now being built in the lake to provide nesting sites for birds. Since construction would run into November, Odiyan requested more workers so that the outdoor crews could finish before the rains started. But instead, a number of senior Odiyan workers were asked to join the sculpture crew in Berkeley. The remaining Odiyan workers had to develop new styles of management and communication, with younger members taking more responsibility. The loss of crew meant work on the additional buildings was delayed.

Through that winter, we began to research ways of repairing the deteriorating coating on the stupa. We considered several different repair techniques for stripping the old coating, and then replating or refinishing the metal surface. Research was quite complex, involving problems of chemical engineering, and we were not always confident we were moving in the best direction.

Rinpoche wrote us a long memo on the importance of developing a broad understanding that could see the details without becoming distracted by them. Although an unemotional approach is best when trying to make careful decisions about complex technical matters, we often do not realize the extent of our emotional involvement in any problems we have helped create. Collecting research and making detailed reports will not bring clarity if we cannot first dispel our confusion. Rinpoche urged us to appreciate what we had learned from experience and to rely upon the confidence we had gained; then intelligence could readily penetrate confusion.

In the spring of 1986 the decision was made to remove the coating and cover the stupa in gold. A Stupa Fund was established to help finance the project, and Odiyan's friends soon responded in a deeply supportive gesture of caring. By summer there was sufficient money to begin, and by October the project was completed. The Odiyan Stupa now radiates a rich golden light even more beautiful than its former sheen of sparkling silver, reminding us of the possibility of transformation.

TNMC student: "There appears to be a rule in our organization that once something goes wrong, it must not only be fixed, but made even better than before. Covering the stupa in gold seemed deeply symbolic to me—a manifestation of transformation. Even if we make mistakes, they can be reversed if we are willing to work at it. If we know how, we can actually extract an advantage of one kind or another out of a mistake; either we learn something valuable, or we can make an unexpected refinement. There seems to be some deep principle at work here which I do not fully grasp, but it runs through much of what we do at Nyingma. Everything can be used and turned to advantage."

Ornamenting the land itself will take many years as we work with the growing rhythms of various kinds of foliage. But the first stages in long-range landscaping plans have been initiated. Parts of the land had been heavily logged and needed reforestation. We began this project in 1976, spending about a thousand man-hours each year since then.

We have added plants and red rock around the lake, and have begun to landscape the temple mound and rim structure gardens. One hundred acres of gardens will extend beyond the rim structure on all four sides; stands of flowering fruit and nut trees within parklike expanses of native and exotic flowering plants are planned. Ringing the stupa will be formal gardens dedicated to world peace, planted with fifty varieties of roses and ornamented with ever-burning lamps.

The peaceful, inspiring Odiyan environment is ideal for retreats and religious practice. Huts have been built for students undertaking traditional three-year retreats.

Several types of group retreats have already been held, and individual and group retreats will continue in the future. Dharma Publishing plans to expand its operation to Odiyan very soon. Plans for various Yeshe De projects are also underway; it will be possible for translations and research results sponsored by the Yeshe De Project to be published through the facilities of Dharma Publishing at Odiyan.

The construction of Odiyan has taken about twelve years. A small, untrained crew has gradually mastered a whole range of building skills, learning to work together in a spirit of cooperation and taking inspiration from a vision that transcends personal interest.

The long work is now nearing completion. Difficulties have been overcome by dedication to the vision and purpose of Odiyan, by making work an offering, a celebration, and a way of learning. Accomplishing something truly worthwhile for oneself and for others has brought us great joy, which we hope to share with others. Odiyan is a living manifestation of the growth of human creativity and the desire to be of benefit. The sheer beauty of Odiyan, made of the finest materials available, with the best skills we could develop, is both an offering to the Dharma and a reflection of the value of the Dharma for humanity. Its teachings open the way to endless human possibilities, unfolding dimensions of beauty and meaning for all people.

DYNAMIC ACTION

1963
THE EARLY YEARS

WORK IN INDIA

Tarthang Tulku founds Dharma Mudranalaya in India to preserve Tibetan texts and art. Tibetan typeface is designed, and over twenty Tibetan texts are reproduced. The reproduction of Longchenpa texts is begun, and Lama Mipham commentaries are brought out.

1969
THE FIRST YEAR

TNMC FOUNDED

After his arrival in New York at the end of 1968, Rinpoche travels to California and offers seminars and classes around the Bay Area. He founds TNMC at Webster Street in March of 1969. TNMC activities include study and practice, as well as traditional ceremonies on the tenth, fifteenth, twenty-fifth and thirtieth days of each lunar month. Some students undertake the traditional Nyingma preliminary practices (Bum Nga).

AID FOR TIBETANS ABROAD

To offer support to Tibetans in India and to help preserve Tibetan culture, Rinpoche initiates the Tibetan Aid project. Rinpoche's first interview in America, published in June of 1969, encourages people to join the Pen Friends Program. An American pen friend could support the needs of a Tibetan refugee for as little as ten dollars per month. TAP coordinates this program while collecting goods and clothing to ship to India.

1970
THE SECOND YEAR

STUDY OF RITUAL ARTS AND CRAFTS BEGINS

Rinpoche begins to encourage the study of art and traditional religious crafts at TNMC and to devise ways to take advantage of Western technology. Modern printing, for example, could provide clear, exact copies of prayers in smaller sizes and in greater volume than older techniques available in Tibet. If TNMC students could gain printing skills, many millions of prayers could be printed and set in motion in prayer wheels. At Webster Street, the first prayer wheels are built: four 35-inch wheels designed to run on electric power. Wheels made in 1970 have been turning continuously for eighteen years, sending the blessings of enlightened knowledge out in all directions.

FIRST SADHANAS

December of 1970 marks the first intensive sadhana practice at TNMC, a three-day Nyung Nay ceremony dedicated to Avalokiteshvara. The first Longchenpa sadhana is held in February of 1971, and is performed each succeeding year.

TNMC BEGINS PRINTING

The first line drawings, short prayers, and invitations to TNMC events are printed by Dharma Publishing using the hand press or donated facilities of printing shops. Students begin to learn the basics of printing.

FIRST ART EXHIBITS

The first art exhibit sponsored by TNMC is held at the California College of Arts and Crafts in Oakland. It attracts large crowds and stimulates newpaper articles on Rinpoche's efforts to preserve the Buddhist tradition, as well as articles on Tibetan art. This and succeeding exhibits introduce many Westerners to the richly symbolic tradition of Tibetan sacred art.

1971
THE THIRD YEAR

PADMA LING

An old fraternity house is renovated by TNMC workers and becomes Padma Ling, "Lotus Ground." A small traditional temple is created, surrounded by spacious rooms, beautiful gardens, and the offices of TNMC, headquarters for the Nyingma Centers. TNMC and Publishing activities are centered at Padma Ling, as well as classes on Buddhist philosophy and meditation. Rinpoche's weekend seminars on the Buddhist teachings attract more people each year.

FIRST THANKAS PRINTED IN U.S.

The first full-color reproductions of Tibetan thankas are printed in America: the Eight Manifestations of Guru Padmasambhava. The catalogue of the art exhibit is Dharma Publishing and Dharma Press's first book.

CRYSTAL MIRROR SERIES BEGINS

The first issue of TNMC's journal, *Crystal Mirror,* is published, offering Americans background and historical information on the Nyingma lineage. We believe that this is the first time that many of the names of great Nyingma masters had been heard in our country.

TEXTS REPRODUCED

Several precious Tibetan texts Rinpoche had brought with him from Tibet are reproduced photographically from woodblock prints, as well as some prayers and Sutra texts for students.

PADMA LING STUDIES

TNMC students intensify their study of Buddhist psychology, philosophy, and Tibetan language. Work on small texts gives students an opportunity to practice translating, and provides study materials for the center.

1972
THE FOURTH YEAR

SUPPORT FOR RELIGIOUS CEREMONIES

At Rinpoche's direction, TNMC sponsors special religious ceremonies at centers of all four schools in India. These ceremonies promote world peace and harmony, offering the blessings of enlightenment to all peoples.

VISITS FROM BUDDHIST TEACHERS

H. H. Dudjom Rinpoche visits Berkeley, giving special talks and ceremonies at Padma Ling. Other lamas are invited to the new center and spend various periods of time in America.

NYINGMA INSTITUTE FOUNDED

With the seminars and programs at Padma Ling attracting many participants, Rinpoche establishes an institute for the public. The Nyingma Institute is founded early in 1972 and formally incorporated in September.

PRESS FACILITIES ESTABLISHED

Dharma Press obtains a 65-inch Harris press and moves its facilities to Emeryville. The inexperienced staff now begins to develop typesetting, printing, and business skills to support Nyingma projects and publications. Students are teaching themselves to run the Big Press, a slow and difficult process.

PRINTING MORE SACRED ART

While students are learning to operate the new equipment, Rinpoche has full-color thankas of the founders of Tibetan Buddhism printed at outside facilities to provide more students and practitioners with authentic images of sacred art.

INSTITUTE BRANCH FOUNDED IN ARIZONA

After several very successful seminars and workshops in Arizona, Rinpoche founds the Nyingma Institute of Phoenix where interested individuals gather to study basic Buddhist teachings.

1973
THE FIFTH YEAR

FIRST LARGE-SCALE PRAYER WHEEL

Following the traditional instructions, craftsmen build the first large-scale prayer wheel for Padma Ling—nearly six feet tall and two and a half feet wide. This first large wheel in America sends forth prayers counteracting unbalanced energies and ignorance.

CONTINUING ART EXHIBITS

TNMC sponsors art exhibits at Lone Mountain College in San Francisco and at locations in Berkeley, supporting the growing interest and appreciation for Tibetan art in America.

LITTLE BUDDHA STATUES

A set of 108 small Buddha statues, designed according to the texts, is cast, covered in gold, and placed in the new temple at Padma Ling.

TEACHERS VISIT PADMA LING

Dodrup Chen Rinpoche and Lama Golog Jigtse spend several months at Padma Ling, their presence deeply inspiring Nyingma students.

PRINTING NEW THANKAS

Rinpoche initiates a project to reproduce color thankas of Buddhas and Bodhisattvas such as Avalokiteshvara, Tara, and Amitabha to preserve these precious images.

THE FIRST TRANSLATIONS

More Tibetan language studies and translations are underway this year. Dharma Publishing brings out two book-length translations, *Calm and Clear* and *Legend of the Great Stupa,* the first books in the Tibetan Translation Series. These books bring Western Dharma students the invaluable advice of Tibetan masters.

GESAR MAGAZINE

Rinpoche founds *Gesar Magazine* to bring introductory teachings and information on the Buddhist tradition to a wider audience. Articles on Buddhism in the West, practical advice on meditation and self-understanding, and essays on art, culture, or history are included in each issue. *Gesar* may offer future historians valuable material for understanding how the Buddhist teachings were brought into our culture.

PRESS EQUIPMENT

The Press purchases a TxT typesetter and aims at developing both printing and typesetting capacities, while producing Dharma Publishing books, *Gesar*, and brochures for the new Institute.

NEW FACILITIES FOR THE INSTITUTE

A new building for the Nyingma Institute is located near the University of California in Berkeley. TNMC students renovate and redecorate it before the first classes begin during this summer.

FIRST HDTP PROGRAM

Rinpoche offers the first Human Development Training Program in the summer of 1973 at the Institute. These Training Programs attract people from far and wide and encourage hundreds of people to explore the Buddhist tradition. That fall seminars and weekends are offered by Dr. D. S. Ruegg, Claudio Naranjo, and others.

1974
THE SIXTH YEAR

SECOND LARGE-SCALE PRAYER WHEEL

TNMC craftsmen begin the creation of a new prayer wheel seven feet high and four feet wide for the Institute shrine room. As classes begin in September, the new wheel radiates the compassionate blessings of all the Buddhas, heightening the peaceful, light atmosphere at the new Institute.

ART EXHIBIT AT GRACE CATHEDRAL

TNMC holds another successful art exhibit of nearly one hundred thankas at Grace Cathedral in San Francisco, where eight hundred people gather to view the fine examples of sacred art. A series of films on Tibetan culture complement the art exhibit and include "Lost Horizons"; a film about the Dalai Lama made in Tibet; a documentary by Lowell Thomas; "Assault on Mount Everest"; and "Requiem for a Faith." Newspapers report this event, informing many people of our other activities and classes at the new Institute.

TIBETAN NYINGMA RELIEF FOUNDATION

TAP is incorporated into the Tibetan Nyingma Relief Foundation, with a board of directors composed of TNMC students and Institute staff. TNRF can now begin active fund-raising. Goals include developing and supporting medical and agricultural improvements for the Tibetan communities, as well as distributing food and supplies, and supporting traditional culture.

PRINTING CRYSTAL MIRROR

Publishing prepares *Crystal Mirror III,* an expanded issue with more articles and news. The Press purchases a small Harris press to provide better printing capacities. This *Crystal Mirror,* which includes photos and line drawings, is the first book off the new press.

GUIDING THE INSTITUTE

Rinpoche offers seminars in Kum Nye relaxation, in Buddhist psychology and philosophy, and meditation, as well as short retreats and a program for educators. He guides a special month-long retreat for Buddhist studies students, and holds the second Human Development Training Program in the summer.

BUDDHIST STUDIES DEVELOP

Following Rinpoche's guidelines, the Institute establishes basic Buddhist studies courses to lay a foundation for further study and practice. Classes are offered by Rinpoche as well as by visiting scholars, including Dr. Herbert Guenther, Dr. Lewis Lancaster, Rev. Leslie Kawamura, Dr. Vanak Paranjipe, Ven. Thich Thien-an,

Ven. Koon Kum-Heng, Dr. Yuichi Kajiyama, and other scholars and teachers.

VISITS BY IMPORTANT TEACHERS

H. H. Gyalwa Karmapa visits Padma Ling where special ceremonies are held. He attends a reception in his honor at the Nyingma Institute, and pays a visit to Dharma Press. Sakya Trizin visits Padma Ling and the Nyingma Institute. Over the next several years, TNMC will sponsor visits from important Tibetan teachers belonging to all the Tibetan schools.

KUNGA LING ESTABLISHED

A ranch is offered to the Arizona Institute as a permanent facility for workshops. Named Kunga Ling, Place of Joy, by Rinpoche, the new center becomes a residential community and soon is offering nine-month training programs in human development.

1975
THE SEVENTH YEAR

FOUNDING OF ODIYAN

After several years of search, beautiful property for a country center is located in the fall of 1974. Purchased during 1975, on August 9th the land is consecrated by Rinpoche for the Dharma. Once building permits are obtained, construction begins on the rim structure. The farmhouse is renovated and a workshop built. Rinpoche works intensively with both architects and engineers to develop a full plan for construction of the temple and the four entryway pagodas.

DHARMA MUDRANALAYA

In March of 1975, Dharma Publishing and Dharma Press are officially incorporated as Dharma Mudranalaya to continue the work of the press Rinpoche established in India and in honor of the great Tibetan printing house of that name in Derge in Eastern Tibet.

ART PUBLICATIONS INCREASE

Dharma Publishing brings out more traditional art, the first sets of twenty thanka reproductions being printed and published in a high-quality gold-embossed portfolio.

NEW BOOKS PRINTED

New books include *Nyingma Annals I, Crystal Mirror IV, Mind in Buddhist Psychology, Golden Zephyr,* and *Reflections of Mind,* the first book in the new Nyingma Psychology Series. The *Jataka Tales* are published, with proceeds donated to support Tibetan Relief activities.

A THIRD LARGE-SCALE PRAYER WHEEL

Following traditional guidelines, TNMC craftsmen build a five-and-a-half-ton prayer wheel for the Institute meditation garden. This wheel contains more than 200,000 large sheets of paper, each printed with 108 different mantras that promote the ending of suffering and the awakening of compassion. Every day this single prayer wheel releases 200 trillion mantras especially selected to be beneficial for America.

BUDDHIST STUDIES PROGRESS

At the Institute the new Buddhist studies program is underway, with courses offered by Rinpoche, Lama Govinda, Dr. Herbert Guenther, Dr. F. A. Bischoff, Lobsang Lhalungpa, Dr. Leo Pruden, Dr. Yeshe Donden, Rev. Leslie Kawamura, Dr. Stephen Beyer, and others. Dhyana Master Hsuan Hua, Rev. Kobum Chino, Kennet Roshi, and Rev. Mokurai Cherlin give special talks.

INSTITUTE SEMINARS

Scientists and health professionals join seminars on East/West medicine, healing, and explorations of relaxation and meditation. Rinpoche holds the third Human Development Training Program and also offers seminars on dreams and emotions.

BUDDHA'S BIRTHDAY

The Institute holds a large and festive celebration of the Buddha's birthday in this and several succeeding years. Elaborate decorations are created, and three hundred guests entertained in honor of the Buddha.

ARIZONA SUPPORT

Interested members of the Nyingma Institute in Arizona form a support group for Odiyan projects: to offer Odiyan workers encouragement, to raise funds, and to recruit new volunteers.

COLORADO INSTITUTE BRANCHES

Under the direction of Rinpoche, students of the Human Development Training Program establish a meditation center and an institute in Denver, Colorado. Classes are offered in basic Buddhist philosophy and meditation.

MANJUSHRI VIHARA

Manjushri Vihara, the library at the Institute, has now collected over 1,500 books on Buddhism and Tibet, and is actively obtaining Tibetan texts.

EIGHT STUPAS

Craftspeople at Padma Ling carve eight three-foot-high stupas commemorating eight important events in the life of the Buddha. Each has a particular shape and special proportions as described in the texts. The stupas are covered in gold and placed in the temple at Padma Ling.

TAP SPONSORS EVENTS

TAP sponsors a two-day seminar given by Rinpoche at the University of Southern California, which is attended by over two hundred psychologists and mental health professionals. Six fund-raising events are organized in the San Francisco area.

SUPPORT FOR PENFRIENDS AND TAP INCREASING

More than six hundred people have joined the Penfriend Program to offer support and friendship to the Tibetan exiles. TNMC Head Lama and TAP are sending regular monthly support to fourteen centers, and make contributions to many other colleges and centers of each of the four schools. TAP is publishing quarterly reports in *Gesar Magazine*.

1976
THE EIGHTH YEAR

TRANSLATIONS AND CULTURAL STUDIES

To make available more teachings by Nyingma masters, Dharma Publishing brings out the trilogy *Kindly Bent to Ease Us* by Longchenpa, translated by Dr. H. V. Guenther, in the Tibetan Translation Series. *Psychocosmic Symbolism of the Buddhist Stupa* by Lama Govinda is also published.

VISITS BY IMPORTANT TEACHERS

In the spring H. H. Dilgo Khentse visits Padma Ling where special ceremonies are held. At the Institute His Holiness gives teachings to four hundred people. He visits Dharma Press and the Odiyan Center, offering his blessings and encouragement to Nyingma students. In the summer H. H. Dudjom Rinpoche visits Padma Ling, the Nyingma Institute, Dharma Press, and Odiyan, offering his blessings and support for the efforts of students.

NYINGMA CENTERS ESTABLISHED

Nyingma Centers Corporation is formed at Rinpoche's suggestion as an umbrella organization to coordinate and oversee the activities of the five organizations. The Board is to be composed of members of each organization and long-time friends of the Centers.

BUDDHIST STUDIES PROGRAMS FLOURISH

The Institute Buddhist studies program is expanding, and includes courses by Rinpoche, Dr. Herbert Guenther, Sonam Gyatso, Geshe Wangyal, Dr. Charlene

McDermott, Dr. Stephan Beyer, and others. Institute staff trained by Rinpoche offer introductory courses in Buddhist philosophy and psychology.

EAST/WEST SEMINARS

East/West studies focus on healing, stress reduction, consciousness studies, and comparative psychology. Rinpoche offers the fourth Human Development Training Program as well as seminars on science and religion, healing, and meditation. A teachers' training program, designed by Rinpoche for Western educators, is held during this summer.

NEW ARIZONA INSTITUTE BRANCH

Nyingma students in Mesa and Phoenix wish to open an institute in Tuscon, and with Rinpoche's permission, establish a new branch. Courses focus on basic Dharma teachings, philosophy, and psychology.

ODIYAN RIM STRUCTURE COMPLETE

The Odiyan rim structure is completed, and a Corten roof added. A foundry is built, and a portable sawmill set up. Large fireplaces for the rim structure are built from rock off the property. The first piece of heavy equipment — a forklift — is purchased.

WORK ON THE ODIYAN LAND

Land clearing, road construction, and reforestation work begin; well and water tanks are installed. Neglected for many years, the land begins to respond to restoration efforts. Much work remains to be done to clean up existing wooded areas.

THE FIRST TSA TSA PROJECT

TNMC students learn how to produce traditional small clay images known as tsa tsas. A set of 100,000 of the Longevity Trinity is created during 1976 and 1977. Painted gold, these tsa tsas are installed in the stupa in 1980 and placed in natural locations to encourage balance and protection from disasters.

1977
THE NINTH YEAR

LARGE SETS OF PRAYER WHEELS

Senior TNMC craftsmen begin the production of 170 three-hundred-pound prayer wheels for Odiyan, the Institute, and Padma Ling, as well as 1,080 hand-held prayer wheels. One large wheel activates over fourteen million mantras; each revolution of a set of thirty-five wheels generates five hundred million prayers for the peace and welfare of all sentient beings.

STUDENTS LEARN RITUAL ARTS AND CRAFTS

Ritual art projects supervised by Rinpoche include the creation of six hundred specially designed prayer flags, an entry gate banner, eight cylindrical chevron banners, and eight auspicious symbol banners for Odiyan.

SCHOLARLY WORKS PUBLISHED

Dharma Publishing brings out *Elegant Sayings,* and several new volumes by scholars: *Revelation in Indian Thought, Tibetan Buddhism in Western Perspective,* and *Buddhist Thought and Asian Civilization*.

GUIDANCE IN BUDDHIST STUDIES AND ART

Rinpoche guides months of extensive TNMC student research necessary for *Crystal Mirror V,* the lengthiest, most detailed volume to date. Experienced TNMC artists create nearly one hundred traditional line drawings for this book, gaining more practice and background for further studies in iconography.

TWO NEW BOOKS BY RINPOCHE

Rinpoche completes both *Gesture of Balance,* a collection of talks on meditation and self-understanding, and *Time, Space, and Knowledge,* a visionary book of great complexity. Student editors gain valuable experience, but the editorial process is very slow, requiring many months of Rinpoche's time.

TEN DHARMA BOOKS

Dharma Press produces ten Dharma books in 1977, including scholarly works, the *Nyingma Annals II,* and the *Odiyan Country Cookbook.* Bindery equipment is purchased this year, making the Press a complete book production facility.

TRANSLATIONS OF DHARMA PUBLISHING BOOKS

This is the first year that Dharma Publishing books are translated into a foreign language. *Calm and Clear* is translated into both German and Italian; *Mind in Buddhist Psychology* and *Legend of the Great Stupa* are translated into Italian. With each passing year, Dharma Publishing titles are reaching a wider audience.

BUDDHIST STUDIES REFINED

The Buddhist studies program at the Institute continues to be refined. Courses are offered by Rinpoche, Dr. Herbert Guenther, Geshe Wangyal, Dr. Roger Corless, Dawa Norbu, and others. Special talks are given by Ven. Hsuan Hua and Ven. Thich Thien-an.

TSK SEMINARS BEGIN

Rinpoche holds several seminars to introduce the TSK vision to scientists and others interested in this new approach to knowledge. Noted physicists and consciousness researchers join Institute staff in a TSK symposium. In December a celebration at the Institute attended by four hundred guests marks the publication of TSK. The first run of 3,000 copies is sold out in one month.

INSTITUTE SPECIAL PROGRAMS

Special programs on healing by guest faculty continue. Rinpoche offers weekend courses on Kum Nye, dreams, and working with emotions, as well as holding the fifth Human Development Training Program.

ODIYAN OPEN HOUSE

Odiyan crews work intensively to prepare for the first Odiyan Open House in June. Four hundred guests attend ceremonies and take tours of the land. Seeing the vision begin to take form, supporters and friends are freshly inspired with the opportunities Odiyan might open for the the West. Bringing an ancient knowledge tradition into modern culture seems deeply worthwhile.

FINISHING THE ODIYAN RIM STRUCTURE

Finishing work is done on the rim structure and kitchen, while the north, south, and west entryways are framed and the dome installed on the north pagoda. A small temple room is created in the rim structure.

GENTLING THE ODIYAN LAND

Crews make some progress with long-term landscaping and planting projects. The four-acre garden is expanded, and more plantings are made in the orchard. Five thousand new tree seedlings are planted around the property. A herd of thirty-five wild mustangs dying of drought is transported from Nevada to pastures at Odiyan where they begin to flourish.

TNRF ACTIVITIES INCREASE

Over one thousand people are now active in the Penfriend Program, bringing support and friendship to many Tibetans. TNRF regularly sends funds and supplies to Tibetan communities in India, Bhutan, Sikkim, and Nepal, while TNMC Head Lama continues to make contributions to sponsor religious ceremonies and to bring more visiting lamas to America.

1978
THE TENTH YEAR

TIBETAN TRANSLATION SERIES

At Rinpoche's suggestion, several professors had undertaken a translation from the French of the biography of Guru Rinpoche, which is now published as *The Life and*

Liberation of Padmasambhava after more than four years of work. The publication of this precious text gives students new inspiration and helps deepen appreciation for the teachings of the Nyingma tradition. The elegant design for these volumes sets the standard for the Tibetan Translation Series.

NEW BOOKS BY RINPOCHE

Rinpoche authors *Openness Mind, Skillful Means,* and the two-volume *Kum Nye Relaxation,* making his talks and advice on study and practice more widely available.

GESTURE OF BALANCE TRANSLATED

Gesture of Balance is translated into Italian this year and into German the following year. Since its publication, this has been our most popular, most widely-read volume, inspiring readers to practice meditation and to take courses at the Institute.

PRESS PROGRESS

After more than six months of effort, Dharma Press successfully produces the complex design of *Life and Liberation,* which includes fifty-eight color thanka plates. A clothbound portfolio of Padmasambhava thankas is printed, making these precious images more widely available to students and practitioners.

STUDYING SACRED ART

TNMC artists begin training to learn the types of line art planned for the *Nyingma Edition:* graceful images of Buddhas, Bodhisattvas, and Arhats, Dharmapalas, Dharma Kings, and Buddhist Masters.

THANKA RESEARCH BEGINS

Research begins to locate thankas for reproduction in the *Nyingma Edition*. TNMC begins to ship thanka prints in large quantities to India for use in meditation and devotional practices.

TNRF RAISES MONEY

A mailing of 25,000 brochures brings in thousands of dollars of support for Tibetans in India. TNMC Head Lama continues to sponsor religious ceremonies conducted for peace and the longevity of the Dharma.

INSTITUTE ADMINISTRATION CHANGES

Rinpoche takes a leave of absence to supervise other projects and to author several books. New officers for the Institute are selected and begin to take more responsibility for administration and teaching.

BUDDHIST STUDIES CONTINUE

Buddhist studies courses continue to be offered by Lama Govinda, Dr. Herbert Guenther, Geshe Wangyal, Geshe Jamspel, Dr. D. S. Ruegg, Dr. David Levin, Dr. Roger Corless, and Dr. Charles Prebish. John Blofeld and Yeshe Donden both give special seminars. Week-long monthly intensives and month-long summer intensives in special topics in Buddhist studies are introduced.

KUM NYE PROGRAMS BEGIN

The focus on Kum Nye increases with the first nine-month training program for Kum Nye teachers. Many students from this program become closely associated with Nyingma over the next several years. Three week-long Kum Nye retreats are offered, as well as workshops and weekends with particular themes.

ODIYAN RETREATS

This spring marks the first retreats held at Odiyan, one in Kum Nye and one in TSK. Participants from all over America and from Europe gather for these special opportunities to practice within the Odiyan mandala. The peaceful natural environment is ideal for retreats.

WORK AT ODIYAN GROWS DIFFICULT

At Odiyan, work begins on the west and south entryways, and the dome for the north entryway is erected. The Odiyan crew begins work on the temple mound and installs foundation piers. Steel for the temple is delivered. Work is growing more difficult and complex, and money is running low. Rinpoche offers continuing support, carefully controlling the Odiyan budget and encouraging the crew to work well together through the discouraging difficulties.

ODIYAN PRAYER WHEEL

TNMC workers begin the production of the ten-ton prayer wheel for Odiyan. This massive wheel, ten feet in diameter and fifteen feet in height, will later become the center of the Odiyan Stupa, which will be built around it. A prayer wheel of this size creates a very powerful source of blessings for our country, generating three hundred million mantras with each rotation.

1979
THE ELEVENTH YEAR

NEW BOOKS FROM PUBLISHING

Dharma Publishing brings out *Tibet in Pictures* and *Buddha's Lions* before beginning work on the *Nyingma Edition*. In the last five years, Dharma Mudranalaya has brought out fifty titles, which are distributed in thirty countries. More than a quarter of a million volumes have been sold since we began publishing and printing less than ten years ago. Our books are becoming much better known, and some are being used in colleges and universities. *Gesture of Balance,* for example, has now been adopted for forty-four different courses.

WORK COMMENCES ON THE NYINGMA EDITION

Rinpoche establishes several canonical research projects, which are underway as printing of the texts begins. The total design concept for the new edition is devised, and a production plan is worked out. Soon, this project takes the full-time efforts of all Publishing staff and demands a tremendous amount of Rinpoche's time to advise, guide, and check each step of the work.

BUDDHIST STUDIES PROGRAM DEVELOPMENTS

The Institute Buddhist studies program continues with courses by Geshe Jamspel, Geshe Gyeltsen, Dr. Charlene McDermott, Gesshin Cheney, and Dr. David Levin. Special weekends are offered by Dr. Andrew Rawlinson, Dr. Claudio Naranjo, and others. The curriculum is further revised to more closely reflect the traditional topics of basic study.

KUM NYE PROGRAMS INCREASE

Long-term Kum Nye programs attract several hundred students. The second nine-month program begins, and summer intensives in Kum Nye are given.

TSK PROGRAMS BEGIN

The first intensive TSK seminar is held this summer, attended by both Americans and Europeans; a one-week retreat is also offered. Rinpoche suggests instructors begin compiling a training manual. TSK is already in its third printing, and by fall there is enough interest for nine-month programs not only in Berkeley, but also in Arizona and at Odiyan. Five TSK retreats are held at Odiyan, drawing many participants.

OUTREACH PROGRAMS BEGIN

The first outreach programs in Kum Nye and meditation are taught by Institute staff members at locations in Europe and Australia.

DALAI LAMA VISITS INSTITUTE

The Dalai Lama visits the Nyingma Institute in October and gives a public address attended by five hundred people. After his talk, participants offer ceremonial scarves and receive blessings. His Holiness then visits Padma Ling where he blesses the work in progress on the new edition of the Kanjur and Tanjur.

RITUAL ART PROJECTS

TNMC craftspeople create 150 prayer flags particularly designed to foster balance in nature, avert earthquakes and other natural disasters, and prevent disease. Over two hundred prayer wheel covers are produced as well as several ceremonial umbrellas in traditional styles.

LAMAS' VISITS SPONSORED

TNMC sponsors visits by Tibetan lamas including Khenpo Palden Sherab, Khenpo Tsewang, Thinley Norbu, and Tulku Thondrup, and Sangyumma, who is the widow of Rinpoche's teacher Jamyang Khyentse.

ODIYAN CONSTRUCTION DELAYED

Financial difficulties at Odiyan require a six-month halt in construction. As work resumes, Nyingma students are freshly appreciative of the importance of creating Odiyan. Work begins on the large prayer wheel, the west entryway is framed, the south entryway is stuccoed and sheetrocked, and the north entryway dome is plastered. When the copper for the west dome is installed, we begin to realize how beautiful the pagodas will be.

PLANS FOR A STUPA IN THE WEST

Rinpoche plans to construct a large stupa exactly proportioned to symbolize the enlightened mind of the Buddha. Such architectural symbols have been built all over Asia for centuries. Building a stupa in America will bring inspiration to Western Dharma students and the blessings for peace and harmony to our culture. As Rinpoche designs the stupa, the Odiyan crew starts to work on the access road to the stupa and installs the foundation piers.

TNMC FOCUSES ON LONG-RANGE PRESERVATION

By 1979 TAP and TNRF had offered many thousands of dollars in assistance to Tibetan refugees. The Pen Friend Program had generated additional support from several thousand Westerners. As conditions improved for the Tibetan communities, TNMC focused its efforts on long-range cultural preservation projects. The Head Lama of TNMC continues to sponsor religious ceremonies at numerous centers, monasteries, and colleges.

1980
THE TWELFTH YEAR

TSK INTEREST INCREASING

The two-volume set of *Dimensions of Thought* includes essays by participants in TSK programs, and by scientists, educators, and psychologists interested in the new vision. The nine-month training program at the Institute is offered again, and workshops are given in many cities in response to reader requests. A six-week retreat as well as four shorter retreats are held at Odiyan.

FULL-TIME WORK ON THE NYINGMA EDITION

The extensive work to produce the *Nyingma Edition* requires Rinpoche's constant guidance and efforts of all the staff of Dharma Publishing as well as support from TNMC and Dharma Press. The new edition includes the complete Derge Edition plus 593 additional texts from other editions. Production of introductory and research materials—charts, maps, chapter lists, and data on authors and translators—for each of 120 volumes is underway. Elaborate title pages in traditional scripts are designed for each sacred text.

FIRST EDITION OF THE GUIDE

A preliminary edition of the *Guide to the Nyingma Edition,* listing all the texts, authors, and translators, is produced in June for the Stupa Celebration held on Padmasambhava's birthday.

TRANSLATIONS OF RINPOCHE'S BOOKS

Translations of Rinpoche's books begin to accelerate: *Gesture of Balance* is translated into Dutch; *Openness Mind, Skillful Means, and Reflections of Mind* are translated into Italian; *Kum Nye Relaxation* into German and Italian; *Openness Mind* into Dutch and Italian; *Time, Space, and Knowledge* into Italian.

SKILLFUL MEANS PROGRAMS

At the Institute, Skillful Means programs and seminars are underway, as this new approach to more creative work begins to reach people in a wide variety of fields. An unusual program combines work at one of the Nyingma Centers with Institute classes.

BUDDHIST STUDIES AND PSYCHOLOGY PROGRAMS

Buddhist studies courses are offered at the Institute by Dr. Leslie Kawamura, Ven. Rewata Dhamma, Dr. Kennard Lipman, and others. Courses in experiential psychology are presented by Dr. Eugene Gendlin, Dr. Claudio Naranjo, and other specialists.

OUTREACH EXPANDS

Institute staff members begin regular visits to study groups in Holland and Germany, offering weekends and week-long retreats in Kum Nye and meditation.

NEW DEANS FOR BRANCH INSTITUTES

New deans are named for the Tuscon, Arizona Institute and the Boulder, Colorado Institute. The new administrations encourage the growth of these two branches and the offering of more courses in Buddhist subjects.

COLLECTING TEXTS

TNMC and Dharma Publishing obtain the Taisho edition of the Canon, the Karmapa's Kanjur edition, the Bo Dong collection, the Gyud Bum, and many hundreds of additional texts.

ART FOR THE NYINGMA EDITION

TNMC artists are now concentrating on artwork for the *Nyingma Edition*. Rinpoche supervises the production of line drawings of 83 Buddhas, 15 Great Bodhisattvas, 28 Arhats and Great Patrons, 9 Manifestations of Guru Padmasambhava, 31 Mahapanditas, 21 Mahasiddhas, 7 Great Dharma Kings, 37 Excellent Tibetan Masters, 31 Wrathful Deities, and 67 Stupas. Permission is obtained to reproduce 231 thankas from museum and private collections around the world.

PRESS OBTAINS NEW EQUIPMENT

The Press obtains the equipment necessary for producing the *Nyingma Edition:* a gilder, a shrinkwrapping machine, a gold foil stamper, and equipment for French-groove binding. A used Miehle press is also purchased.

BUDDHA STATUE PROJECT

TNMC craftspeople begin work on a life-sized Buddha statue carved in clay. The original is placed in the temple at Padma Ling, and a likeness is cast to place in the stupa at Odiyan. This beautiful, large statue of the Buddha is deeply inspiring to students, most of whom have never seen a life-sized sacred statue. The second statue is ready in time for the Stupa Celebration.

ODIYAN STUPA

Though work on the *Nyingma Edition* requires much of Nyingma Centers' time and effort, the Odiyan Stupa is completed this same year. A monument 113 feet high on a 60-foot-square base, the magnificent white stupa is completed in June. Rinpoche places many precious objects within the stupa in a special ceremony, which is followed by a celebration with hundreds of guests and friends. The presence of the stupa seems to initiate a new phase in the development of Odiyan; long-time supporters and Odiyan workers feel new appreciation for the deep vision guiding the Nyingma Centers' efforts.

WORK BEGINS ON ODIYAN TEMPLE

The steel is erected for the temple, the temple walls are framed, and the roof waterproofed. Rinpoche designs a cupola for the temple roof, which brings the temple height to eighty feet. The construction of the specially designed temple would prove complex, costly, and time-consuming, but with the completion of the stupa, we felt a new confidence and inspiration.

1981
THE THIRTEENTH YEAR

FINISHING THE NYINGMA EDITION

Dharma Publishing completes the *Nyingma Edition* of the Kanjur and Tanjur: 108 sets of 120 volumes each, nearly 13,000 volumes in all, specially designed with high-quality paper and binding, custom-made satin slip-covers, gold-stamped covers, and gilded pages. Checking and finishing procedures at the Press require six months for four to ten people to complete. With the inspiration and guidance of Rinpoche and the blessings of the Nyingma lineage, we are able to accomplish a truly worthwhile project that will have lasting benefits for many years into the future.

CATALOGUE/BIBLIOGRAPHY

Intensive work now begins on the *Research Catalogue/ Bibliography* for the new edition of the Kanjur and Tanjur. Following guidelines for collecting full bibliographic information on each text, the staff assembles valuable data that will support translators' and researchers' efforts in studying the tradition.

HIDDEN MIND OF FREEDOM

Hidden Mind of Freedom, a new collection of talks by Rinpoche on meditation and awareness, is brought out. These useful essays, which had appeared over the years in other Nyingma publications, are now easily available to the many readers of Rinpoche's books.

NEW INSTITUTE STAFF

The administration of the Institute is rotated, a new dean being named and the former dean beginning a three-year retreat at Odiyan. This is the first year an American Nyingma student has undertaken the long-term traditional retreat.

KUM NYE PROGRAMS FLOURISH

The Kum Nye nine-month and three-month programs continue to attract many students. Special Kum Nye workshops in stress reduction are offered, and new Kum Nye instructors are trained.

TSK PROGRAMS GROWING

The ten-month Dawn of Knowledge TSK program enrolls fifty American and European participants. The first issue of the TSK journal is published.

BUDDHIST COURSES

Special courses are offered at the Institute by U Silananda, Swami Sivananda-Radha, and Dr. Jagannath Upadhyaya, while basic Dharma classes and meditation are given particular emphasis.

RITUAL ART PROJECTS

Following textual guidelines, TNMC craftspeople produce 556 prayer flags designed to prevent disaster and to promote healing energies in nature.

SILK SCREENING SACRED ART

A large set of 7,590 copies of line drawings chosen from the *Nyingma Edition* is silkscreened by TNMC craftspeople; 320 silkscreened thankas and 100 thankas on paper are framed in the traditional Tibetan style.

CONSTRUCTION ON THE TEMPLE

At Odiyan work on the temple is underway, including the installation of 72,000 square feet of copper roof, the addition of a radiant heating slab, and the plastering of the dome using specially constructed movable scaffolding. Temple gallery columns and precast moldings are fabricated and installed.

ORNAMENTING THE TEMPLE BEGINS

Two thousand pieces of temple ornamentation are designed and cast in concrete. The temple mound is now regraded and landscaping begins. We can sense a new atmosphere emerging at Odiyan as the temple takes shape in the center of the rim structure. With the support and guidance of Rinpoche's long-range vision, we are beginning to see results that surprise us all. The design of the temple conveys great power and delicacy in an unusual blend of Eastern and Western motifs.

STAINED GLASS PROJECTS

During 1979, a new art project had been initiated, the creation of stained glass windows for the temples and stupa at Odiyan. By 1980 sixteen plum blossom windows for the entryway pagodas were complete; by 1981 sixteen semicircular windows are finished. Another project is a set of twenty-four leaded windows for the temple.

A stained glass Buddha image eight by five feet made of many hundreds of separate pieces is installed in the window of the Buddha Room in the stupa.

1982
THE FOURTEENTH YEAR

WORK ON THE CATALOGUE

Eight of the large volumes of the *Research Catalogue/Bibliography* are completed at the end of 1982, and printed and bound in the same high-quality format as the *Nyingma Edition*. Producing the *Nyingma Edition* had preempted all of Publishing's other work for more than three years and required vast outlays of funds. Now we could begin other projects.

MICROFICHE PROJECT

This year we obtained the necessary equipment to preserve materials on microfiche, and Publishing began a project to preserve the new *Nyingma Edition* in this form. Thirty-three complete sets (120 volumes each) were made, each stored in cases specially designed to guarantee long life.

NEW PRAYER WHEELS FOR ODIYAN

TNMC craftsmen begin the production of new prayer wheels containing longer prayers and even entire texts. TNMC workers produce 112 prayer wheels for Odiyan, plus a set of identical prayers in microfilm for smaller prayer wheels. Installed in 1983, each large wheel is encased in copper imprinted with mantras in Lantsa script, and topped with a smaller microfilm wheel to offer additional blessings.

RITUAL ART PROJECTS

TNMC craftspeople produce 1,245 prayer flags made in eleven different designs for balancing energies in nature, relieving the suffering of sentient beings, and supporting the awakening of enlightened attitudes. Over 90 Lantsa prints for thankas are silkscreened and framed; more than 360 covers for *Nyingma Edition* volumes are made; 60 thankas are framed in traditional cloth hangings. These efforts will help preserve many fine examples of sacred art for the future.

THANKAS PRINTED

This year the Press printed a set of twenty-four thankas, nine of Padmasambhava, seven of the Buddha, and eight of Bodhisattvas and protective deities. This particular series was painted by TNMC artists who had spent years studying with Rinpoche and could now skillfully carry out thanka designs.

EXHIBITION OF NEW EDITION AT INSTITUTE

An exhibition of the *Nyingma Edition* is held at the Nyingma Institute, including a full set on display, an hour-long video tracing the history of the Dharma, and a presentation of more than seven hundred framed prints of thankas, line drawings, and maps. Over five hundred people attend, and local newspapers and radio stations cover the event.

LONG-TERM PROGRAMS

The nine-month Kum Nye training program continues to be very popular. The three-month program is also successful; both attract new students from Europe.

BUDDHIST STUDIES

A year-long evening program focuses on Buddhist studies for students who have completed a long-term experiential program such as Kum Nye or TSK. Classes based on reading Sutras and works by Tibetan masters in translation are especially stressed. Special lectures offered by Jagannath Upadhyaya are attended by over a hundred people.

DAWN OF KNOWLEDGE CONFERENCE

In the spring, the Dawn of Knowledge conference, "New Visions," is hosted jointly with the physics department of U.C. Berkeley. Over five hundred people attend. *Time, Space, and Knowledge* is translated into Dutch this year.

1983
THE FIFTEENTH YEAR

ORNAMENTING THE TEMPLE

During 1982 and 1983 ornamenting work continues at Odiyan as twenty-five tons of granite veneer are hung on the temple exterior. Marble is installed on temple stairs and gallery, and a terrazzo floor is created for the Dharma Hall. Black walnut exterior doors are constructed as well as two thousand copper ornaments.

New stained glass is installed in the temple, an ornamental spire is added, and painting of the temple exterior is completed. Handmade wooden cabinets are finished, silkscreened wallpaper and curtains are hung. Hydronic and solar heating systems are installed.

ODIYAN LANDSCAPING

The perimeter fence is erected around the property, landscaping is expanded around the stupa, and a marble floor is laid in the stupa. Retaining walls are built for the temple mound and plantings are added to the mound. Framing of the east entryway pagoda is finished, roofs are installed on the north and south entryways, and entry doors are built in walnut.

TEMPLE CELEBRATION

In June a celebration is held to commemorate the development of Odiyan and the temple mandala. Friends and supporters gather to see the progress made on the temple and to view a special exhibit of the Kanjur and Tanjur. The temple is deeply impressive—three stories topped with flying copper roofs against blue sky. The news media are invited to this celebration, and scores of articles about Odiyan begin to appear.

ODIYAN WINDOW PROJECT

The stained glass window project is expanded during 1982 in order to create a total of over 500 windows for the Odiyan temple and entryway pagodas. Techniques are developed that include silkscreening and sandblasting. By 1985 hundreds of windows are completed: 56 of important Tibetan masters; 90 Buddhist symbols;

64 Buddhas, Bodhisattvas, Herukas, and Dharmapalas; 16 plum blossom windows; 16 semicircular windows; 64 blue glass panels with Buddhas, Bodhisattvas, and manifestations of Padmasambhava imprinted in gold; 77 temple windows including Buddhas, Bodhisattvas, mantras, eight auspicious symbols, and Dharma symbols. More than 50 panels for library cabinets are also silkscreened, and over 50 stained glass lampshades are created for the temple.

TRANSLATIONS OF SPIRITUAL BIOGRAPHIES

Dharma Publishing brings out three new volumes in the Translation Series: *The Voice of the Buddha* (The Lalitavistara Sutra), *The Marvelous Companion* (Jataka Tales), and *Mother of Knowledge* (biography of Yeshe Tsogyal). These spiritual biographies, which reveal deeper dimensions of the nature of the Buddha and the lives of great masters, are very important foundation texts for the study and practice of the Dharma.

RINPOCHE'S BOOKS IN TRANSLATION

Hidden Mind of Freedom is translated into Dutch and Italian; *Skillful Means* is translated into Dutch; *Time, Space, and Knowledge* is translated into German.

REVISED GUIDE

A revised and enlarged *Guide to the Nyingma Edition* is finished after the *Catalogue* volumes are printed.

RITUAL ARTS PROJECTS

TNMC art projects for Odiyan are increasing in volume: 18 hanging temple banners, 114 framed silkscreened thankas of Rinpoche's teachers, 8 round chevron hangings, over 1,100 feet of meditation runners, 250 specially designed meditation cushions for the temple, and 4 victory banners. Designs for 70 prayer wheel casings are silkscreened onto copper, and designs for curtains are silkscreened onto fabric.

DHARMART DESIGNS

A new subdivision of Dharma Publishing is formed to create distinctive lines of greeting cards, calendars, and various gift items. TNMC artists provided many unusual designs for the new project.

SPECIAL PROGRAMS AT THE INSTITUTE

Numerous new weekend courses are offered on meditation, self-healing, emotional balance, self-image, and Skillful Means. One-month intensives in Kum Nye and introductory Buddhist teachings are stressed. Kum Nye weekends are held in many cities across the country.

TRIP TO ASIA

During the summer, Rinpoche travels to Asia, together with a few members of the TNMC staff. Monasteries and temples are visited; rare pieces of art are located for the Odiyan temple.

SUPPORT FOR TARTHANG MONASTERY

Rinpoche spends several months in Tibet at Tarthang Monastery, visiting friends and family and encouraging the rebuilding efforts. TNMC is inspired to offer support for these efforts and hopes to send the monastery texts and art.

THE YESHE DE PROJECT

The Nyingma Institute together with Dharma Publishing and TNMC sponsor a long-range project named after the great Tibetan translator Yeshe De. We hope to encourage translations of Buddhist texts by qualified scholars and research into Buddhist civilizations. Yeshe De projects will be supported by staff and facilities of Dharma Publishing.

1984
THE SIXTEENTH YEAR

NEW INSTITUTE STAFF

Administration of the Institute is rotated. The former dean begins a traditional three-year retreat at Odiyan, and the dean from the Boulder, Colorado Institute becomes the new dean at Berkeley. A long-time instructor from Berkeley becomes dean of the Boulder, Colorado Institute. At Berkeley an Associate Membership is introduced to encourage long-time students and friends to participate more directly in the Institute planning.

NEW INSTITUTE PROGRAMS

The five basic Institute programs are arranged into a unified mandala program: Psychology and Philosophy, Meditation, Kum Nye, Skillful Means, and Tibetan. New programs are initiated at Rinpoche's suggestion: a Nyingma practices program, a four-month and two-month program. Long retreats are now particularly emphasized. A one-month Nyingma practice intensive is held in the summer.

KUM NYE PROGRAMS GROWING

The Kum Nye training programs continue to be very successful; Kum Nye outreach programs are held at prisons, senior centers, and other locations.

OUTREACH PROGRAMS EXPAND

Institute staff members begin to make regular visits to study groups in Brazil. Twice yearly outreach programs continue to be held in Holland and Germany, focusing especially on Kum Nye and TSK.

TSK PROGRAMS

Advanced TSK retreats and seminars are held at the Institute, while instructors offer eight-week programs at different locations around the San Francisco area.

TWO NEW CRYSTAL MIRRORS

Publishing brings out *Crystal Mirrors VI* and *VII,* each of which contains research materials from *Nyingma Edition* projects. Though staff skills are improving, a great deal of Rinpoche's time and energy is still required in discussion of research topics, setting guidelines, and reviewing each publication.

KNOWLEDGE OF FREEDOM

Knowledge of Freedom comes out at the end of the year after more than two years of work. New programs based on these teachings begin immediately at Odiyan and at the Institute.

MORE TRANSLATIONS OF RINPOCHE'S BOOKS

Gesture of Balance is translated into Portuguese this year; *Kum Nye Relaxation* is translated into Dutch and Portuguese.

RITUAL ARTS PROJECTS

TNMC craftspeople create 413 prayer flags designed to bring the blessings of the enlightened lineage into this land. The silkscreening crew makes 132 sets of curtains with the eight auspicious symbols. Sewing projects include 70 thankas mounted, 16 large temple hangings, an 80-foot-long temple banner, 5 large yolwas, and 200 altar cloths, and framing of 253 silk-screened prints and 260 silkscreened mandalas.

SUPPORT FOR ODIYAN

As Odiyan expenses continue to rise, and more elaborate ornamentation is created, Nyingma Institute and Dharma Press pledge to increase their support for Odiyan in whatever ways they can, with workers, funds, and encouragement. Individuals continue to provide small but much-appreciated contributions for the many special art projects underway for Odiyan.

MANDALA PLATING PROJECT

Rinpoche initiates a huge project to reproduce sets of a famous collection of 132 mandalas. Two complete sets of mandalas are etched into copper plates and plated in gold and silver patterns designed by Rinpoche. One set is destined for the temple dome and one for the stupa.

MANDALA SILKSCREENING PROJECT

Five sets of the mandala collection are silkscreened onto duraleen; one set is hand colored. Five sets are silkscreened onto silk; one silk set is sent to Tibet, and two sets are framed. One set is silkscreened onto ricepaper.

ADDITIONAL SILKSCREENING PROJECTS

Silkscreening projects overseen by Rinpoche include 960 line drawings from the Canon, 14,000 mandalas on paper, 65 portraits of Buddhist masters, and wallpaper for the temple.

ART AND TEXT PLATING PROJECTS FOR THE STUPA

The original plating project is now expanded to include 577 sacred texts from the Kanjur for the purpose of ornamenting the stupa. Rinpoche also selects precious texts, prayers, and art for plating: mantras and Longchenpa texts and prayers, images of the 35 Buddhas of Forgiveness, deities, stupas, guardians, dakinis, as well as the eight auspicious symbols and the seven royal symbols. These large-scale projects will require several years of effort to complete. In all 2,800 plates are produced for the stupa, preserving the Buddha Dharma in a beautiful and long-lasting form. As the sunlight falls upon the stupa and the breezes move across its surface, the words and symbols of the Dharma will spread their blessings in all directions.

MORE PLATING FOR THE TEMPLE

Rinpoche sponsors the etching of an entire copy of the Bhadrakalpika Sutra, in addition to the Manjushri Namasamgiti, for installation in the dome of the temple.

He also chooses mantras, rare Nyingma texts, mandalas, and Longchenpa texts for this project.

NEW SET OF PRAYER WHEELS

Senior TNMC craftspeople begin production of 484 prayer wheels for Odiyan: 364 large wheels and 120 smaller ones. Each large wheel contains three sets of precious Kanjur texts that were often memorized and recited in Tibet, as well as hundreds or thousands of repetitions of special dharanis and mantras. These new wheels generate two billion mantras a minute. With the completion of this project, 886 wheels have been produced over the years for Nyingma Centers.

THE ODIYAN LAKE

Excavation begins on a lake to encircle the rim structure. Ninety feet from bank to bank, the lake places the temple and rim complex on an "island." Over 60,000 cubic yards of dirt are moved, and the original entrance road is now rerouted.

ADDITIONAL BUILDINGS AT ODIYAN

Excavations begin on additional buildings near the rim structure for Dharma Publishing projects and to provide space for meetings and for storage.

MURALS FOR ODIYAN TEMPLE

TNMC artists create murals for the Dharma Hall, following instructions in the texts for the placement of various elements and figures. The eight murals, each three feet by seven-and-a-half feet, represent the Birth of the Buddha, the Life of Prince Siddhartha, the Buddha's

Renunciation, the Enlightenment, Turning the Wheel of the Dharma, the Descent from Tushita, and the Parinirvana. An eighth mural depicts Padmasambhava together with the Vidyadharas and Masters of the Nyingma lineage.

NEW EQUIPMENT FOR THE PRESS

New computer systems are researched and purchased for Press and Publishing. A new Heidelberg press, which offers very high-quality printing, is purchased, as well as a second film processor and more modern platemaking equipment. Though such equipment is expensive and our budget is always tight, having the best equipment we can afford allows us to produce books and art reproductions of great beauty.

1985
THE SEVENTEENTH YEAR

NEW BOOKS

Dharma Publishing brings out *Nyingma Annals III*, documenting many of Nyingma Centers' more recent projects, and *550 Books on Buddhism*, a valuable bibliographic resource for students of the Dharma. A new translation of the Buddhist classic, the Dhammapada, includes a useful glossary of Sanskrit, Tibetan, and English terms for students of Tibetan.

COPPER MOUNTAIN MANDALA

Rinpoche authors *Copper Mountain Mandala: Mystic Land of Odiyan*, gathering together hundreds of photos to document the history of Odiyan. The complex design requires months of work to complete. A supplement will document art and landscaping projects over the last two years, revealing the full beauty of Odiyan. With each year, the mandala grows more meaningful, embodying both the sacred and the natural realms.

THANKAS FOR INDIA AND TIBET

TNMC ships thousands of thanka reproductions produced by Dharma Mudranalaya to Tibetan communities in India, Nepal, Sikkim, Bhutan, and Tibet. Similar shipments are made during 1986 and 1987, bringing the total number of thanka prints sent abroad to more than 60,000 over the last fifteen years.

TRANSLATIONS OF DHARMA PUBLISHING BOOKS

Hidden Mind of Freedom is translated into German and Portuguese; *The Marvelous Companion* is translated into Italian.

RITUAL ARTS PROJECTS

Large art projects are established to create 484 prayer wheel covers, 99 Tibetan book covers, 16 victory banners, 27 Lantsa yolwas, 27 temple door covers, 44 appliqué designs for the temple gallery, a Ye Dharma banner for the temple cupola, and 32 large appliqué hanging medallions. To support the Dharma in the West and to bring the blessings of universal harmony, 200 prayer flags are produced. This set of flags brings the total number of flags created by TNMC to 3,800.

THANKA PRINTING

Between the autumn of 1985 and the summer of 1987, Dharma Publishing and TNMC research museum collections and obtain permission to reproduce 139 thankas, including images of the Sixteen Great Arhats and the Nine Manifestations of Padmasambhava together with the Eighty-Eight Siddhas.

PADMASAMBHAVA STATUES

A set of Padmasambhava statues is cast in metal in the Odiyan foundry using the lost wax technique. The delicate steps entail much practice, and a three-man crew would require five years to cast a set of one thousand statues. Research is underway to find more efficient techniques. By 1987 many more small Padmasambhava statues have been cast in various materials.

SKILLFUL MEANS PRESS

Skillful Means Press is founded to support the efforts of Nyingma in the West and to promote the principles of the Dharma in the American workplace. Skillful Means makes very valuable contributions to Nyingma projects, especially to Odiyan, while its workers continue to use their jobs as a way of practicing the Dharma and bringing benefit to others.

GESTURE OF BALANCE PROGRAM

The Gesture of Balance Program is underway at the Institute. Numerous prayer flags, 1,080 small stupas, 100,000 tsa tsas, and 143 Buddha statues with haloes are produced from forms in the traditional style. Institute students begin to learn more about Tibetan Buddhist iconography, developing a new appreciation for sacred art, new skills, and better ways of working together.

LONG-TERM INSTITUTE PROGRAMS

The two-month and four-month programs continue, while a new nine-month Nyingma practice program is begun. Because it focuses on a different theme each year, such as topics from *Gesture of Balance* or *The Voice of the Buddha,* this program can be repeated by students. The Knowledge of Freedom course is expanded into a nine-month program.

ART EXHIBIT

Nyingma Institute sponsors an art exhibit of a selection of Dharma Mudranalaya art publications. The exhibit helps Institute students develop a broader perspective on Tibetan art, while offering the public a rare opportunity to view a large collection of sacred art.

CHANDELIER PROJECT

Rinpoche designs chandeliers for the main temple as well as for the four small entryway temples. The north pagoda chandelier is completed in 1985; the remaining ones are finished during 1987. The chandelier for the main temple is nine feet across and seventeen feet high, while the smaller ones are about four feet across and seven feet high. More than 70,000 crystals specially ordered from Europe are used to complete the intricate designs. The large chandelier is shaped like a vase of immortality, radiating sparkling light from the heart of the mandala.

1986
THE EIGHTEENTH YEAR

CLASS ADOPTIONS

By 1986 many Dharma Publishing books, particularly those by Rinpoche, have been adopted as class texts in over 500 American universities and colleges. *Gesture of Balance* is most popular, with 129 adoptions. Others include *Calm and Clear,* 16; *Crystal Mirror,* 12; *Kindly Bent to Ease Us,* 17; *Kum Nye,* 45; *Mind in Buddhist Psychology,* 19; *Openness Mind,* 32; *Reflections of Mind,* 15; *Skillful Means,* 60; TSK, 106.

INSTITUTE PROGRAMS FLOURISH

The eighth nine-month Kum Nye training program is held; the two-month and four-month programs are attracting participants from all over America as well as from Europe and South America.

TSK UPDATE

By this year TSK has been translated into German, Dutch, and Italian, and study groups are active in Germany, Holland, and in Japan.

TEMPLE JEWELS PROJECT

To decorate the temple ceilings, TNMC craftspeople create 108 looped feet of strung jewels. In Tibet jeweled patterns were usually painted on the temples, but the Odiyan temple will have hanging faceted beads and crystals — a tapestry of 54,855 jewels.

ODIYAN STATUE PROJECT

To create original life-sized statues for the Odiyan temple, students at TNMC learn traditional sculpture and Buddhist iconography. Nine original clay statues are created from which seventy-five plaster and resin statues are cast. With Rinpoche's constant guidance and inspiration, the first set of large-scale Buddhist statues made in America is completed: fifteen Buddhas, five Manjushris, five Taras, five Vajrapanis, five Dhyani Buddhas, eight major Bodhisattvas, two Four-armed Avalokiteshvaras, two Avalokiteshvaras with one thousand arms, nine Padmasambhavas, five Amitabhas, two Maitreyas, eight Herukas, and four Dorje Drolods.

RITUAL ORNAMENTATION AND JEWELRY

TNMC craftspeople produce many hundreds of ritual implements and ornaments for the Odiyan statues by etching and hammering copper, which is then covered in gold: long and short necklaces, earrings, crowns, bracelets, anklets, scarves, ritual implements such as bowls, beads, staffs, and dorjes.

RITUAL ARTS PROJECT

Though most students' time and energy is devoted to the statue and ornamentation projects, TNMC creates 800 prayerflags and 535 victory banners according to traditional designs to increase peace and happiness.

DHARMA PUBLISHING BOOKS IN EUROPE

Openness Mind is translated into Portuguese this year. Ten of our books are available in European languages; translations offer European readers a wealth of new material for Dharma study and support the Institute's outreach programs.

YESHE DE PUBLICATIONS

Under the auspices of the Yeshe De Project, Publishing brings out the first English translation of the famous Bhadrakalpika Sutra, a four-volume set with Tibetan facing the English. *Ancient Tibet,* an introduction to ancient Tibetan history, contains valuable background information and resources for those interested in research into Tibetan history.

VISITING LAMA

Khentse Rinpoche, the reincarnation of Rinpoche's root Guru, Jamwang Khentse Wangpo, visits Padma Ling where he offers blessings to students. At the Institute he gives a long Dharma talk and encourages students to study and practice.

ART EXHIBITS

An art exhibit entitled "Sacred Images" is held at the Nyingma Institute in the summer, followed by the "Path of Beauty" exhibit in the fall. We are fortunate to have an opportunity to view so many sacred images; even in Tibet few people had access to such a large collection of sacred art. Throughout the exhibition, special classes, lectures, and workshops encouraged a deeper appreciation of Tibetan art. The thanka prints, framed in the traditional way, will eventually be housed at Odiyan, adding to the treasury of art and ritual objects in the Odiyan collection.

THREE-YEAR RETREATS

Another Nyingma student begins the traditional three-year retreat at Odiyan, bringing the number of participants up to four. As we see American students complete this traditional training, more students are beginning to consider doing a long retreat.

NYINGMA EDITION GIFTS

TNMC Head Lama offers five gift sets of the *Nyingma Edition* to Nyingma centers in Europe, Asia, and in Tibet. Sixty-nine copies of the *Guide to the Nyingma Edition* are sent to major Nyingma centers in India, Bhutan, Sikkim, and Nepal to support study and research in Buddhist subjects.

GOLDEN ODIYAN STUPA

A project to refinish the stupa in gold begins in the summer and is completed in the fall. Though very time-consuming and expensive, and requiring much detailed research, the results are worth the effort. The first gold stupa in the West now shines brilliantly in the sunlight by day and glows in the moonlight by night. Gold as a symbol of the Buddha has been used in the art, sculpture, and monuments of Buddhist lands for centuries. The new set of tsa tsas is now placed in the Buddha Room in the stupa, adding special blessings and prayers for harmony and peace. Covering the Odiyan Stupa with gold seems deeply significant to Nyingma students. The power and beauty of the stupa seem to hold forth the possibility that in the future the Dharma will find a true home in our country.

GOLDEN STATUES

In the spring, seventy-five statues produced at Padma Ling are taken to Odiyan to be painted or covered in gold. The opportunity to participate in creating sacred art is remarkable to us; the results far surpass what we had ever imagined possible. Rinpoche instructs students in creating obelisks for each statue to hold prayers and mantras he selects. When the obelisks are placed inside the forms, these statues will become true treasures of the Dharma.

LANDSCAPING PROJECTS

A ring of Serbian spruce trees as well as oriental bamboos are planted around the lake, while Japanese maples are planted between the lake and the rim structure. A perimeter road is built to encircle the lake, and a footwalk is added around its inside edge. Many truckloads of red rock quarried from the property are laid along the banks. More than 3,000 cuttings are planted in various locations throughout Odiyan. Foundations are poured for four specially shaped islands in the lake.

LARGE PRAYER FLAGS

Special large permanent prayer flagpoles are designed to surround the rim structure with flying flags. Thirty-two poles each thirty-two feet high are built and installed, each holding three very large flags. Atop each pole is a jewel shape filled with precious treasures to surround the temple complex with prayers and to bring the blessings of the Dharma into America for the benefit of all people.

VICTORY BANNERS

Following traditional guidelines, TNMC craftspeople build twenty large metal victory banners in cylindrical form to turn on the wind, sending forth blessings that promote peace and harmony. Eight are installed at the stupa and the rest at the rim structure.

PLATES MOUNTED IN TEMPLE

Copper plates etched the previous year with texts in silver and gold are mounted in the temple dome and bell. Nyingma students are impressed with the great beauty and power of the results. Though we do not yet understand the meaning of many of the texts and images, we can sense the deep value they hold. Preserving them for the future while also bringing such beauty into the temple seems a most fitting combination, and a wonderful use of modern technology for the Dharma.

GARDENS AROUND RIM STRUCTURE

Original plans to create gardens of different kinds on each of the four sides of the rim structure have gradually been modified over the years as harmonious designs have been worked out. Lawns and hedges are being added as well as magnolias and other flowering species. In time, each side of the rim structure will manifest a distinctive beauty of its own, reflecting the particular light and qualities of each direction.

WINDOW PROJECTS

To provide improved lighting for the new buildings at Odiyan, clerestory windows are built. Twenty-one semi-circular stained glass windows for these buildings are also created. Other stained glass projects include four colorful lanterns for outside the temple and four for the stupa, and six desk lamps for the temple library.

ART FOR THE TEMPLE

TNMC craftspeople create 112 door mantras etched in copper for the temple, in addition to silkscreening 56 portraits of Buddhist teachers onto glass. Elaborate frames are constructed with fine wood and stained glass. One hundred and thirty nine thankas are framed as well as a set of Padmasambhava and the Eighty-Eight Siddhas thankas framed in traditional Western style; 120 small thankas of Padmasambhava and the Buddha are framed. Three hundred and eleven large copper medallions are etched with canonical art, as well as several hundred gift plaques etched with five different mantras in ornate Lantsa script.

TEMPLE APARTMENTS

Finishing work is completed on the apartments within the temple, adding furniture and appliances. Carpeting, tile, and other amenities are installed.

TEXT PRESERVATION

Rinpoche initiates a large-scale project to preserve on microfiche the Rinchen Terzod, a precious collection of Terma assembled by the nineteenth-century Buddhist master Kongtrul. By recording these rare texts on film, Dharma Mudranalaya hopes to assure their long life and make them more widely available.

1987 THE NINETEENTH YEAR

ADDITIONAL ODIYAN LAND

In January 112 acres of land, not far from the rim structure, were added to the Odiyan property. This land had been tentatively included in the original plans for the Odiyan mandala, but was not available for purchase until this year. The new property will afford space for special Dharma projects soon underway.

YESHE DE TRANSLATIONS

Dharma Publishing offers two new translations under the auspices of the Yeshe De Project. *Master of Wisdom* is a collection of Nagarjuna texts translated by a well-known scholar, published with Tibetan and Sanskrit editions. *Joy for the World* is a translation of a play by Candragomin, the seventh-century Buddhist master.

NEW EQUIPMENT FOR DHARMA PROJECTS

In order to have complete facilities for projects at Odiyan, Dharma Publishing obtains new high-quality equipment, guaranteeing our capacity to produce fine Dharma books and publish research.

TEXT PRESERVATION

Rinpoche continues to focus on preserving Buddhist texts, hoping to publish as many sacred texts as possible in the future, especially rare Nyingma teachings. Dharma Publishing plans to compile as many editions of the Nyingma Canon as possible, though this project would eventually be twice the size of the Kanjur and Tanjur publication.

STUPA PRAYER WHEELS

Two rings of prayerwheels are added around the stupa, with 60 new wheels being created to complete the two sets. The last three series of wheels have used nearly 400 miles of paper for millions of prayers and mantras, about one mile of paper for each wheel. Roofed walkways enclosing the prayer wheels are being constructed around the stupa, and additional landscaping is being added. These new projects have created a beautiful and inspiring environment that radiates innumerable blessings into the world.

MORE ORNAMENTATION AND RITUAL ART

Two pairs of large doors are created for the south and west entryways of the rim structure. Built of walnut, the new doors are intricately carved with square patterns. All four gates into the rim structure now have formal doors. Special Hor Yig Mantras and Longchenpa texts are plated and installed above the inner temple doors. Four new door hangings are made and 550 book covers. Nine new thankas are being created by TNMC artists.

LANDSCAPING EFFORTS CONTINUE

The orchard is expanded by 400 trees. Seven hundred maples, chestnuts, jasmine, and camellias are added to the rim structure gardens. By 1987 over 50,000 trees had been planted in the reforestation project. An irrigation system is built for the stupa gardens. The four bridges across the Odiyan lake are finished, one in each direction. Special stupa forms are being created for each island. Landscaping around the stupa continues as plans are made for a Peace Garden with fifty varieties of roses and ever-burning lamps.

PROGRESS ON THE NEW BUILDINGS

Both the south and the west buildings are roughed in. Concrete walls are poured; Bernhold sheets are erected to make large arched ceilings without using columns. Waterproofing, drainage, and sealing of roofs are underway. Rough plumbing and electrical wiring are installed.

BEAUTIFYING ODIYAN

Rim structure rooms are redecorated. A new balcony railing is added, and railings around the temple are painted. Doors are varnished, temple rooms and gallery walkways cleaned. Four entryway storage rooms are enclosed. Pedestals and ornamental borders are added to the lake. Mosaic tilework is placed around walkways. To empower statues, 4,480 gzungs are prepared.

LOVE OF KNOWLEDGE

Ten years after the publication of TSK, Rinpoche brings out a sequel, *Love of Knowledge,* requiring several years of intensive work. This latest analysis, supplemented with exercises and TSK graphics, promises to give readers new access to the TSK vision and is eagerly anticipated by TSK teachers and students. Additional volumes on TSK are planned for the future.

TNMC SUMMARY

Over eighteen years, TNMC has focused on the production of ritual arts and crafts to make a contribution to the preservation of traditional Tibetan culture. TNMC has actively supported Dharma Mudranalaya's efforts to publish thankas and other art forms: Over sixteen hundred line drawings, thankas, and photos have been made available in books and as reproductions. Thousands of prayer flags and nearly one thousand prayer wheels have been produced. The opportunity to participate in traditional Buddhist art has been deeply rewarding to each of us as individuals and has enabled us to help bring the wisdom and compassion of the Buddhas to our land. May the merit that flows from such actions deepen the appreciation of the Dharma in the West for future generations.

DHARMA MUDRANALAYA

Though we began with only a vision of possibilities, Dharma Mudranalaya has been able to make substantial contributions to the Dharma over the last eighteen years. The texts of the Kanjur and Tanjur are reprinted, and hundreds of thankas have been preserved. With the passing of each year, our publications and art prints have reached a wider audience. By 1987, 42,000 copies of *Gesture of Balance* have been sold; 35,000 copies of TSK; 30,000 copies of *Kum Nye;* 11,000 copies of *Kindly Bent to Ease Us*; 15,000 copies of *Calm and Clear;* 24,000 copies of *Skillful Means;* and 12,000 copies of *Knowledge of Freedom.* The staff of Publishing and Press are grateful for the opportunity to have learned so many skills and contribute to sharing and preserving Dharma teachings that bring lasting benefits to individuals and our societies.

NYINGMA INSTITUTE SUMMARY

In the fourteen years since Rinpoche founded the Institute, we have been able to offer courses in Buddhist studies and practice, long retreats, and programs in relaxation and experiential pyschology to foster deeper self-understanding. Over fifteen hundred people attended the HDTP; more than fifty thousand participants have benefited from other programs, finding helpful ways of working and living with greater openness and balance. We are deeply grateful for the remarkable opportunity afforded us by working at the Institute. The longer we study and practice, the more we begin to appreciate the depth of the Dharma and the benefits it might bring to the West.

ODIYAN MANDALA SUMMARY

Twelve years of dedicated work guided by Rinpoche have resulted in the creation of a beautiful and deeply meaningful mandala of possibilities. The work of the last two or three years has required funds which more than equal the expenses of the first ten years. But somehow it has been possible with Rinpoche's constant support and the blessings of all the Buddhas. Remarkable ritual art has been obtained and created; facilities and equipment for Dharma Publishing will be available; landscaping and lake projects have evoked new beauty and harmony within the mandala. Odiyan workers have had a rare opportunity to learn and to contribute something of enduring value at the same time. We have seen a vision of great beauty become a reality before our very eyes.

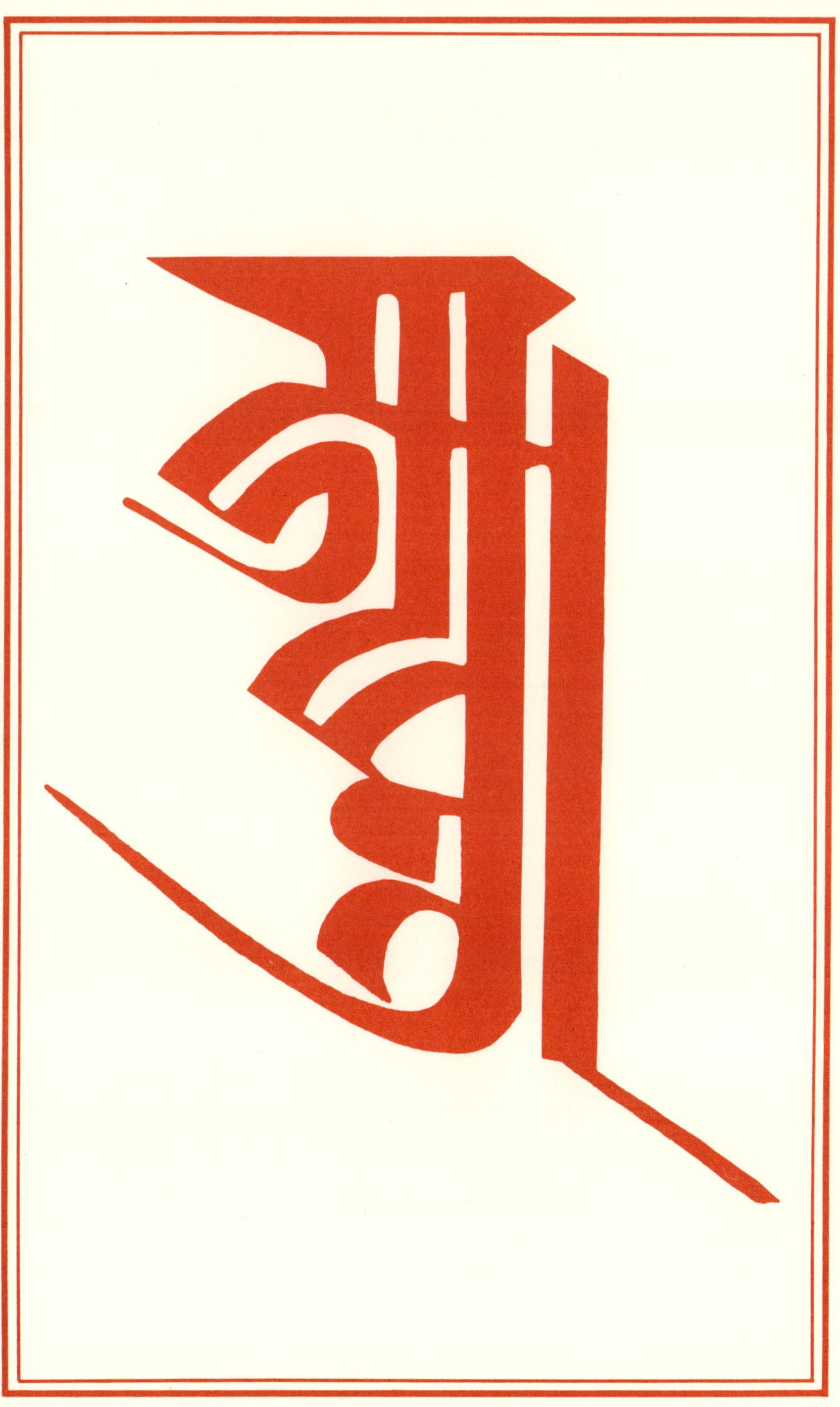

The ancient Lantsa script symbol of the Sanskrit word Jayantu:
May all people find happiness and freedom.